THE WAY OF CHRIST

Theodore G. Stylianopoulos

THE WAY OF CHRIST

GOSPEL, SPIRITUAL LIFE AND RENEWAL IN ORTHODOXY

Holy Cross Orthodox Press
Brookline, Massachusetts

The publication of this book was made possible through a generous gift by Constance Vrionis in loving memory of her husband, Milton Gerasimos Vrionis.

© Copyright 2002 Holy Cross Orthodox Press
Published by Holy Cross Orthodox Press
50 Goddard Avenue
Brookline, Massachusetts 02445

On the cover: Mosaic of Palm Sunday (1100 AD). The Monastery of Daphni, Northern Vault of the Cross .

Library of Congress Cataloging–in–Publication Data
Stylianopoulos, Theodore G.
The way of Christ: Gospel, spiritual life, and renewal in orthodoxy / Theodore Stylianopoulos, Demetrios Trakatellis
p. cm.
Includes bibliographical references and index.
ISBN 1-885652-59-3 (paper)
1. Orthodox Eastern Church – Doctrines. 2. Theology, Doctrinal. I. Trakatellis, Demetrios. II. Title.

BX320.3.S 79 2002
281.9 – dc21

2002068456

For

Archbishop Iakovos

churchman, visionary, noble soul

"Jesus came into Galilee, preaching the Gospel of God, and saying, 'The time is fulfilled, and the kingdom of God is at hand; repent, and believe in the Gospel.'" Mark 1:14-15

"By this we may be sure that we are in Him: he who says he abides in Him ought to walk in the same way in which He walked." 1 John 2:5-6

"The standard of Christianity is imitation of Christ in the measure of His incarnation according to the duty of each person's calling." Saint Basil the Great, *Monastic Rules II, Question 43.1*

"A Christian is an imitator of Christ in thought, word and deed, as far as this is humanly possible." Saint John Climacos, *The Ladder of Divine Ascent*, Step 1.

CONTENTS

FOREWORD

Then He said to them: "Therefore every scribe instructed in the kingdom of heaven is like a householder who brings out of his treasure what is new and what is old." Matthew 13:42

The author of the present work is like the scribe whom Jesus Christ the Lord describes in the above passage from Saint Matthew's Gospel. In this book, the Very Reverend Professor Theodore Stylianopoulos brings out of his remarkable priestly, academic and human treasure truly invaluable new and old insights, ideas, experiences and visions. Readers will discover here an amazing spiritual wealth, generously displayed under the title *The Way of Christ: Gospel, Spiritual Life and Renewal in Orthodoxy.* The material is indeed rich, covering vast areas of vital significance for Orthodoxy – as Church, as theology, as history, as worship, as a way of life, as personal piety, as spiritual *askesis*, as past, present and future.

The definitive characteristic of this book is its unwavering focus. At every step, in each chapter, in every page, regardless of the specificity and variety of content, the focus is always one and the same: Jesus Christ. The book exalts the priority of Christ, the uniqueness of Christ, the centrality of Christ and His Gospel. Readers of this exceptional work will be frequently reminded of Saint Paul's words that "Christ is all and in all" (Col. 3:11) and that "we take every thought captive to obey Christ" (2 Cor. 10:5).

At the same time, however, as we progress through the book, we enjoy a refreshing spiritual and intellectual achievement, a clear and strong synthesis of a rich variety of contents. Insights and images from the New Testament, the classical Fathers, the ascetic authors, the history of the Church, the liturgical practice, pastoral studies and contemporary theology – all blend harmoniously with each other to form an integral unity of highly edifying and educational quality. This work provides a synthesis in which the core idea of "continuity and renewal" finds a cogent and inspiring expression.

On behalf of the Greek Orthodox Archdiocese of America, I congratulate and thank Fr. Theodore, an esteemed friend, for offering to Orthodox believers and others, a book which constitutes both a spiritual challenge and an invitation to the world of Orthodoxy as a Gift and a Treasure.

Archbishop Demetrios of America
New York, N.Y.

PREFACE

Christianity is a religion of continuity and renewal. The dynamic interplay between tradition and newness is a definitive aspect of the ministry of Jesus, the early Church, as well as the history of Christianity. While rooted in the religious tradition of the Jewish people, Jesus saw His mission as a renewal of Judaism. He came not to abolish the law and the prophets but to fulfill them (Mt. 5:17). The good news of God's kingdom, the "new wine" that He brought to the world, was the fullness of the personal presence and power of the living God as Father, Son and Holy Spirit, who is to be worshiped, as Jesus said, "in spirit and truth" (Jn 4:23-24). The New Testament authors lived and wrote with a distinct sense that in Christ "the old has passed away, behold, the new has come" (2 Cor. 5:17). Yet they were open to embrace "whatever is true, whatever is honorable, whatever is just, whatever is pure, whatever is lovely" (Phil. 4:8) from both the Jewish and Greek traditions. Later, the Church Fathers were engaged in a similar task of proclaiming the Gospel, interpreting the new faith, and applying its truths to new situations. At a time of controversies, heresies, and schisms, Saint Basil the Great in particular provides a powerful and irenic example of the renewal of Church life and monasticism on the basis of Christ, the Gospel, as well as the early Church as a loving and sharing community.

The present book is offered as a collection of reflections on "what is old and what is new" in Eastern Orthodoxy. Addressed mainly to theological students, priests, Christian educators, and informed laity, its overarching theme is continuity and renewal as the Orthodox Church confronts new situations in the modern world. The book consists of mostly published retreat talks and conference papers, all of them now revised and arranged in what I hope is a coherent whole, but not without some repetitions and recurring themes. Representing a kind of harvest of my theological and pastoral labors during the last ten years, this work in character is thematic rather than analytic, suggestive rather than definitive, invitational rather than prescriptive. If you are looking for either a blueprint for change, or for discussion of specific issues in current ecclesiastical affairs, you will not find them here. Rather, my purpose is to engage you in conversation about our common task of defining the spiritual treasures of Orthodoxy and actualizing them in our personal and corporate lives.

Orthodoxy today finds itself in the paradoxical situation of attracting a significant number of converts while not being adequately successful in keeping all of its own people. This is particularly true of our youth, newly married couples, and many adults totally involved in the contemporary world of business, the professions, government, economics, entertainment, sports and various forms of family recreation. What are the dynamics behind this paradox? On the one hand, earnest seekers with spiritual interests perceive the power of the Orthodox Liturgy, the beauty of Orthodox worship, the balanced and wholesome vision of Orthodox theology and spirituality. On the other hand, those who are born into the Orthodox Church, and are inevitably exposed to the Orthodox liturgical forms and to the patterns of Orthodox parish life from childhood, often remain existentially unmoved by the spiritual treasures in and behind those forms and patterns. It seems that by many baptized Orthodox Christians, even those who maintain regular connections with the Church, Orthodoxy is seen as a religious system of ritual ceremonies and ecclesiastical structures with little substantial impact on their lives. Of course, it may well be that we, Orthodox theologians, priests, teachers, leaders, and parents, have not done an adequate job teaching and living the transforming elements of Orthodoxy, a job at any rate equal to the powerful forces shaping modern and post-modern life.

Apart from hand wringing and finding blame, however, what is really the answer to the above paradox fraught with promise and peril? The answer cannot be simply the appointment of more committees and task forces, or the publication of more books and programs, or even the undying hope of the rise of future, brilliant leaders to guide the Church to unseen golden horizons, although these things are good in themselves and are welcome. Nor is the answer in quick and mindless changes pertaining to liturgical forms and ecclesiastical policies without a renewed, deep theological and spiritual vision. Rather, the essential answer can be no other than recovery and energizing of the vital resources within Orthodoxy by directing focused attention to them and by communicating them with clarity, consistency, and personal commitment. What are the timeless and vital resources within Orthodoxy? They are: the Gospel, spiritual life, and a balanced vision of faith, tradition and renewal.

The proclamation of the Gospel leads to focus on Christ, the living center and foundation of the Church. When proclaimed effectively with the living voice and an evangelical spirit, the unique attribute of the Gospel is that it awakens faith in God's saving power and action both in the past and the present, stirring human hearts toward commitment and change. Spiritual life as worship, prayerfulness, and sincere Christian living brings about a deeper sense of conversion of the heart and mind, an increased receptivity to the mystery of divine love, an experience of freshness and spiritual energy for service in the name of Christ. However, in Orthodox perspective, this process of transformation is not merely subjective and individualistic, but is measured and guided by the Church's tradition. Only a balanced vision of personal faith, tradition, and renewal can serve as the context of the fullness of Orthodox faith and life, a context where the "new creation" in Christ blossoms by God's grace. All these elements together are the generative forces within Orthodoxy that can enliven the worship of the Church, its Liturgy, and its ministries for the nurture of its membership as well as the fulfillment of its world mission. And this is a task to be accomplished by all of us working in harmony with the Holy Spirit and by being true simply to our respective callings – as bishops, priests, theologians, educators, lay leaders, parish council members, choir members, parents, and parishioners young and old. In this grand vision of synergy and of being co-workers with God, we plant and water as did Paul and Apollos, but God gives the growth (1 Cor. 3:5-6).

I am delighted to dedicate this book to Archbishop Iakovos, a great churchman, an inspired visionary, and a man of noble sentiments. As a seminarian, I experienced his preaching of God's word as burning fire. As a priest, I have been uplifted as many times as I have had the honor to participate in the Liturgies celebrated by him. As a theologian, I am deeply grateful for his guidance and support over many and trying years.

Many thanks to Dr. Anton Vrame and his staff at the Holy Cross Orthodox Press for their labors in bringing this book to the light of publication.

Fr. Theodore G. Stylianopoulos
Holy Cross Greek Orthodox School of Theology
Brookline, Massachusetts
August 28, 2001

INTRODUCTION

THE GIFTS OF ORTHODOXY

What is distinctive about Orthodoxy? What features define Orthodox identity in the context of contemporary pluralism, secularism and post-modernism? These questions are of enormous significance for the future of Orthodoxy and its effective mission in the world. They have to do with our own self-understanding: who we are, how we see ourselves, what values we hold, what are the distinctive aspects of our common life, what traits or features define our character and behavior. The issue of identity is integrally connected to our mission: who we are guides us in what we are to do, and how to do it. The dynamic task of defining both identity and mission apply equally to individual Orthodox Christians, specific parishes and the Church as a whole.

It is especially important today to be clear about these weighty matters because the modern world has an overwhelming influence on all of us. Our pluralistic and secular society no longer supports Christian existence in any sense except for the exercise of the right of freedom. In fact the modern world undermines Christianity at every turn, while at the same time, paradoxically, many men and women deeply hunger for God and authentic expressions of Christianity. The more clearly our identity is defined, the more focused our mission is, the more effective the success of our witness becomes. And we trust that the words of Christ remain equally true for our society today: "Lift up your eyes, and see how the fields are already white for harvest" (Jn 4:35).

Some have attempted to define the essence of Orthodoxy in terms of single elements or themes. In a book first published in German (1957) and later translated into English under the title *The Eastern Orthodox Church* (1967), the German theologian Ernst Benz brilliantly introduced western readers to Orthodoxy through the symbol of the icon. The Orthodox dogmatician John Karmiris and other noted Greek theologians of the twentieth century located the quintessence

1

of Orthodoxy in the Nicene Creed and the Seven Ecumenical Councils. Still other theologians have put the emphasis elsewhere: the Eucharist, the understanding of the Holy Trinity, the ethos of freedom, the centrality of love, the teaching of salvation by divinization (*theosis*). These approaches have highlighted valuable aspects of Orthodoxy. However, one-sided focus on particular themes or topics is inevitably reductionistic and narrow. It proves inadequate to the task of grasping Orthodoxy in its fullness of faith and life, a task appropriate to its confession of being the One, Holy, Catholic and Apostolic Church.

At the opposite end of the spectrum are those who would advocate an ideal "Holy Orthodoxy" in all its historical particulars to be presented to the world as a seamless whole. For some who have followed this approach, there are really no problems except that most Orthodox Christians lack the zeal to observe all the traditions and canons of the Church. On a visit to Mount Athos many years ago, the writer briefly met an elderly monastic who seemed sublimely innocent of Church and family issues in America. He was incredulous that Orthodoxy could exist in America. With sincere conviction, I am sure, he came quickly to the point: "Why don't you leave America," he said. "Leave your work, your wife and your children, and come here to the Holy Mountain. It is here where you can find (true) Orthodoxy and see the glory of Byzantium that remains!" For him, Orthodoxy and the glory of Byzantium were one reality reflected in the monastic culture of Mount Athos.

The well-meaning monastic's vision of Orthodoxy was understandable because he had been on Mount Athos from childhood. However, similar views by those who live in the world, although understandable as a reaction to the modern world and the fear that Orthodox Christians are losing their moorings, are not at all justifiable. Efforts at a reenactment of "Holy Byzantium" or "Holy Russia," or a type of monastic culture in the parish, are not only historically impossible but also theologically indefensible. They are uninformed about the interplay between Christianity and culture throughout the ages. They ignore the struggle of the great Church Fathers who wrestled with Hellenism in order to christianize it. They forget the mission of the Church to engage the world directly as the Lord himself engaged it through His incarnation and said to the disciples: "As the Father has sent me, even so I send you" (Jn 20:21). In the end, the option of a "Holy Byzantium" distorts the universal, dynamic character of Orthodoxy, surrendering it to sectarianism, legalism, authoritarianism and obscurantism. It tends to foster an unloving, cultic and fanatical religiosity that once stood in mortal opposition to Christ Himself.

We find a different vision in the thought of Father Thomas Hopko, of St. Vladimir's Orthodox Theological Seminary. In an article on Orthodoxy and culture,[1] Father Hopko is forthright, almost to the point of pessimism, about the grave dangers of Orthodoxy in the post-modern world. Nevertheless, he insists that to deny engagement with contemporary society by escaping to a world of our own making is to live "for illusions and delusions." His vision of the task of Orthodoxy today is a clarion call to action. In his own language, which he describes at one point as "violent but true," Father Thomas advocates numerous urgent priorities. Chief among them are to: 1) put Christ and His Gospel at the center our concerns; 2) think and act in truly conciliar spirit apart from narrow agendas, whether as individuals or parishes or entire Churches and patriarchates; 3) abandon the lie that the universal truth of Orthodoxy can equally be served while fully retaining our ethnic cultures and even the set forms of ecclesiastical institutions; 4) resist the temptation of viewing Orthodoxy as an ideology, a sort of hypostatized entity, unconnected with how we actually think and live, and 5) be wisely open and vulnerable to the world, both witnessing to the truth and accepting criticism because "wherever truth is, Christ is there."[2] Father Hopko's perspective is as challenging and instructive as it is candid and courageous.

In what follows I present my own proposal about five characteristics or dimensions of Orthodoxy that are at the forefront of Orthodoxy's engagement with the modern society of which Orthodox Christians themselves, like it or not, are full members. What I develop is not in contrast to Father Hopko's vision. It is only another way of casting the issue and suggesting the groundwork for further reflection. I choose to call these five characteristics "the gifts of Orthodoxy." Far from being separate from each other, they in fact overlap forming a cohesive whole. These are precious gifts which ought to be presented first of all to Orthodox Christians themselves as ways of understanding the identity of Orthodoxy, and as ways of living joyously the fullness of its faith and life. Only then can they be offered to the world, as well, in a loving, positive, intelligible, and convincing manner. In each case, I also raise questions about whether or not we as Orthodox Christians truly practice what we preach. This is necessary in order not to be found wanting while appearing to instruct others. Authenticity is nothing else but life in conformity with one's truth claims with a sense of genuine, self-critical integrity.

ORTHODOXY AS TRUE FAITH

The greatest gift of Orthodoxy is its conviction of being the true faith, that is, a way of faith and life which possesses and proclaims the truth as a gift of God. At the heart of this awesome claim is Christ Himself who said: "I am the way, the truth and the life" (Jn 14:6). Based on the truth of the person and saving work of Christ, the Apostles and Church Fathers have bequeathed to Orthodox Christians a remarkably coherent and universal vision of truth pertaining to God, man, creation, salvation, Church, ethics, society, family, marriage, vocations, and so on. This theological vision, resisting all sectarian dichotomies, moves toward a harmonious balance on such matters as Bible and tradition, faith and reason, grace and will, faith and works, word and sacrament, prayer and action, clergy and laity, hierarchy and conciliarity, body and soul, man and woman, religion and culture, church and state. According to Orthodox theology, all these elements constitute aspects of the universal truth of Orthodoxy to be interpreted and presented to the world in deed and word precisely as objective and living truth, yet apart from both blind faith and naive rationalism. Following the great Cappadocian Fathers, Saint Basil, Saint Gregory the Theologian and Saint Gregory of Nyssa, Orthodox Christians are to engage life not only with deep faith but also with sound reason, the highest attribute of man created in the image and likeness of God. For the Cappadocian Fathers our minds are a way of sharing the mind of God. Without the gift of reason, there would be no free will, no moral responsibility, and no freely chosen progress toward God.[3]

There is a growing awareness in the world today, both among scholars and lay people, that Orthodoxy preserves the most authentic expression of classic Christianity. The problem is that many sincere seekers do not see glowing and tangible evidence of it among the Orthodox themselves. Our urgent task is to integrate truth and life – orthodoxia and orthopraxia. However, right faith (orthodoxia) is not only correct doctrine registered in the mind as theological information. It is also sound spirituality, a true Christian spirit and way of thinking (*phronema*) reflecting the mind of Christ. Nor is right practice (*orthopraxia*) simply the correct performance of liturgical rubrics. It is also, and above all, a right way of living (*bioma*) according to Christ. "The standard (*kanon*) of Christianity is the imitation of Christ (*mimesis Chrestou*)," writes Saint Basil.[4] Are we living and promoting the centrality of Christ and the Gospel? Are we applying Orthodox truths to our own ecclesial and personal existence as bishops, priests and lay Orthodox? Or are we merely satisfied with triumphal claims while denying these truths in practice? Are we transformed and liberated by the knowledge and practice of these truths in order to share them? Or are we quick to judge and show disdain toward others? In imitation of Christ, who came to save rather than to judge, we ought to rejoice in whatever elements of truth others may possess and humbly offer to them the fullness of faith and life in the name of Christ. In a free and open society, the truth itself is the most powerful force. The presentation of truth, enacted in word and deed, will determine the viability of Orthodoxy and the success of its mission.

ORTHODOXY AS TRUE CHURCH

A closely related gift of Orthodoxy is its embodiment in historical communities, the true Church, One, Holy, Catholic and Apostolic, identified with the family of Orthodox Churches throughout the world. The Church is the Body of Christ. The Church is wholly centered on Christ and the Gospel, nurturing its communal faith and life by the power of the Spirit through sacrament, proclamation, teaching, practice and witness. Its unity is confirmed by a common faith and life, not by one world organization controlled by a single center. It is a Church which rejects both clericalism and congregationalism. It is shepherded by a hierarchy defined by conciliarity and the synodical system. The Church lives by a synergy of gifts and talents of clergy and laity, together making up God's people, all mutually supportive and accountable, all serving as the conscience of the Church, all being the guardians of the faith. As a family of Churches, the universal Orthodox Church welcomes all nations to join the family according to the principle of one Church in one region, without enslaving them or prohibiting them from retaining their cultures and governing their lives. Today there are about fifteen independent Orthodox Churches throughout the world. There could be fifty or a hundred and fifty, provided they are united striving together toward the fullness of faith and life in God.

Once again, the challenge for Orthodox Christians is to integrate theory and practice in ecclesiology, eschewing on the one hand the spirit of institutionalism, authoritarianism and factionalism, and showing on the other hand that the Church is truly the redeemed community, a witness to the new creation in Christ, an image of unity in love which God offers to the world. Our respective cultural and ethnic treasures are advanced by inspired work, and not by rhetoric or polemics against those perceived to be less ethnic-minded. According to Saint Paul we are to welcome all to the Church, for there is no Jew, Greek, barbarian or slave in the Body of Christ. We have the strength and creativity to cooperate and establish effective ways of perpetuating our respective ethnic traditions while allowing the Church to focus on saving souls and manifesting its catholicity. We have the wisdom and patience in Christ to discuss the issue of jurisdictional unity in a timely and appropriate manner. We want to foster personal freedom, dignity and justice in the Church because, while the Church is not a democracy, it is far more and not less than a democracy. The Church is a loving community of brothers and sisters ready to lay down their lives for each other.

ORTHODOXY AS TRUE WORSHIP

Because worship is a primary expression of Orthodox life, "Orthodoxia" is often interpreted as "right glory" or "right worship." The essence of worship is the adoration of the Triune God worthy of all praise and thanksgiving in His majesty, goodness and saving activity. The Divine Liturgy, the jewel of Orthodox worship, is a celebration of the saving work of Christ, a festival of the new creation in the Spirit, a joyful reception of the blessings of God's kingdom. To the degree that the Orthodox Church has survived and flourished throughout the centuries, it has done so largely by the sacred majesty and spiritual power of its worship. A scholar once remarked that while Western Christianity attempts to analyze and comprehend God, Eastern Christianity seeks to praise and adore the mystery of God. Innumerable converts have embraced Orthodoxy because of the beauty, the transcendence, and experienced holiness of Orthodoxy as true worship.

The challenge here, according to Christ's teachings, is to foster worship "in spirit and truth" (Jn 4:23-24), worship as fervent communal prayer, as a spiritually transforming event, not merely a formal performance of ceremonies. The complexity of worship services, the richness of hymnology, the difficulties of language, all unwittingly discourage congregational participation by voice and soul. A massive part of hymnology and seasonal services are never heard by many faithful, and when they are heard, they are not understood. The necessary reliance on chanters and choirs often puts worshipers in the position of observers and spectators. Much work is needed in liturgical instruction. We must teach each other how to pray. We must encourage active engagement in worship by the congregation. We must come to appreciate more deeply the liturgical services, not only as beautiful ceremonies but also as vibrant prayers of the entire community. The gift of true worship is actualized when, in the words of St. John Chrysostom, Orthodox Christians come out of worship like "lions breathing fire" and ready to do God's work in the world.

ORTHODOXY AS TRUE LIFE

Saint Eirenaios taught that the glory of God is a person fully alive and that true life is the experience of God. "If I love the Lord, how can I let even a shadow of evil into my heart?" asked Saint John of Kronstadt. Christ commanded that we should love one another as He loved us. He promised that if we obey His teachings, He and the Father will come to dwell in our hearts by the power of the Spirit. Saint Isaac the Syrian held that hell was created not by God but by His creatures and their refusal of His love, and that God equally loves those in hell, but His love is inoperative where it is rejected. Orthodoxy as true life testifies to the most beautiful and sublime teachings worthy of the message and spirit of Christ. Called to ascetic struggle against all personal, social and cosmic wickedness, we nevertheless rely on the saving grace and power of God. Called to obedience, we practice obedience in the spirit of Christ's love, truth and righteousness. Called to "theosis," we know that the way to it is through service to the least of the brothers and sisters by fervent prayer and humble action.

The challenge is to achieve what the saints call *bioma* – the personal experience of Christ testified by love and humility – over against the dangers of secularism, nominalism, minimalism and hypocrisy. Secularism is worshiping the gods of the present age, while being totally indifferent or even hostile toward the true God. Nominalism is being a Christian in name only, a colossal hoax. Minimalism is lukewarm Christianity to suit our selfish interests and convenience. Hypocrisy is religiosity without spirituality, a pharisaical attachment to external forms while denying the inner substance of the faith. St. Symeon the New Theologian writes that all efforts that do not attain to love in a contrite spirit are in vain. The challenge is to transform secular life into spiritual life, formal faith into living faith, religious zeal into divine love by God's grace.

ORTHODOXY AS TRUE WITNESS

Someone has said: "Faith cannot be imposed on anyone because it has to be freely given and freely embraced; but faith will not be easily received if the new life it creates is never seen or heard." Orthodoxy cannot successfully preach love, righteousness, justice, unity and peace to others without convincing evidence of these realities within its own bosom. Jesus' words ring out: "You are the light of the world . . . let your light shine before others, so that they may see your good works and give glory to your Father in heaven" (Mt. 5:14,16). Orthodoxy is endowed with the gift of true witness. It proclaims Christ and the Gospel in its fullness, and it gives of what it freely has received, but without coercion, manipulation, or dissimulation. Orthodoxy takes an incarnational approach to the world, showing profound love and respect for all people in their own cultural contexts, ignorance, even sin. Its deepest intention is to let the truth speak for itself and to attract people to Christ, not merely to "Orthodoxy" as a self-contained ideology or a religion of exotic externals.

The challenge for Orthodox Christians is to recover more of our evangelical spirit through genuine repentance, deep prayer and spiritual renewal. The evangelical spirit, kindled by the grace of God, is the vital energy behind the Church's ministries. We must plan and define objectives in the light of Christ and the Gospel. We must meet in boardrooms and conferences in the presence of the Holy Spirit as if were conducting a Liturgy. We must face issues of leadership, education and administration with the eyes of God. We must come out of our committee meetings and our liturgical assemblies transformed and ready to share the "more" of Orthodoxy as fullness of faith and life. Orthodoxy is the fulfillment of all things in order that God's glory may shine in all creation. The living tradition of Orthodoxy is creative and liberating, not merely protective and preservative. The message of Orthodoxy is one of love, joy and generosity; it has nothing to do with defensiveness, narrowness, self-righteousness, hostility or negativism toward others. Respectful of other faiths and religions, and gracious toward all people and their backgrounds, we witness to the fullness of the mystery of Christ shining in the gifts of Orthodoxy for the glory of the Father and the Son and the Holy Spirit.

NOTES

[1] Thomas Hopko, "Orthodoxy in Post-Modern Pluralistic Societies," *Orthodoxy and Culture*, ed. Ioan Sauca (Geneva: World Council of Churches, 1996), pp. 137-150.

[2] Hopko, pp. 143-146.

[3] For an excellent book on faith and reason in the Church Fathers, and the interaction of Christianity and Hellenism in antiquity, see Jaroslav Pelikan, *Christianity and Classical Culture* (New Haven: Yale University Press, 1993).

[4] Saint Basil the Great, *Monastic Rules II, Question 43.1.* In the context St. Basil lifts up Christ's example of love and humility to be practiced especially by Church leaders. Saint John Climacos, *The Ladder of Divine Ascent*, Step 1, similarly writes: "A Christian is an imitator of Christ in thought, word and deed, as far as this is humanly possible." In 1 Jn 2:6 we read: "He who says he abides in Him ought to walk in the same way in which He walked."

PART ONE

THE GOSPEL

CHAPTER ONE

THE GOSPEL IN SAINT JOHN CHRYSOSTOM

An important factor behind the vitality of the Church as it stands at the beginning of the twenty-first century is its own confidence in the saving message with which it has been entrusted. The tremendous success of early Christianity in the pluralistic world of antiquity was due in large measure to the invincible conviction of the early Christians, the Christian martyrs, and the Church Fathers about the intrinsic truth and power of the Gospel grounded in the self-revelation of God in salvation history. In this chapter we shall reflect on Saint John Chrysostom's understanding of the Gospel.

Saint John Chrysostom (ca. 350-407) is an heir of this early Christian confidence in the truth of the Gospel to which he devoted his life and work both in Antioch as presbyter (381-397) and Constantinople as archbishop (398-404). In his treatise *On the Priesthood*, as well known, Saint John expounds at length on the ministry of preaching, a task requiring talent as well as diligence. In this famous work one finds a classic patristic contribution to the understanding of preaching as a skilled and disciplined ministry in the proclamation of the good news, while refuting errors and heresies. The focus of the present chapter, however, is another. It falls neither on the preacher nor the ministry of preaching but rather on the theological meaning and spiritual power of the Gospel itself. It explores basic questions such as, how does Chrysostom define the Gospel? What is the content of the Gospel? What is the power of the Gospel and what determines its efficacy in the world?

The sources used for this chapter are Saint John's homilies on Matthew, John, Acts, Romans, 1 Corinthians and Galatians, as well as his work *In Praise of Saint Paul*. The methodological approach is both descriptive and analytic, that is to say, reporting Chrysostom's views in diverse homilies and simultaneously seeking to assess the overall structure of his thought concerning our topic.

THE NATURE OF THE GOSPEL

Saint John does not anywhere take up the Gospel as a systematic topic of discussion. We must glean his ideas about the Gospel from various parts of his writings. An analysis of his understanding of the nature of the Gospel will show that he moves within three related concentric circles dealing with the following major subjects: (a) Scripture as the word of God, (b) the earthly ministry of Christ as recorded in the Gospels, and (c) the person of Christ Himself, the Incarnate Word of God, who is the supreme revelation of truth and life. Each of these invites closer examination.

An appreciation of Chrysostom's convictions about the Gospel must begin widely with his view of divine revelation as a whole. The patristic perspective on the unity of revelation made it possible for the Antiochean Father to link the Church's saving message with both the Old and the New Testaments. In its widest scope, therefore, according to Chrysostom, the good news of salvation is associated with the word of God, a salvific word of truth and life, expressed everywhere in Holy Scripture. Insofar as Scripture is the recorded revelation of divine truth, it constitutes the richest and most authoritative source of salvific truth for humanity.

Chrysostom draws an interesting distinction between oral and recorded revelation, the unwritten and written word of God. The great biblical figures of revelation such as Abraham and Moses were, according to Chrysostom, living bearers of revelation because of their privileged direct communication with God. Their intimacy with God excluded the need for books. So, too, the apostles, on the day of Pentecost became "living books and laws" (*biblia kai nomoi empsychoi*), pouring forth treasures of teachings and gifts to the world. However, subsequent generations of both Jews and Christians lost the purity of teaching and life of their spiritual leaders and had to receive God's truth in written words now recorded in the Old and New Testament.[1] This concept of oral and written revelation is traditional among the Church Fathers and goes back to Philo of Alexandria, the Jewish biblical interpreter and philosopher of the first century AD. According to this view, Holy Scripture is an expression of God's condescension or accommodation to human weakness. A corollary insight is that the highest mode of knowledge of God is not dependent on books but rather on charismatic leaders of the people of God who are in intimate communion with God.

However, according to Saint John Chrysostom, the nature of Scripture as an accommodation to human weakness diminishes neither the truth nor the authority of God's written word. For Saint John, what the Evangelist Matthew wrote in his Gospel is not his own but belongs to Christ.[2] All of recorded revelation, inspired by the Holy Spirit, is God's word. This authoritative view of the Bible is the basis for Chrysostom's numerous exhortations about the primacy of hearing and reading the Bible as the divine, all-sufficient source of truth and healing. To quote him:

> Let us then also learn therefore to consider all things secondary (*parerga*) to the hearing of the word of God, and to deem no season unseasonable. . . Let food and baths and dinners and the other things of this life have their appointed time; but let the teaching of the heavenly philosophy have no separate time, [but] let every season belong to it.[3]

And again:

> Great is the profit of the divine Scriptures, and all-sufficient is the aid which comes from them. . . For the divine oracles are a treasury of all manner of medicines, so that whether it be needful to quench pride, to lull desire to sleep, to tread under foot the love of money, to despise pain, to inspire confidence, to gain patience – from them one may find abundant resource.[4]

Secondly, while Chrysostom views all of the Bible as a source of truth and a treasure of heavenly blessings, he associates the Gospel more closely with the four written Gospels and the ministry of Christ. According to Saint John the title "evangelist," properly speaking, applies to the authors of the Gospels who have recorded the Lord's salvific ministry. Although Saint Paul as a proclaimer of the good news can also be called an evangelist, he is primarily an apostle, whereas Matthew is preeminently an evangelist.[5] Of course, for Saint Paul the two terms, evangelist and apostle, were closely related. As an apostle he was called and sent out precisely to be an evangelist – to preach the Gospel (1 Cor. 1:16). Nevertheless, Chrysostom and the Christian tradition were correct to stress the importance of the Gospels as primary sources of the good news. The Gospel is grounded in the historical ministry of Jesus. The fullness of the good news as saving truth for humanity embraces the entire life of Christ from incarnation to ascension. This view is behind the Antiochean Father's point that the preeminent evangelists are the Gospel writers.

Saint John celebrates the Gospel in terms of two elements: its blessings and essential truths. In terms of its blessings, he asks the
question: Why did Matthew call his work good news (*euangelion*)?
The answer is because of its spiritual benefits. The Antiochean Father enumerates these blessings as follows: removal of punishment,
remission of sins, righteousness, sanctification, redemption, adoption, inheritance of heaven, and an intimate closeness to the Son of
God (*syggeneian pros ton uion tou Theou*). He goes on, waxing eloquent about the blessings flowing from Christ's earthly ministry:

> God on earth, humanity in heaven; all mingled together, angels join-
> ing the choirs of humanity and humanity having fellowship with
> angels. . . . reconciliation between God and our nature, the devil brought
> to shame, demons in flight, death destroyed, paradise opened, the
> curse blotted out, sin put out of the way, error driven off, truth re-
> turning, the word of godliness everywhere sown, and flourishing in
> its growth, . . . and hope abundant touching future things.[6]

All these constitute good news because they are secure blessings
and undeserved gifts given on account of God's great love toward
humanity. Chrysostom further comments: "For [it is] not by laboring and sweating, not by fatigue and suffering, but merely as being
beloved of God, [that] we received what we have received."[7] Although the Saint emphasizes the role of free will and moral striving
in the attainment of virtue, he never forgets that all are part of God's
gifts, all are dependent on grace.

In terms of the contents of the Gospel, Chrysostom draws a distinction between the variety of incidental descriptions and the
essential features of Christ's ministry. He concedes that the plural-
ity of the canonical Gospels displays a certain discordance in the
details (*en mikrois diaphonia*) pertaining to time, place and exact word-
ing. But such discrepancies actually carry positive implications. For
one thing they dispel any suspicion of pernicious collusion on the
part of the sacred authors. For another they underscore the veracity
of the essentials of Jesus' ministry on which the Gospels agree and
on which Christian life and the good news are grounded (*en tois
kephalaiois tois synechousin hemon ten zoen kai to kerygma synkrotousin*).
What are these central truths that form the foundation of Christian
life and preaching? Saint John states:

> That God became man, that He performed miracles, that He rose,
> that He ascended, that He will judge, that He has given saving com-
> mandments, that He has introduced a law not contrary to [but in

fulfillment of] the Old Testament, that He is a Son, only-begotten, a true Son, that He is of the same essence with the Father, and as many other truths as are like these.[8]

While Saint John wisely does not try to compile a definitive list of agreed essentials, nevertheless the distinction is extremely significant. It provides a way of appreciating the diversity of the Gospels apparent to any careful reader but also affirms their unity based on the essential aspects and events of Christ's ministry.

Thirdly, Chrysostom identifies the Gospel with the living Christ Himself. The person of Christ is ultimately the essence of the Gospel in terms of both its content and blessings. Among many passages which express this truth, two may be cited, one from his *Homilies on First Corinthians* and one from his *Homilies on the Gospel of John*. The Antiochean offers a magnificent extended exhortation based 1 Cor. 3:11, combining the images of Christ as the Foundation and the Vine, as follows:

> Upon this then let us build, and let us be connected to this foundation, as a branch to a vine; and let there be no interval between us and Christ. For if there be any interval, immediately we perish. For the branch by its adherence draws in the richness, and the building stands because it is cemented together. Since, if it stand apart it perishes, having nothing whereon to support itself. Let us not then merely keep hold of Christ, but let us be cemented (*kollethomen*) to Him, for if we stand apart, we perish.[9]

In the same homily Chrysostom continues to expound lyrically on the theme of intimate unity between Christ and Christians. He writes:

> He [Christ] brings us into unity by means of many images . . . He is the Head, we are the body; . . . He is the Foundation, we the building; He the Vine, we the branches; He the Bridegroom, we the bride; He the Shepherd, we the sheep; He is the Way, we they who walk therein; again, we are the temple, He the Indweller (*enoikos*); He the First-begotten, we the brothers; He the Heir, we the co-heirs; He the Life, we the living; He the Resurrection, we those who rise; He the Light, we the illuminated. All these things indicate unity; and they allow no void interval, not even the smallest. For he who removes himself but a little, will go on till he has become very far distant.[10]

The other reference is a reflection on Jn 1:29 and Nathaniel's jubilant confession to Christ: "Rabbi, you are the Son of God, you are the King of Israel!" The Antiochean Father, appealing rhetorically to

his hearers, comments on Nathaniel's eager acclamation and connects it with one of his favorite themes – seeing Christ in the face of
the poor and the needy:

> Do you see how his soul is filled at once with exceeding joy, and em-
> braces Jesus with words? . . . How he leaps and dances with delight?
> So ought we also to rejoice, who have been thought worthy to know
> the Son of God; to rejoice, not in thought alone, but to show it also by
> our actions . . . When He is hungry, let us feed Him; when He is thirsty,
> let us give Him drink; though you give Him but a cup of cold water,
> He receives it; for He loves you, and to one who loves, the offerings
> of the beloved, though they be small, appear great.[11]

For Chrysostom it is the person of Christ who provides the secure ground of the unity of the Gospel. The written Gospels are many,
yet the Gospel is one, and is centered on Christ, His incarnation,
death and resurrection. For the Antiochean Father this same Gospel
was anticipated and proclaimed by human and angelic beings in
the Old and New Testaments:

> For the sum of the [written] Gospels had its origin hence, from God
> having become man and having been crucified and having risen. This
> gospel also Gabriel preached to the Virgin, this also the prophets
> [preached] to the world, this also the apostles all of them [preached
> to the world].[12]

In his work on the Epistle to the Galatians, Chrysostom presents
the same truth in another striking way. Does not Saint Paul state
that there can be no other Gospel except the one which he preached
(Gal. 1:7)? How then can there be four Gospels? St. John knew and
rejected the position of the Marcionites who had taken these words
of Saint Paul literally and had canonized only the Gospel of Luke,
and that expurgated of what Marcion regarded as Jewish elements.
Saint Paul, so Chrysostom counters, had in view not the number of
written Gospels but the discrepancy of doctrines circulating among
the Galatians. Saint John concludes:

> We assert, therefore, that, although a thousand Gospels [would be]
> written, if the contents of all were the same, they would still be one,
> and their unity no wise infringed by the number of writers . . . For the
> oneness of a work depends not on the number of its authors, but on
> the agreement or contradictoriness of its contents. Therefore it is clear
> that the four Gospels are one Gospel; for, as the four say the same
> thing, its oneness is preserved by the harmony of the contents and
> not impaired by the difference of persons.[13]

Saint John Chrysostom's words presuppose a perspective which is especially significant for the Orthodox theological tradition. The Gospel as a saving message is finally not to be tied in a literalistic way to the Bible alone or even to the Gospels. Rather it constitutes the central Christian good news which can be proclaimed and celebrated in its integrity by others means, too, such as the creed, the liturgical texts, and the writings of the Church Fathers.

THE POWER OF THE GOSPEL

The story of the expansion of Christianity in the ancient world is the story of a great triumph. The early Christian apostles and missionaries, as well as the later Church Fathers, such as Saint Ignatios of Antioch, Saint Justin Martyr, Saint Eirenaios, and others, were aglow with an amazing confidence that they possessed universal saving truth and had a sacred calling to proclaim and teach it to all. No human or demonic power could impede the progress of the Gospel of Christ. Even during the fourth century, when Arianism rocked the Church and when paganism was by no means dead, Christian authors seemed to be imbued with a spirit of confidence about the truth and power of the Gospel which they saw as the primary reasons behind its success.

For comparative purposes one might cite the case of Saint Athanasios. In his essay *On the Incarnation of the Word*, which C. S. Lewis has called a masterpiece, Saint Athanasios shines with confidence not only in expounding theological truth but also in demonstrating the power of that truth from historical evidence, including the ongoing triumph of Christianity during his own times. For example, after discussing the theological meaning of the resurrection, Saint Athanasios goes on to support its reality by pointing to what the risen Christ was doing in the very days of the Alexandrian Father:

> The Savior is working mightily among people; every day He is invisibly persuading numbers of people all over the world, both within and beyond the Greek-speaking world, to accept His faith and be obedient to His teaching. Can anyone, in face of this, still doubt that He has risen and lives, or rather that He is Himself the Life?[14]

Toward the end of his work, after a sustained exposition on the success of the Christian faith over against various opposing forces, Saint Athanasios sums up his whole argument with these words:

Since the Savior's advent in our midst, not only does idolatry no longer increase, but it is getting less and gradually ceasing to be. Similarly, not only does the wisdom of the Greeks no longer make any progress, but that which used to be is disappearing. And demons, so far from continuing to impose on people by their deceits and oracle-givings and sorceries, are routed by the sign of the cross, if they so much as try. On the other hand, while idolatry and everything else that opposes the faith of Christ is daily dwindling and weakening and falling, see, the Savior's teaching is increasing everywhere! Worship, then, the Savior, who is above all and mighty, even God the Word, and condemn those who are being defeated and made to disappear by Him. When the sun has come, darkness prevails no longer; any of it that may be left anywhere is driven away. So also, now that the divine epiphany of the Word of God has taken place, the darkness of idols prevails no more, and all parts of the world in every direction are enlightened by His teaching.[15]

We find similar sentiments in Saint John Chrysostom who may well have read Saint Athanasios. Saint John, too, is an heir of this glorious tradition of the triumph of Christianity. He is distinctly conscious of the victorious legacy of the Christian faith which he promotes with all his pastoral and rhetorical energies. He does not try to hide the failings of Christians. On the contrary, he untiringly seeks to expose and cure them like a skillful surgeon, to use one of his favorite images. However, neither the shortcomings of his flock, nor those of the Church at large, seem to have diminished either his assurance about the power of the Gospel or his ardor about preaching and teaching the good news. Just as in the case of Saint Athanasios, so also in the case of Saint John, we meet the glowing conviction that the success of the Christian faith is not the result of human talents or favorable historical circumstances, but rather the achievement of divine grace at work in history. Saint John associates this achievement very closely with the proclamation of the Gospel. In a striking passage in his fourth homily *In Praise of Saint Paul* he echoes the words of Saint Athanasios and uses the same image of light dispelling darkness to celebrate the resounding success of the Gospel:

Just as the rays of the rising sun put darkness into flight, and make the wild beasts seek shelter and rest, causing thieves to take to their heels, murderers to seek refuge in caves, pirates to disappear, . . . and everything becomes bright and luminous on earth and sea as the rays beam down from above the waters, mountains, villages, and cities; so, too, in the clear light of the Gospel as it was disseminated by Paul, error was banished, truth introduced in its place . . . and shameful practices associated with pagan rites in the temples came to a complete standstill . . . The flame of truth rose in splendor over the ashes and towered to the heavens.[16]

How did the Antiochean Father understand the workings of this divine power behind the triumph of the Gospel? In what ways was it evident in history and the lives of people? Answers to these questions are provided by Saint John's homilies on the Book of Acts and on 1 Corinthians.

As he contemplates the scope of Acts, Saint John sees God's power manifested in two essential events: the resurrection of Christ and the pentecostal gift of the Spirit. These two direct experiences of the apostles, the assurance that Christ lives and the infusion of the Spirit, empowered them to conquer the world. For Saint John the Book of Acts is, on the one hand, a great testimony to the truth of the resurrection. He writes:

> For this, in fact, is just what this Book is: a demonstration of the resurrection. This being once believed, the rest would come in due course. The subject then and entire scope of this Book, in the main, is just what I have said [the resurrection].[17]

On the other hand, it is also a Book of the Holy Spirit. The words and actions of the apostles are words and actions of the Holy Spirit. Just as Christ is the primary figure in the Gospels, so also the Spirit is the primary figure in the Book of Acts. Chrysostom states: "The Gospels, then, are a history of what Christ did and said; but the Acts, of what that other Comforter [the Holy Spirit] said and did."[18]

These twin foci of revelation, the resurrection of Christ and the gift of the Spirit, according to the Antiochean, are the sources of divine power at work in the proclamation of the Gospel, the mighty deeds of the apostles, and the whole triumph of Christianity. It is on these grounds that he argues in rhetorical fashion with unbelievers in his first homily on Acts. If Christ did not rise from the dead and so unequivocally convince his disciples, how could they possibly perform miracles, and most of all, the greatest miracle of the establishment of the Christian religion by poor and illiterate fishermen? It was not because of material wealth, human wisdom, or any such thing that the apostles prevailed. Objectors to Christianity must, even against their own will, admit that a divine power was at work in these men, for no human power could possibly account for such great results of mass conversions. In a later homily on Acts, Saint

John lifts up the example of the Apostle Peter speaking with great boldness to the crowds about the resurrection, the same Peter who formerly had cowered in fear at the question of the servant girl on the night of Jesus' passion. For Chrysostom only one explanation was adequate. Peter was now filled with the power of the Holy Spirit. "For wherever the Holy Spirit is present, He makes men of gold out of men of clay."[19]

The theme of the divine power behind the work of the apostles and their proclamation of the Gospel receives greater attention in Saint John's homilies on 1 Corinthians. The theme appears especially in the early chapters of this Epistle, where Saint Paul writes about the foolishness and weakness of the Gospel centered on the crucified Lord (1 Cor. 1:18-2:5). Saint Paul does not concede that the Gospel of the crucified Christ lacks either power or wisdom, but only that it appears to do so by the standards of the world. However, in Saint Paul's own view "Christ [is] the power of God and the wisdom of God" (1 Cor. 1:24). Nor does Saint Paul try to diminish the scandal of the cross. As he says, he himself came to Corinth, humanly speaking, in weakness, fear and trembling, resolved to know "nothing . . . except Jesus Christ and Him crucified" (1 Cor. 2:2). Yet, while not counting on rhetorical eloquence or philosophical wisdom, Saint Paul nevertheless preached the Gospel by the power of the Holy Spirit. The faith of the Corinthian Christians was grounded not in human skill or wisdom but in the power of God (1 Cor. 2:4-5).

In his third homily on 1 Corinthians, Chrysostom comments at length on 1 Cor. 1:18, where Saint Paul states that Christ sent him to preach the Gospel "not with eloquent wisdom, lest the cross of Christ be emptied of its power." According to Chrysostom, Saint Paul's intent behind these words was to deflate the pride of the Corinthians who argued and boasted about their spiritual gifts in a worldly manner. The fact that the apostles themselves did not claim human eloquence and wisdom, and that unlearned men established God's word in the world, is sufficient to check such arrogance and compel modesty. The reason that the apostles did not prove humanly wise was not because of any weakness of the gift but only that the Gospel, the heralding of the good news, might not be harmed or diminished in value. That Apollos was an eloquent Christian shows that God embraces everyone and does not discriminate against the learned of the world. Nevertheless, the basic fact remains that the apostles were what the Book of Acts states of them: "uneducated and common men" (*agrammatoi kai idiotai*, Acts 4:13).[20]

But what of the Apostle Paul? Was he unlearned, too? Here Saint John somewhat presses the point. Let no one say that even Paul was humanly wise, at least not in comparison with such philosophers as Plato. Saint John tells how he once had heard a Christian debating in a ludicrous way with a pagan about Paul and Plato. While the pagan argued that Paul was hardly educated as compared to Plato, the Christian erroneously claimed that Paul was more eloquent than the great philosopher. Thus, the argument was won by the pagan. For Chrysostom, however, that Christian's point should have been the opposite of what it was because, if Paul was indeed unlearned and yet overcame Plato in results, the victory was brilliant. It showed that "the Gospel was the result not of human wisdom, but of the grace of God." The Antiochean sings the praises of the unpolished and illiterate apostles in order to underscore the supernatural power (*hyper physin ischyn*) behind their glorious achievement:

> The fisherman, the tentmaker, the publican, the ignorant, the unlettered, coming from the far distant country of Palestine, and having beaten off their own ground the philosophers, the masters of oratory, the skilful debaters, alone prevailed against them in a short space of time; in the midst of perils; against the opposition of peoples and kings, the striving of nature itself, length of time, the vehement resistance of inveterate custom, demons in arms, the devil in battle array and stirring up all, kings, rulers, peoples, nations, cities, barbarians, Greeks, philosophers, orators, sophists, historians, laws, tribunals, diverse kinds of punishments, deaths innumerable and of all sorts.[21]

How could the apostles think of and attempt such great things? If they had so little courage when Christ was with them during his earthly ministry, how could they take on the whole world if they knew that He was now dead? Would they not say to themselves, if our Master could not save Himself, how could He now defend us? From all this it is evident, so Chrysostom concludes, that Christ arose, spoke to the apostles and infused them with the courage to do things that they could not have imagined. Christ's resurrection is the great proof (*megiste apodeixis*) of the divine power behind the apostolic proclamation (*kerygma*) and mission.[22]

THE RESPONSE TO THE GOSPEL

An assessment of Chrysostom's understanding of the nature and power of the Gospel would be incomplete without consideration of the indispensable element of the human response to the good news. Saint John possessed an unshakable confidence in the divine power behind the evangelistic mission of the Church. Yet, according to the Antiochean Father, the grace of the Spirit neither operates by compulsion, nor will it penetrate stony hearts. Divine grace requires the synergy of human freedom. The power of the word of God is released in the act of reception by responsive souls. The proclamation of the Gospel takes hold and bears rich fruit where it finds fertile ground.

The most important aspect of the human response to the Gospel is, according to Chrysostom, the act of personal faith. A true, living faith, for Saint John, is "a great blessing . . . [which] arises from glowing feelings, great love, and a fervent soul; it makes us truly wise, it hides our human meanness, and leaving reasonings beneath, it philosophizes about things in heaven."[23]

Chrysostom turns time and again to the theme of faith. The first characteristic of faith, the mother of all good things, is its appropriate disposition in grasping the basic mysteries of revelation. Truths which transcend human reasoning, such as the incarnation, the virgin birth, the power of the cross, the heavenly birth of which Jesus spoke to Nicodemus, and the like, require faith alone. To try to offer rational explanations of these and similar mysteries would be to invite derision, not because of the weakness of these truths themselves but because heavenly matters cannot be brought under the scrutiny of earthly reasonings.[24] The human mind is useful in interpreting and applying revelation, exactly as the Antiochean does in his homilies. Nevertheless, human reasonings left alone are like "webs of spiders," weaving such madness as to say sometimes that there is nothing real in the world and that all things are contrary to what they appear to be.[25] The second characteristic of faith is its capacity to receive God's gifts, such as righteousness revealed through the preaching of the Gospel (Rom. 1:17). This righteousness, so Saint John states, is not [our] own, but that of God . . . "for you do not achieve it by toilings and labors, but you receive it from above, contributing one thing only from your own store, believing."[26] Here again we catch a clear view of Chrysostom's underlying supposition, despite his emphasis on moral works, that Christians are justified and saved by grace through faith (cf. Eph. 2:8-10).

An example of Saint John's understanding of the synergistic relationship between grace and faith is his interpretation of Jn 1:12:

"But to all who received Him, who believed in His name, He gave power to become children of God." Chrysostom comments that, whether slave or free, Greek or barbarian, male or female, young or old, rich or poor, all are deemed worthy of the same privilege through faith. Faith and the grace of the Holy Spirit remove inequality and stamp all believers with a royal seal. What can equal the mercy of Christ who shared His very nature with publicans, sorcerers, slaves, and those suffering with many ills? Yet Christ works not by compulsion but requires free will (*autoexousion*). Christ has done His part, He has made the marriage, has prepared the table, and has sent messengers to call us. It falls to us, both before and after baptism, to supply faith, and not only faith but also zeal and earnestness of a pure life.[27] Chrysostom is aware of no tension or contrast between faith and good works; both are vital elements in one's response to grace. But faith is primary.

Another aspect of the human response in appropriating the power and blessings of the Gospel is, according to Chrysostom, serious and regular engagement with the Scriptures. To enter into one of the Gospels is to enter a city of gold; it is to hear the words not of an earthly king but of the Lord of angels.[28] Hearing and reading the message of the Scriptures with appropriate receptivity has the power to lift human beings from earth to heaven.

In a particular way, Saint John concentrates on this theme of the earnest hearing and reading of Scripture in his first homily on the Gospel of Saint John. Chrysostom first calls for zealous and earnest attention to God's word. If people long to know what is going on at the palace, what the king has said or done, or what thoughts he has about his subject, how much more should they be concerned about Christ's message which He brings from the Father. The attention required is not for one day but for all of life. It is not merely external, requiring orderly behavior. It is above all internal, the hearing of the soul, requiring a deep silence which the Antiochean Father elsewhere calls "mystical silence" (*mystike sige*).[29]

A second element in the transforming reception of the word of God is spiritual cleansing. The words of the Gospel can mean nothing to him who has no desire to be freed from a "swinish life." Christ instructed the disciples not to give holy things to the dogs, nor to cast pearls before swine (Mt. 7:6). Nothing is sweeter nor more precious than the words of Scripture (Ps. 19:10). Yet this is true only for those who are in good spiritual health. The cleansing and healing power of God's word is given to receptive souls by the power of the Holy Spirit. Where receptive souls gather to read and hear the Bible, that place becomes a "house of spiritual healing" (*iatreion pneumatikon*).[30] The Spirit Himself burns away the evil elements, making hard and stubborn hearts soft and yielding to divine grace.

A third element is a firm resolve or earnest will (*espoudasmene boulesis*) which leaves behind the desires and ways of the multitude. Armed with earnest will, it is possible, not in five days but in one moment, to change the course of one's whole life, even to change suddenly like the robber on the cross.[31] Evil and wickedness are grounded in free will and distort human beings into wilful beasts and many-faced monsters.[32] But let no one despair. If human fierceness (*agriotes*) is caused by choice and not by nature, then the words of Scripture empowered by the grace of the Spirit can tame a human being far more effectively than human words can tame a beast. Saint John exhorts:

> Let then the man who despairs of himself. . . come continually to this house of healing (*iatreion*), let him hear at all times the laws of the Spirit, and on retiring home let him write down in his mind the things which he has heard; so shall his hopes be good and his confidence great, as he feels his progress by experience. For when the devil sees the law of God written in the soul, and the heart become tablets to write it on, he will not approach any more.[33]

A final aspect of the response to the Gospel is related to society at large and to the witness of Christians within it. Saint John was concerned not only about the impact of the Gospel upon believers but also about its success in terms of the Church's mission in the world. The stress that Saint John places on this theme can hardly be exaggerated. The frequency and manner with which he returns to it shows that Christianity in his day was still involved in a widespread confrontation with paganism over the true "philosophy" of life that can be shown only by persuasive conduct. In his homilies on the early chapters of 1 Corinthians, Saint John develops a continuous case demonstrating the power of the Gospel. It is there that he also builds up a series of appeals to Christians on the theme of the evangelistic value of their lives. He cries out to his hearers:

> Let us astound them [the pagans] by our way of life rather than by words. For this is the main battle (*megale mache*), this is the unanswerable argument, the argument from conduct. For though we give ten thousand precepts of philosophy in words, if we do not exhibit a life

better than theirs, the gain is nothing.[34]

If the Gospel has had such amazing success since the days of the apostles, Chrysostom asks, why do not all believe in his own day? The answer rests with the quality of life Christians display. The Antiochean candidly exposes and censures the failings of Christians. He comments that in his day "a dark night" (*batheia nyx*) seemed to prevail among Christians with respect to both teaching and life.[35] For him the greatest critique of Christianity was not so much a good pagan as a corrupt Christian. The sharpest censure of the contemporary Church is perhaps to be found in his reflections on 1 Corinthians, chapter 14. As he contemplates the vigor of early Christian worship and of the charismatic phenomena reported by Saint Paul, Chrysostom bewails the conditions of the Church of his own days. Now, he laments, the Church has only empty signs and memorials of those things. He continues:

> The Church now is like a woman who has fallen from her former prosperity and in many respects retains the symbols only of that ancient good estate; displaying indeed the cases and boxes of her golden ornaments but bereft of her wealth. . . And I say not this concerning [special] gifts, for it would be nothing terrible if it were this only, but also life and virtue.[36]

These words, however, are not a counsel of resignation and despair. They are part of a prophetic critique based on the conviction that God's word is to be preached to all and that it is the responsibility of the hearers to pay heed. The personal failures of Christians and the shortcomings of the Church challenged Saint John all the more to preach and teach the good news of Christ with fervor and urgency, trusting that the grace of the Spirit would do its invincible work in willing and receptive hearts.

In his seventh homily on 1 Corinthians Chrysostom sums up his long and detailed exposition in demonstration of the triumph of the Gospel during the early centuries. It is clear that he had given much thought to the ongoing encounter between Christianity and culture. He wanted Christians to be keenly aware of this struggle and to be knowledgeable, confident and effective in their daily interactions with pagans on behalf of the cause of Christianity. It may be instructive to enumerate his major points by way of conclusion: 1) the overcoming of the tyranny of ancient custom through a new religion; 2) the courage of the apostles in the face of many perils; 3) the requirement of higher moral standards; 4) the scandalous nature of the Christian message concerning a crucified God; 5) the persuasion of the masses to truths that even philosophers like Plato could not comprehend; 6) the promise of future rather than immediate rewards, and 7) the fulfillment of Christ's prophecy that the gates of hell would not prevail against the Church. But Saint John also admonished Christians to convince pagans by the quality of their lives: "Of all these things then . . . let us speak to the Gentiles, and again, let us show them the evidence of our lives, that by both means we ourselves may be saved and they drawn over by our means to the glory of God."[37]

Receiving and enjoying the blessings of the Gospel, Christians ought to celebrate all of time as a festival. The Antiochean Father, rightly surnamed "Chrysostomos" ("Golden-mouthed"), offers to all these golden words:

> The whole of time is a festival for Christians, because of the abundance of good things that have been given. . . The Son of God was made man for you; He freed you from death and called you to a kingdom. Therefore, you who have obtained and are still obtaining such things, how can it be less than your duty to keep the feast all your life? Let no one then be downcast about poverty, and disease, and craft of enemies. For it is a festival, even the whole of our time. For this reason Paul said: "Rejoice in the Lord always, again I say, rejoice."[38]

NOTES

[1] See *The Homilies of Saint John Chrysostom on the Gospel of Saint Matthew, Homily 1.1-3.* For the convenience of the general reader, the English translation for all the cited works of Chrysostom in this chapter, except for his *In Praise of Saint Paul*, is that of *The Nicene and Post-Nicene Fathers*, edited by Philip Schaff and reprinted by Wm B. Eerdmans Publishing Company over the past several decades. I have consulted the original Greek in the series edited by P. Christou and Th. Zisis, *The Greek Fathers of the Church* and published in Thessalonike.

[2] *On Matthew, Homily 1.13.*

[3] *On John, Homily 18.4.*

[4] *On John, Homily 37.1.*

[5] *On Romans, Homily 1* (Rom. 1:1).

[6] *On Matthew, Homily 1.4.*

[7] *Ibid.*

[8] *On Matthew, Homily 1.6.*

[9] *On First Corinthians, Homily 8.7.*

[10] *Ibid.*

[11] *On John, Homily 20.3.*

[12] *On First Corinthians, Homily 38.2.*

[13] *On Galatians, Chapter 1* (Gal. 1:7). Chrysostom's work on Galatians is arranged according to commentary notes rather than developed homilies.

[14] Saint Athanasios, *On the Incarnation of the Word,* translated and edited by a Religious of C.S.M.V. with an Introduction by C. S. Lewis (London, 1953), Chap. 30, p. 61.

[15] *Ibid., Chap. 55, pp. 93-94.*

[16] St. John Chrysostom, *In Praise of St. Paul,* translated by Thomas Halton (Boston, 1963), pp. 69-70.

[17] *On Acts, Homily 1.*

[18] *Ibid.*

[19] *On Acts, Homily 4.*

[20] *On First Corinthians, Homily 3.7-8.*

[21] *On First Corinthians, Homily 3.8.*

[22] *On First Corinthians, Homily 4.8.*

[23] *On John, Homily 63.3.*

[24] *On John, Homilies 4.2* and *24.3.*

[25] *On First Corinthians 5.4.*

[26] *On Romans, Homily 2.*

[27] *On John, Homily 10.2-3.*

[28] *On Matthew, Homily 1.17.*

[29] *Ibid.*

[30] *On John, Homily 2.11.*

[31] *On John, Homily 1.5.*

[32] *On John, Homily 2.11.*

[33] *On John, Homily 3.1.*

[34] *On First Corinthians, Homily 3.9.*

[35] *On First Corinthians, Homily 4.11*

[36] *On First Corinthians, Homily 36.7.*

[37] *On First Corinthians, Homily 7.20.*

[38] *On First Corinthians, Homily 15.6.*

CHAPTER TWO

The Gospel in the Orthodox Tradition

The aim of this chapter is to present an understanding of the Gospel in a comprehensive Orthodox perspective including worship, preaching, teaching, theology, and spirituality. Three initial remarks may provide a helpful context for consideration of the topic. First, the adjective "Orthodox" is meant not merely as a socio-cultural religious designation but as a referent to the classic and universal Christian tradition. It applies not only to the Orthodox with a capital "O" but to all who regard themselves as orthodox with a small "o," that is to say, those who are committed to a way of life and thinking, and a way of teaching and worship, which reflect authentic Christianity everywhere and in all times. In this sense, to be Orthodox necessarily implies to honor Holy Scripture as the supreme record of God's self-revelation and to cherish the Gospel of Christ as the very soul of the Church.[1]

Second, authentic Orthodoxy has nothing to do with rigidity, narrowness, legalism, formalism, and ritualism. Rather it is signaled by life, catholicity, love, integrity, and prayerfulness. Authentic Orthodoxy fosters unity which does not stifle variety, and rejoices in variety which does not injure unity. But vitality and creativity also require grounding and direction. Thus Orthodoxy seeks to express its dynamic coherence of life and thought through what Thomas Torrance has aptly called "fidelity to truth" and "respect for mystery."[2] Fidelity to truth is being rightly related to the Gospel of the apostolic tradition – the full truth of God's saving work through Christ and the Spirit, lived, celebrated, and proclaimed by the Church. Respect for mystery entails reverent recognition that the living God transcends doctrines. As important as doctrines are for the explication of Christian truth and the maintenance of Christian unity, they are nevertheless only pointers to the mystery of Christ and the mystery of the Holy Trinity to which the Church and each Christian relate existentially by faith and grace.

Third, the Orthodox people themselves have not always lived up to their own ideals. Church history tells of the faithfulness of the martyrs, the radiance of the saints, the suffering of the rank-and-file believers. But it also scores the presumptuousness of the powerful, the bickerings of the contentious, the divisiveness of the proud. Every age has had its saints and sinners; every generation has seen righteousness and wickedness. There has been no time when the light of the Gospel did not shine, nor a time when God's truth has not been suppressed. And the struggle continues. Today Orthodoxy is striving to define and affirm its true character in the encounter with the modern and post-modern world. The contest is hardly engaged in a clear way as Orthodoxy meets the onrush of Western pop culture in traditional Orthodox lands, the chaotic promises of democracy in countries behind the former iron curtain, and the secular pluralism of the West where Orthodoxy has taken root.

However, the good news of salvation abides and has always thrived in challenging times, provided it is faithfully received and genuinely proclaimed. As Orthodoxy stands at the beginning of the third millennium of its history, an enormously opportune time – a *kairos* in the biblical sense – presents itself for reflection on its nature and mission. Such reflection cannot but be centered on the apostolic Gospel concerning Christ who "is the same yesterday and today and forever" (Heb. 13:8). For no other foundation can suffice than that laid by the apostles – Jesus Christ himself, crucified and risen (cf. 1 Cor. 3:11). The New Testament plainly testifies that Christ is the essential content and invincible power of the Gospel which is called, in the language of the Epistle to the Colossians, the word of truth, the mystery hidden for ages but now made manifest, God's mystery of Christ, in whom are hid all the treasures of knowledge, and who is our hope of glory (Col. 1:5,26-27; 2:2-3). The New Testament also bears clear witness that the fullness of the mystery Christ embraces His Church as the historical and mystical body of Christ, vivified and guided by the Holy Spirit (1 Cor. 10:16-17; 12:4-31). The Epistle to the Ephesians notably exalts the mystery of the Church, which it celebrates as the new household of God, the redeemed universal humanity, built on the foundation of the apostles and prophets, with Christ himself as the cornerstone – the Church growing in maturity and unity, and manifesting the treasures of God's blessings (Eph. 2: 19-22; 3:4-10). The Gospel of Christ, which is the foundation of Christian existence, should be attested by all interrelated and interactive aspects of the Church's life – its worship, preaching and teaching, theology and spirituality, as well as daily practice and administration.

THE GOSPEL IN WORSHIP

The attacks by critics before and after Harnack against the externalism of Orthodox worship as mere ritual are well-known and still crop up in Protestant circles. They are partly justified insofar as they refer to ignorant and superficial practices by Orthodox Christians. They are largely misplaced and pernicious insofar as they express a deficient view of Christianity and the biblical way of the adoration of God. It is not my intention here to launch into a defense of the liturgical, sacramental, and yes, material, aspects of Christian worship. The Book of Acts and the Letters of Paul abundantly testify that to be a Christian has meant from the outset to engage an ecclesial praxis of hearing and accepting the Gospel, of repenting and being baptized, of celebrating the Lord's Supper and sharing in the entire communal life of the apostolic Church. After all the studies on early Christian worship, it is no longer possible to separate word from sacrament, the proclamation of the crucified and risen Lord from the bread and wine of the Eucharist. Rather it is now the case that a sound biblical ecclesiology must take into account the constitutive reality of the Church, the creative power and authority of tradition, the sacramental efficacy of Baptism and Eucharist, as well as the communion of the saints.

The Gospel in the worship of the early Church is reflected in numerous hymnological passages of the New Testament itself, such as the prologue of the Gospel of John, Philippians 2:6-11, and the doxologies of the Book of Revelation. To these should be added the sacramental passages of John 6, Romans 6, and 1 Corinthians 10 and 11, as well as much of 1 Peter which resounds with baptismal overtones. All of these texts attest to the liturgical confessions of faith pertaining to the good news of God's saving work through Christ. The liturgical tradition in subsequent centuries developed extraordinary riches in the hymnological presentation of the Gospel. Most Christians may be familiar with some of these treasures of Christian antiquity still used in Orthodox worship. One of these is the Trisagion Prayer – "Holy God, Holy Mighty, Holy Immortal: have mercy on us" – a doxological song to the Holy Trinity with a penitential element echoing the Prophet Isaiah's experience and sentiments according to Isaiah 6. Another is the hymn entitled "Only-Begotten Son" which proclaims the incarnation, death and resurrection of Christ and exalts Him as "one of the Holy Trinity."[3] The basic eight-week hymnological cycle according to eight musical modes which has developed over centuries in the Orthodox Church now constitutes a huge collection of hymns contained in the liturgical book called *Parakletike*, meaning Book of Intercession and Consolation. Especially the hymns for Saturday Vespers and Sunday Matins, called *Anastasima*, that is, "Resurrection Hymns," set forth the Gospel of the death and resurrection of Christ with a certain concentration going back to the emphasis of the great Apostle Paul.

Here is a medley of *Anastasima* from the Matins of the first musical mode which praise the death as well as the resurrection of Christ, the two being held together in the Orthodox tradition:[4]

Though the tomb was sealed by a stone and soldiers guarded Your pure body, You arose, O Savior, on the third day, giving life to the world. Therefore, O Giver of life, the heavenly powers praise You: glory to Your Resurrection, O Christ, glory to Your kingdom, glory to Your plan of redemption, O loving God.

You were nailed upon the cross willingly, O Merciful One, and were placed in a grave as dead, O Giver of life. You trampled the power of death by Your death, O Mighty One. The gates of hell trembled before You and You raised with You those who were dead for ages, O loving God.

As God You rose in glory from the grave, raising the world with You. All mortal nature praises You as God; death is destroyed and Adam dances, O Master, while Eve, now freed from bondage, rejoices saying: It is You, O Christ, who gives resurrection to all.

Not infrequently these doxological hymns, evangelical in content and spirit, contain practical exhortations. The Easter service of Matins explodes with countless lyrical praises to the crucified and risen Lord. Yet even on Easter night references to the practical implications of the saving events are not lacking. The following hymns of the Easter service may serve as an illustration:

The angels in heaven praise Your resurrection, O Christ, our Savior. Make us on earth also worthy, with pure hearts, to glorify You.

O divine, beloved, and sweet Voice! You, O Christ, have truly promised that You would be with us to the end of all ages. Wherefore, we,
the faithful, rejoice, holding these Your words as an anchor of hope.

This is the day of the resurrection. Let us be glorious in splendor for
the festival and let us embrace one another. Let us speak even to those
who hate us and forgive all things in the resurrection. And so let us
sing: Christ is risen from the dead, by death trampling upon death,
and granting life to those in the tombs.

This liturgical proclamation of the Gospel is not restricted to Saint
Paul's focus on the death and resurrection of Christ. It takes into
comprehensive view Jesus' whole ministry. The basic structure of
the Orthodox liturgical year is anchored in twelve major feasts, most
of which have to do with the key events of the ministry of Jesus as
recorded in the Gospels, namely, the events of the annunciation, the
birth of Jesus, His baptism, transfiguration, death and resurrection,
ascension, gift of the Spirit, and second coming in glory. Thus the
liturgical year itself encompasses the entire life of Christ from con-
ception to his glorious return as Judge.

Moreover, the periods of the Great Lent and Easter seasons have
their separate hymn books which are thoroughly biblical and evangelical. The Lenten hymn book called *Triodion* (literally, "Book of the
Three Odes") features the following topics and themes from the
Gospels: The Parable of the Publican and the Pharisee, the Prodigal
Son, the Last Judgment, Jesus's call to mutual forgiveness, the confession of Jesus as the Christ and Son of God, the veneration of the
cross, and the triumphal entry of Jesus into Jerusalem. The Pentecostal hymn book called *Pentecostarion* ("Book of Pentecost") embraces the period from Easter to Pentecost and celebrates, in addition to Easter, the following events: the confession of Thomas, the
women myrrh-bearers coming to the empty tomb, the healing of the
paralytic of John 5, Jesus' meeting with the Samaritan woman, the
healing of the blind man of John 9, the ascension of the Lord, and
Pentecost itself. Each of these biblical events and topics becomes the
center of liturgical attention and is proclaimed as part of the saving
work of Christ by means of virtually hundreds of hymns which both
recount and expand on the meaning of these salvific events. The
above liturgical books, together with the daily lectionary, provide a
comprehensive account of Jesus' ministry, reflecting a time when,
without the benefit of printing and general education, the people of
God depended primarily on worship for their knowledge and cel-

ebration of the good news of Christ.

In addition, the liturgical presentation of the Gospel is not limited to the New Testament but comprehends the saving message of the Bible as a whole. Rich liturgical traditions have developed around numerous biblical witnesses of the Old and New Testaments who served God's purposes in the history of salvation. These include not only the major figures such as Adam and Eve, Abraham and Sarah, Moses, King David, the Prophets, the Virgin Mary, John the Baptist, Peter and Paul, and the Twelve Apostles, but also lesser known figures such as Job, the Patriarch Joseph, the seven Maccabean martyrs, the co-workers of Paul such as Timothy and Silas, and the seventy apostles. All these are esteemed as saints by the Orthodox tradition, which affirms the active presence of grace in the Old Testament, not only the New. Hymns and prayers bring before the worshipers the total scope of God's dealings with human beings, exalting especially God's great acts of deliverance which Scripture calls the marvelous deeds of God. Thereby the liturgical proclamation of the good news is linked with the larger saving message of the Bible as the word of God and prompts the worshipers to engage the entire horizon of the biblical tradition.

For the Orthodox, the most profound liturgical presentation of the Gospel is the Holy Eucharist or Divine Liturgy itself, the central act of worship in the Orthodox Church. The Liturgy is understood as a continuation of the Last Supper in which Jesus, by means of solemn words and actions, anticipated His redemptive death and resurrection. The Apostle Paul is a firm witness of the eucharistic tradition deriving "from the Lord," who commanded: "Do this in remembrance of me." And Saint Paul adds: "For as often as you eat this bread and drink this cup, you proclaim the Lord's death until he comes" (See 1 Cor. 11:23-26).

Whatever the historical and exegetical complexities of the New Testament eucharistic texts, these texts must be taken as they stand in their canonical context. The innocent reader perceives that they relate to the heart of the Gospel and that they presuppose a realistic view of the efficacy of the eucharistic celebration. Biblical scholarship has long taught us that the essential meaning of biblical remembrance (*anamnesis*) has to do with making present the reality of the saving events in the context of communal prayer and worship. In antiquity the ritual acts among Jews and Christians were not taken as merely figurative, a modern notion, but rather they were seen as bearing divine powers and having decisive consequences, according to the words of Saint Paul. Just as the preaching of the word of God carries intrinsic power and transformative impact on receptive hearers, so also, and indeed more so, the ritual acts of Baptism and the Eucharist, in the context of the Church's living faith and the power of the Holy Spirit, make present the saving reality and blessings of the death and resurrection of the Lord. Surely the Apostle Paul did not view the Lord's Supper as merely metaphorical in 1 Cor. 11, any more than he viewed Baptism as figurative in Rom. 6. The Gospel of John which declares that true worship is "in spirit and truth" (Jn 4:24) also contains references to Baptism and the Eucharist as determining one's entry into the kingdom (Jn 3:5) and one's sharing in the divine life of the Incarnate Lord (Jn 6:52-58).

Seen from this perspective, the Orthodox Eucharist is not only a proclamation but also an actualization of the good news of Christ and his saving work. An inspired preacher can proclaim the Gospel with words, voice inflections and gestures, impacting the congregation with the power of God's word. A prayerful liturgist not only proclaims but acts out the contents of the Gospel, actualizing its blessings amidst God's people. The Liturgy constitutes the most profound *anamnesis* of the events of the Gospel and their efficacious power. The Liturgy is the enactment of the Gospel through sacramental action.

The word "sacramental" in the Orthodox tradition means something different than the legal notions of sacrament in the Western medieval tradition. The very word "sacrament" does not sit well within Orthodox vocabulary, which employs the biblical term "mystery" (*mysterion*) to refer to the central liturgical acts. According to the Orthodox understanding, the efficacy of the sacred mysteries is entirely the work of the Holy Spirit in the context of living faith, and is not dependent on the precision of a particular formula of words and actions. The invocation of the Holy Spirit (*epiklesis*) in the consecration prayer of the Liturgy of Saint John Chrysostom, a prayer directed to the Father, reads as follows:

> Once again we offer to You (God the Father) this rational (*logiken*) worship without the shedding of blood, and we ask, pray, and entreat You: Send down Your Holy Spirit upon us and upon these gifts here presented. And make this bread the precious Body of Your Christ. Amen. And that which is in this cup the precious Blood of Your Christ. Amen. Changing (*metabalon*) them by Your Holy Spirit. Amen. Amen. Amen.[5]

The same prayer offers thanks to God the Father for all the work of salvation but especially for the redemptive work of Christ. The centerpiece is the John 3:16, which is recited in the consecration prayer as a prayer to the Father: "You so loved Your world that you gave Your only-begotten Son so that whoever believes in Him should not perish, but have eternal life" (*Liturgy of Saint John Chrysostom*).

The Gospel in Preaching and Teaching

The presentation of the Gospel in preaching and teaching is an immensely important ministry. The great commission of Mt. 28:16-20 calls for making disciples not only by baptizing them but also by catechizing them regarding Jesus' commandments. Among the Church Fathers for example, Saint Basil taught that the aim of preaching is to bring people under the lordship of Christ, to draw them into the life of the Church, and to build up their personal lives in the likeness of the new creation in Christ. The ministry of evangelization applies not only to outsiders but also to Christians themselves. Evangelization lifts up and exalts the person of Christ, heightening the awareness of hearers not only to the blessings but also to the demands of the Gospel such as to repent of their sins, to seek first the kingdom and its righteousness, to practice self-denial and to serve others in His name. Sound evangelization implies constant alertness regarding integrity and renewal in all expressions of the life of the Church, the primary antidote against the all-too-human tendency toward routine, professionalism and ritualism. Worship in spirit and truth cannot occur apart from evangelization through preaching and teaching. An integral part of the Liturgy itself is the reading of Holy Scripture, the preaching of God's word, and its practical application in the lives of God's people. The prayer for the lectionary lesson in the Liturgy of Saint John Chrysostom asks the Lord to grant not only understanding of the Gospel message but also obedience to his commandments:

> Shine within our hearts, loving Master, the pure light of Your divine knowledge and open the eyes of our minds that we may comprehend the message of your gospel. Instill in us also reverence for your blessed commandments, so that having conquered sinful desires we may pursue a spiritual way of life, thinking and doing all those things that are pleasing to You.

But what does it mean to present the Gospel in preaching and teaching? How is the Gospel understood, interpreted, and expounded? In Protestantism the main preoccupation is with Saint Paul's teaching concerning justification by faith and not by works of the Law. The Reformers took their stand on the principle of justification by faith as opposed to that of meritorious works. Justification by faith alone – the word "alone" being a considerable addition to the Pauline expression – became Protestantism's defining doctrinal position from which ensued the catch phrases "Scripture alone," "Christ alone," "Gospel alone," and "me and God's word alone," leading not infrequently to "my interpretation alone." The strength of traditional Protestantism is the unremitting focus on Scripture, the Gospel, as well as personal faith, concerning which Protestants have taught much to Roman Catholic and Orthodox Christians. The weakness lies in ecclesiology, doctrinal coherence, and a polemical overemphasis on the "alone" which, though justifiable as a corrective in the medieval context, appears reductionistic as an interpretive key to the witness of the whole Bible in its own historical and theological context.

Whatever ways these matters are argued, the point is that the definition and presentation of the Gospel in preaching and teaching is inescapably influenced by one's confessional background and doctrinal position. Strictly speaking, there is no such thing as pure "grace alone," "Scripture alone," "Christ alone," or "faith alone," whether in antiquity or in modern times. Revelation did not occur in a vacuum apart from the receptivity of human subjects. Scripture as a canonical entity developed over many centuries, not without disputes of course, and it did so in conjunction with decisions involving ecclesial tradition, doctrine, and councils. Christ and the Gospel were promoted by His followers, not by His enemies, nor by some other objective observers. And what is faith apart from reason and conduct? However it may be perceived, truth itself, including that which is perceived from the perspective of the "alone" language, is grounded in community. Thus all Christians encounter one another as communities of faith. They are called by Christ and the Spirit to dialogue with mutual respect and faithful openness for the sake of the glory of Christ and the potential unity of the Church.

The Orthodox bear testimony to their own stream of tradition, which is largely unencumbered by the dichotomies of Scripture and tradition, word and sacrament, Gospel and law, grace and will, faith and works, faith and reason.[6] In the Orthodox tradition all these elements have been held together as parts of the same truth in which

unquestionably the revealed initiative and saving action belong to
God, yet require the positive response of human beings. The sovereign efficacy of grace is confessed, while the active role of the receptive will is recognized. The primacy of faith is declared, while the
necessity of works according to which believers will be judged is
affirmed. The supreme authority of Scripture is unquestioned, but
the obvious necessity of its discerning use and normative interpretation is acknowledged.

For the Orthodox the authoritative witnesses to the presentation
of the Gospel in preaching and teaching are the great Church Fathers, who were preeminently preachers of God's word and biblical
theologians. The most notable example is John Chrysostom (ca. 350-
407), the man with the "golden mouth" (*Chrysostomos*), whose works
glow with immense zeal for the Scriptures as well as with focus on
their practical application. Chrysostom's favorite apostle was Saint
Paul, in praise of whom he wrote several homilies[7] and on whose
entire corpus of letters he bequeathed to us valuable commentaries.
Paul was his supreme example of a fearless preacher of the Gospel
who, according to Chrysostom, took up the cross and proclaimed
the good news in the face of the gates of hell itself. Saint John
preached the message of Scripture with equal courage and died in
exile on account of his uncompromising witness to the word of God.[8]

Although Chrysostom nowhere discusses the Gospel as a separate subject, for him the good news in its widest scope is associated
with the entire Scriptures, Old and New Testaments, as the revelation of divine truth.[9] But in particular the four canonical Gospels bear
testimony to the supreme source of truth and heavenly blessings,
including remission of sins, righteousness, sanctification, inheritance
of heaven, and intimate closeness to the Son of God. These blessings
are undeserved gifts on account of God's great love for humanity. To
quote him: "For [it is] not by laboring and sweating, not by fatigue
and suffering, but merely as being beloved of God [that], we received
what we have received."[10] While he is aware of certain apparent discrepancies among the Gospels, he grounds their veracity in their
agreement on the essentials of Jesus' ministry, the basis of Christian
life and proclamation (*ten zoen kai to kerygma*). What are these essentials? According to Saint John, they are the incarnation, the miracles
of Jesus, His death and resurrection, His ascension and glorious return as Judge, His ethical commandments, and the conviction that
He is the true Son sharing the same essence with the Father.[11]

For Chrysostom, the very heart of the Gospel is the living Christ, His saving work, and the blessings He bestows upon those who receive Him. Along with an apostolic boldness about possessing the truth, one meets in Saint John a call to proclaim and teach the Gospel to all. While he hides the failings neither of individual Christians nor of the Church as an institution,[12] he shines with the conviction that the success of the Christian faith is not the result of human talents or favorable historical circumstances but is rather the achievement of divine grace at work in history. The power of the Gospel derives from the risen Christ and the Pentecostal gift of the Spirit. And the victorious legacy of Christianity is linked to the proclamation of the Gospel. The model preacher is the Apostle Paul, whose proclamation of the Gospel Saint John exalts as the rising of the sun dispelling the darkness from the world.[13]

Chrysostom has been erroneously accused of moralizing. It is true that he untiringly calls for practical application of the demands of the gospel, with recurrent attention to the needs of the poor, and he is routinely critical of the temptations of city life such as the chariot races and the theater. He is also the heir of classical education based on earnest will and disciplined effort toward character formation, over against other philosophical and religious currents advocating blind fate and determinism. Nevertheless, it would be erroneous to see his moral emphasis as "righteousness by works." A contextual and holistic reading of Chrysostom prove him to be a preacher and pastor with a balanced biblical vision pertaining to family life, occupations, social relationships, and civic duties. After all, he could not forget that the Master commanded his followers to be doers, not merely hearers, of his words. He read the Gospel of Matthew as well as that of John, and the Book of James as well as that of Galatians. In fact a close reading of Galatians shows that the problem in the Galatian churches was not "moralizing" but "Judaizing," as Chrysostom is quite aware. Thus Saint Paul's contrast between faith and works pertained to the ritual obligations of the Mosaic Law, notably circumcision (Gal. 2:3; 5:2-3,6,11-12; 6:12-13), not to good works, which Paul everywhere deems necessary for Christians under pain of God's judgment.[14]

Chrysostom, like the Eastern Fathers generally, envisions a synergistic relationship between grace and will, faith and works, with the accent unerringly falling on grace and faith. In the Orthodox tradition the notion of synergy implies no more and no less than what the biblical idea of covenant requires. The initiative and saving activity belong to God, while the free and active response of human beings is also required, indeed demanded. For Chrysostom this response included a number of things such as faith, the receptive hearing of the soul, firm resolve, regular reading of the Scriptures, inner cleansing, and right conduct. According to him, Christ has done His part – He has made the marriage, prepared the table, and sent messengers to call the guests. It falls to us, both before and after Baptism, to supply faith, and not only faith but also zeal and earnestness of a pure life.[15]

Saint John Chrysostom praises faith in numerous places. For him, living faith is a great blessing, the mother of all good things. Faith grasps the mysteries of revelation. Rational explanation of such mysteries as the incarnation, the virgin birth, the power of the cross, and the heavenly birth of which Jesus spoke to Nicodemus invite derision – not because of the weakness of these truths themselves, but because heavenly matters cannot be brought under the scrutiny of human reasoning.[16] Faith has the capacity to receive God's gifts, such as the righteousness revealed through the preaching of the Gospel (Rom. 1:17). This righteousness, Chrysostom states, "is not your own, but that of God . . . for you do not achieve it by toilings and labors, but you receive it from above, contributing one thing only from your own choice, believing."[17] It is his confidence in the accomplished work of God and the blessings of the Gospel that leads Chrysostom to view the whole of life as a continuous festival, despite its inevitable troubles and sufferings.

THE GOSPEL IN THEOLOGY AND SPIRITUALITY

What has been said above concerning the Gospel in worship, preaching and teaching already involves essential theological matters. I have defined the content of the Gospel as being the crucified and risen Lord, and His entire ministry, matters which are linked to the saving message of the whole Bible of which Christ is the center. I have also broached the topic of justification by faith, a chief theological concern of Protestants. In what follows, I shall offer additional thoughts pertaining to the relationship between Gospel and theology, the participatory view of salvation called *theosis* ("divinization" or "deification"), and the role of the Gospel in Orthodox spirituality.

In the classic Orthodox tradition, a theologian is not one who has received a formal degree in theology and has become an expert in any given theological discipline. A theologian is someone who is deeply grounded in the life of the Church, who is advanced in the life of prayer, and whose knowledge of Scripture and the Christian tradition reflects profound wisdom. A dictum of Evagrios was, "If you are a theologian, you will pray truly; and if you pray truly, you are a theologian."[18] Properly speaking, theology has to do with personal knowledge of the mystery of the Triune God, the mystery of Christ, and the mystery of Pentecost as attested by the Scriptures and celebrated in the worship of the Church. To be a theologian presupposes living faith, true repentance, inner cleansing, spiritual illumination, and growth toward perfection in Christ-likeness.

Saint Athanasios the Great is a prime example of the centrality of the Gospel in Orthodox theology. His masterful work, *On the Incarnation of the Word,*[19] powerfully expresses the close relationship between Gospel and theology in the Orthodox tradition. Reading this splendid treatise, one enters into the world of early Christian proclamation, teaching and mission. Its chief source and authority is the Bible. Written for a certain Makarios, perhaps a recent convert, its purpose is to explicate the person and work of Christ as the self-disclosure of His divinity. For Athanasios, the incarnation is not just the birth and childhood of Christ, but the adult Christ as the fullness of God on earth. The mystery of Christ's divinity continues to be revealed through His activity as risen Lord. Makarios is instructed to study the Scriptures himself in order to test the truth of the treatise, while being reminded that biblical study must be accompanied by a righteous life and purity of soul.

Three aspects of this work are notable for the present discussion. First, it glows with assurance concerning the Christian mission and the transformative power of Christian truth. Athanasios is not merely expounding an abstract Christology; he is proclaiming Christ. He observes the expansion of the Christian mission, how the Savior's teaching is increasing everywhere, and how men and women disdain even death in the face of martyrdom. According to Athanasios, it is Christ himself as One living and working in the very present who brings people to the Christian faith, thus manifesting His deity and the power of His resurrection. Secondly, Athanasios draws from the whole story of the Bible – creation, fall, redemption, and consummation. He points to God's love and goodness in reaching out to save and restore sinful humanity, especially through the ministry of Christ. And thirdly, he focuses on the reality of Jesus Christ as the eternal and preexistent Word, the same agent who created the world and is now redeeming it. Athanasios does not discuss the infancy narratives. His attention is on the adult ministry of Christ as the One who was fully God and fully man. The Alexandrian's theological perspectives are both Johannine and Pauline. The incarnate Word was living a human life and at the same time – this is the wonder – He was in union with the Father sustaining the life of creation. The chief acts by which He accomplished His redemptive work were through His death and resurrection, to which Athanasios devotes supreme attention.

Saint Athanasios was one of the first Christian theologians to use the language of *theosis* or deification. He is known for the statement: "He [the eternal Word] became human so that we may become deified" (*theopoiethomen*).[20] This is a bold and to some minds perhaps an impossible concept, one which can linguistically be traced back to Plato. However, while acknowledging the Greek philosophical origins of the word, the Orthodox teaching about *theosis* is thoroughly Christian. It is rooted in the New Testament itself, especially the Gospel of John and the Epistles of Paul, which clearly speak of a mystical union with Christ and a personal dwelling of the Holy Spirit in the believer. The Church Fathers elaborated this teaching based on the reality of the incarnation, the full union of the divine and human natures of Christ, to which especially the Fourth Gospel bears testimony.

Like the Evangelist before him, Saint Athanasios viewed the incarnation in its full reality. Through the incarnation, the eternal Word put Himself at the disposal of humanity, manifesting His radiant life and glory. Recall the opening words of the First Epistle of John: "That which was from the beginning, which we have heard, which we have seen with our eyes, which we have looked upon and touched with our hands, concerning the word of life..." (1 Jn 1:1). In a similar way Saint Athanasios stresses the reality and tangibility of the incarnate Word, who fully entered the sinful world of humanity in order to rescue it from corruption and death. Salvation occurs through a new birth, just as Jesus declared to Nicodemos (Jn 3:3ff.), signifying the gift of the Spirit and restoration of intimate communion with God. The Alexandrian Father, as well, uses Pauline language and concepts to expound the overcoming of sin, corruption, mortality, and death through the incarnate presence of divinity, whose supreme goal was the resurrection, the great victory of the Word of Life over the powers of corruption. He cites 1 Cor. 15:53-56 as a key text: "This corruptible (*phtharton*) must put on incorruption (*aphtharsian*) and this mortal (*thneton*) must put on immortality (*athanasian*). . . Then shall come to pass the saying that is written, 'Death is swallowed up in victory. O death, where is your victory? O death, where is your sting?'"

Saint Athanasios brings his readers to the core of the patristic understanding of soteriology, a view of salvation based on the revelation of the incarnate Christ, and the unity of his divine and human natures. This view presupposes the biblical concepts of the solidarity of humanity, the corruption of human nature by transgression and sin, and the human need for healing and transformation through sharing in divine grace and life. It is a soteriology which treats the problem of sin primarily not in legal but in existential terms. Though produced by transgression, sin is a sickness, a blight on humanity. Sick humanity needs divine healing by an infusion of grace, penetrating all of human existence, just as evil had penetrated and engulfed all life, according to Athanasios. The full solution to sin is not only forgiveness from heaven but also recreative sharing in the divine life in union with the crucified and risen Lord. It is a "participatory" view of salvation according to which believers are united with Christ as the branches are united to the vine (Jn 15:1ff.). It is by such intimate union that believers "are being transformed into the same image [of the glory of the Lord] from one degree of glory to another" (2 Cor. 3:18). Thus patristic soteriology is anchored on Johannine and Pauline categories of thought such as union and communion with God, the indwelling of Christ and the Spirit, and the transformation and glorification of all things (2 Cor. 5:17; Rom. 8:18ff.). The most appropriate biblical term for *theosis* is simply *glorification* by means of divine grace.[21]

However, the language of deification is certainly not exclusive among the Church Fathers. When reflecting on the death of Christ, Athanasios himself uses a number of legal or forensic biblical terms and images. The sacrifice of Christ was to free humanity from its Adamic transgression as a result of which a debt had to be paid. The death of the Lord was a ransom for all. By dying Christ became a sufficient exchange for all, a substitutionary offering and sacrifice.[22] Similar terminology and ideas appear in other Church Fathers, although they are never developed into a system as in the case of Anselm in the West. Remarkable as well is the fact that Gregory Palamas, known for his theology of *theosis,* never mentions the term nor deals with the theological concept in his sermons addressed to the ordinary faithful where the usual biblical vocabulary and exhortations prevail.[23]

Let us turn now to some remarks on the Gospel in Orthodox spirituality. This tradition is represented by an astonishingly rich literature dating from the Egyptian Desert Fathers (fourth century and later) to contemporary writers on the Holy Mountain in Greece. The preeminent record is *The Philokalia,*[24] a collection of diversified treatises on the spiritual life covering a period roughly from the fourth to the fourteenth century.

A number of contemporary western scholars have given attention to this tradition of Orthodoxy.[25] Most recently a substantial volume appeared by Douglas Burton-Christie entitled *The Word in the Desert: Scripture and the Quest for Holiness in Early Christian Monasticism.*[26] The thesis of this book is to demonstrate the central role that Scripture played in the life of the ancient monastics whose hearts and minds were shaped by biblical reading and meditation. The emphasis was, according to Burton-Christie, on a hermeneutic of praxis, the release of the power of God's word through the application of the sacred texts with the conviction that they inherently carried the power to transform and sanctify life. By means of study and memorization of the sacred texts, as well as rumination on their meaning, the biblical word penetrated the deepest recesses of the soul. It stripped away layers of ego-centric deceptive concerns and opened up new possibilities for the actualization of the evangelical virtues such as humility, love, and the fervent expectation of the coming kingdom. The ultimate expression of the desert hermeneutic, Burton-Christie concludes, was not doctrinal interpretation but the saintly elder as a *person,* a "Christ-bearer," who embodied the sacred texts and who drew others out of themselves into a world of personal and corporate transformation by means of the practice of the biblical word.[27]

A striking witness to Orthodox spirituality is Saint Mark the Ascetic (fifth century), whose treatises appear in *The Philokalia.* One of them is entitled *On Those Who Think that They Are Made Righteous by Works.*[28] One thousand years before Martin Luther, this erudite monastic affirmed the biblical position in the clearest terms. His opening statement includes the following declaration:

> Wishing to show that to fulfill every commandment is a duty, whereas
> sonship is a gift given to people through His own Blood, the Lord
> said: 'When you have done all that is commanded you, say: "We are
> useless servants: we have only done what was our duty"' (Lk 17:10).
> Thus the kingdom of heaven is not a reward for works, but a gift of
> grace prepared by the Master for his faithful servants.[29]

A few more aphorisms from Saint Mark the Ascetic, given according to their numbering in *The Philokalia*, will provide aspects of his
understanding of spiritual life, especially as related to grace, faith
and works:

> 12. Even though knowledge is true, it is still not firmly established if
> unaccompanied by works. For everything is established by being put
> into practice.

> 22. When Scripture says 'He will reward every man according to his
> works' (Mt 16:27), do not imagine that works in themselves merit
> either hell or the kingdom. On the contrary, Christ rewards each man
> according to whether his works are done with faith or without faith
> in Himself; and He is not a dealer bound by contract, but God our
> Creator and Redeemer.

> 57. He who does something good and expects a reward is serving
> not God but his own will.

> 117. To him who hungers after Christ grace is food; to him who is thirsty,
> a reviving drink; to him who is cold, a garment; to him who is weary,
> rest; to him who prays, assurance; to him who mourns, consolation.

The most prophetic and evangelical voice in Orthodox spirituality is Saint Symeon the New Theologian (949-1022), a learned abbot
of a monastery in Constantinople who shook the religious establishment of his time by his teachings, was persecuted and died in
exile. Some of his works, including *The Disourses*,[30] have been translated into English. In *Discourse 22* Saint Symeon tells how, while seeking as a young man the forgiveness of his sins through fervent prayer,
he unexpectedly beheld the risen Christ in the radiance of His
uncreated light. This sublime experience of renewal marked a new
stage in Saint Symeon's life. He became a zealous preacher of Christ
and insisted that the very life of the apostles could be lived by every
Christian in any epoch. For Saint Symeon, the luminous presence of
Christ, the burning fire of His grace and love, was always eager to

ignite a receptive soul, just as fire is always eager to consume dry wood. What was required was the exercise of the gift of faith, attention to conscience, an awareness of one's blindness and the need for enlightenment, fervent prayer, and faithful obedience to the Lord.

Appealing to the witness of Scripture, especially the Evangelist John and the Apostle Paul, Saint Symeon proclaimed in bold terms the necessity of an adult experience of conversion and renewal, a "new birth," just as Jesus had proclaimed to Nicodemos in the Gospel of John. According to Saint Symeon, most people by adulthood have reached a state of spiritual insensibility, their baptismal grace inactive and concealed by all manner of evil desires and passions. He did not address only lay people but clerics and monastics as well. All needed a profound sense of repentance, a deep conversion of heart and mind, indeed a new "baptism of the Holy Spirit" to rejuvenate baptismal grace. To some Saint Symeon's apostolic message smacked of heresy. His teaching once provoked some of his own monastics to rush at him in order to inflict bodily harm. Although rejected by officials and exiled, he was soon acknowledged as one of the greatest charismatic saints in the Orthodox tradition and was accorded the rare honorary title "Theologian."[31]

The biblical and evangelical dimension in Symeon is simply astonishing. A loyal follower of the great Church Fathers, and deeply respectful of the Church's tradition, Saint Symeon lived and breathed the Scriptures. In *Disourses 28-36* he expounds the new life in Christ presenting "the truth from divine Scripture and from experience."[32] He tells of leaving every other preoccupation in life to labor day and night "excavating" the Scriptures until, by Christ's luminous intervention, they yielded their spiritual treasures.[33] Though being accused of pride and arrogance, he boldly parallels his witness to that of the apostles and the Church Fathers who possessed the mind of Christ. He viewed his work as "a ministry of the Spirit"[34] against which resisters committed the unforgivable sin of blasphemy. According to Symeon, without the renewed life in conscious union with Christ and the Spirit, all are slaves of this world and sit in darkness, whether they be emperors or patriarchs, prelates or priests, monks or lay persons.[35] He viewed himself as no more than "a poor, brother-loving beggar" (*ptochos philadelphos*), who out of love for his fellow beggars ran about the streets calling all beggars to the door of an amazing Master freely dispensing His wealth to all. Nevertheless, as a prophet, he also challenged his hearers to test the truth of his witness with these words:

You, on your part, must see and test that which we say. If we have views different from those of the Apostles and of the holy and God-inspired Fathers, if we speak contrary to what they said, if we fail to repeat what the Holy Gospels say about God, then let me be anathema from the Lord God Jesus Christ.[36]

CONCLUSION

Orthodoxy is gifted with precious treasures. A rich liturgical tradition, a profound theology of communion, a joy in prayer, a depth of spiritual wisdom, a catholic vision of faith and reason – all are part of the Orthodox inheritance. At the core of the Orthodox tradition, whether we turn to the Eucharist or the lives of the great saints, the same truth has primacy, namely, Christ and the Gospel. We have examined above aspects of the grand legacy of Orthodoxy pertaining to the Gospel. However, Orthodoxy also has long exhibited tendencies toward "institutionalization." The problem is not so much that the Church is inevitably a historical institution, and endures by means of its institutional forms, but that because the Church is also an institution it can lose sight of the immediacy of God. The Church as a sociological reality may allow the life in Christ to diminish in various aspects of its existence with the result that a variety of institutional, professional, and cultural norms and forms take prominence. Then the Church risks being a religious institution with primary reference to itself and its survival, rather that to the risen Lord and its mission in the world. The challenge of rediscovering the centrality of the Gospel, as well as of energizing the evangelical ethos deeply enshrined in the Orthodox tradition, is the topic of our next chapter.

NOTES

[1] I borrow this expression from the title of Joseph A. Fitzmyer's book *Scripture, the Soul of Theology* (New York: Paulist Press, 1994).

[2] Thomas Torrance, *The Relevance of Orthodoxy* (Stirling: Drummond Press, n.d.), pp. 10-11.

[3] The complete hymn reads as follows: "Only-begotten Son and Word of God, although immortal, You humbled Yourself for our salvation, taking flesh from the holy Theotokos and ever virgin Mary and, without change, became man. Christ, our God, You were crucified but conquered death by death. You are one of the Holy Trinity, glorified with the Father and the Holy Spirit – save us!"

[4] Sometimes one hears or reads about a false generalization that Eastern Orthodoxy features a "theology of the resurrection" as compared to the "theology of the cross" of the Western Christian tradition. In fact Ortho-

doxy has a profound vision of the cross both in worship and spirituality. Orthodoxy knows no resurrection without the cross and no cross without the resurrection, viewing these redemptive events as inseparable.

[5] For an interpretation of the mode of Christ's presence in the eucharistic gifts in Orthodox perspective, see my article "Christ, Church and Eucharist," in *Diakonia* 18 (2, 1983) 100-127 and reprinted in a collection of essays entitled *The Good News of Christ* (Brookline: Holy Cross Press, 1991), pp.52-79.

[6] Two illuminating studies on the patristic tradition pertaining to some of these topics are by Jaroslav Pelikan, *Christianity and Classical Culture* (New Haven: Yale University Press, 1993) and Philip Rousseau, *Basil of Caesarea* (Berkeley: University of California Press, 1994).

[7] See St. John Chrysostom, *In Praise of St. Paul*, translated by Thomas Halton (Boston, 1963).

[8] A recent thorough account of Saint John Chrysostom's life and struggles, including his commitment to Christian truth and his missionary interests, can be found in J. N. D. Kelly, *Golden Mouth: The Story of John Chrysostom* (Ithaca: Cornell University Press, 1995).

[9] For a fuller account of Saint John Chrysostom's understanding of the Gospel, see Chapter One.

[10] *Homilies on Matthew 1.4.*

[11] *Ibid.* 1.6.

[12] One of Chrysostom's sharper critiques of the Church is to be found in Homily 36 on First Corinthians, where he reflects on the vigor of early Christian worship and the charismatic phenomena mentioned by Saint Paul in 1 Cor 14. In contrast, Chrysostom bewails the conditions of his contemporary Church which he likens to a woman fallen from her former prosperity and now exhibiting empty signs of her previous good estate.

[13] *In Praise of St. Paul*, pp. 69-70.

[14] Saint Paul's whole point is that the Galatian Christians have begun to practice Jewish customs, not that they were overly ethical, something which Paul requires as intrinsic to Christian life (Gal. 5:16-6:10). The practice of sinful deeds excludes one from inheriting the kingdom (5:21; cf. 6:7). Overall the Apostle Paul seems to distinguish three kinds of "works:" 1) "works of the flesh," that is, rejectable sinful deeds (Gal. 5:19; Rom. 13:12; 1 Cor 6:9-11); "works of the law," that is, the ritual injunctions of the Mosaic Law (Gal. 2:3,12-16; 4:10; 5:2), which are no longer required for salvation; and 3) "good works," that is, ethical deeds (Rom. 2:6-16,21-26; Gal 5:6; 6:7-10), on the basis of which Christians, too, will be judged by God (1 Cor 6:9-10; Gal 5:21; 2 Cor 5:10). Thus Paul's contrast between faith and works fundamentally concerns faith in Christ and specifically "works of the law," namely, the ritual law, not the moral commandments of the Old Testament which remain valid and are fulfilled by Christ (Rom. 2:21-26; 8:4; 13:9; 1 Cor. 7:19). Christ, the Gospel, and Christian existence fulfill, and do not reject or destroy, the moral law of the Old Testament (Mt. 5:17; Rom. 8:4; Gal 5:14). Still, salvation is "by grace. . . through faith" in Christ and it is a "gift of

God" (Eph. 2:8). Faith in Christ and good works are integrated, not contrasted, much less opposed, by Paul who everywhere exhorts and demands necessary ethical obedience. Paul teaches not only justification by faith but also judgment by the criterion of good works.

[15] *Homilies on John 10.2-3.*

[16] *Ibid.* 4.2 and 24.3.

[17] *Homilies on Romans* 2.

[18] Evagrios the Solitary, *On Prayer: One Hundred and Fifty-Three Texts in The Philokalia: The Complete Text,* Vol. 1, ed. by G. E. H. Palmer and others (London & Boston: Faber and Faber, 1979), p. 62.

[19] Saint Athanasios, *On the Incarnation.* See Chapter One, n. 14.

[20] *Ibid.,* p. 93 and Chap. 54 of Saint Athanasios' work..

[21] For use of this word I am indebted to Father John Romanides, who has regularly employed the term "glorification" as a biblical term in order to avoid the Platonic philosophical implications of the term *theosis.* A recent attempt to relate the Orthodox teaching of *theosis* to the Protestant understanding of salvation has been made by Risto Saarinen, "Salvation in the Lutheran-Orthodox Dialogue: A Comparative Perspective" *Pro Ecclesia* 5 (2, 1996), pp. 202-213.

[22] See *On the Incarnation,* pp. 33-37, 48-49, 54-56 and Chaps. 8, 10, 20, and 25 respectively in the same work.

[23] I owe this observation to George Mantzarides, a Greek Orthodox scholar of Palamite studies.

[24] See above, n. 18 for the first volume. Volumes two and three appeared in 1981 and 1984.

[25] For example Margaret R. Miles, *Fullness of Life* (Philadelphia: Westminster, 1981); Roberta C. Bondi, *To Love God as God Loves* (Philadelphia: Fortress Press, 1987), and several books by Henri Nouwen.

[26] Published by Oxford University Press, New York and Oxford, 1993.

[27] *Ibid.,* pp. 297-300.

[28] *The Philokalia: The Complete Text,* Vol. 1, pp. 125-146.

[29] *Ibid.,* p. 125.

[30] *Symeon the New Theologian: The Discourses,* translated by C. J. deCatanzaro (New York: Paulist Press, 1980). A recent doctoral dissertation by Helen Criticos Theodoropoulos, *Love of God and Love of Neighbor in the Mystical Theology of St. Bernard of Clairvaux and St. Symeon the New Theologian, Vols I-II,* submitted to the University of Chicago (1995), provides a full bibliography on Symeon the New Theologian.

[31] The only other Christian authors formally called "Theologians" in the Orthodox tradition are John the Evangelist and Gregory (Nazianzen) the Theologian.

[32] Saint Symeon, *Discourses,* p. 353.

[33] Saint Symeon, *Discourses,* p. 355.

[34] Saint Symeon, *Discourses,* p. 350.

[35] Saint Symeon, *Discourses,* p. 298.

[36] Saint Symeon, *Discourses,* p. 354.

CHAPTER THREE

THE GOSPEL IN THE PARISH

About twenty years ago Bishop Anastasios Yannoulatos, now Archbishop of the autocephalous Church of Albania, published an article with the striking title "Discovering the Orthodox Missionary Ethos."[1] The thrust of the article was to underscore what he saw, during the sixties and seventies, as "a rekindling of missionary interest" in the Orthodox Church. Highlighting Orthodox missionary activities particularly in Africa, where he himself was a pioneer, the Archbishop emphasized that "the awakening of the Orthodox missionary conscience" was "no innovation but a rediscovery" of an essential dimension of the Church.[2] Today, thanks to the work of His Beatitude and others, both clergy and laity, including graduates of our own Holy Cross School of Theology, many more Orthodox have not only been awakened to but are now strongly supportive of missionary work in distant lands, what we usually think of as "external mission." Our own Orthodox Christian Mission Center in Florida, a vital and growing panorthodox ministry, is the administrative and inspirational center through which Orthodox clergy and laity of America channel their sense of missionary resurgence.

The thesis of the present chapter is that, as the new millennium beckons us forward, a parallel rekindling and rediscovery of another closely related ministry of the Orthodox Church is needed, having to do with the "internal mission" of the Church, namely, the evangelization of rank-and-file Orthodox Christians at the level of each parish. The crux of the matter is the ministry of evangelism to the baptized. We are talking about not only the proclamation but also *the actualization of the Gospel in the parish*. At stake is the discovery of the inner evangelical spirit of the Orthodox Church by which the Church may be empowered to continue to fulfill its mission in North America.

It may be rather startling to suggest that, after twenty centuries of Church history, Orthodox clergy and laity need to reawaken to the Gospel of Christ, the core message of salvation. And yet it is precisely true in the sense of Archbishop Anastasios' words: it is a matter not of "innovation" but of "rediscovery" – the rediscovery of a precious and dynamic treasure already enshrined in the Holy Scriptures, the Divine Liturgy, the hymnology, the theology and tradition of the Church. But the treasure is not adequately appreciated, nor sufficiently effective, unless it is brought out into full view so that its beauty and power may be released by God's grace.

In our generation a significant number of formerly evangelical Protestant Christians joined in mass the Orthodox Church in the United States and now constitute one of the fastest growing parts of the worldwide family of the Orthodox.[3] Over the last decade they have stirred up things in Orthodoxy, bringing with them a fervent personal faith, a zeal for the Scriptures and the Gospel, and a high level of Christian commitment sometimes discomforting to Orthodox Christians born into the Orthodox faith. At the same time, they have earnestly sought to live and express the gifts they have brought with them in terms of an authentic liturgical and doctrinal Orthodox mindset (*phronema*). We so-called "cradle" Orthodox have been learning from them and they have been learning from us, sometimes in creative tension.

Whatever our reciprocal lessons and perceptions, whatever our mutual gifts and tensions, the substantive task is clear and decisive for all: What is the direction and shape of the Orthodox Church in America that we should strive for as bishops, priests, and laity? What is the enduring message of Orthodoxy according to its own authentic identity as the One, Holy, Catholic, and Apostolic Church? What is the dynamic spirit by which to build up the spiritual character of our parishes and to help them become local missionary centers across America? Certainly, one of the major tasks that lie ahead is that of the evangelism of the baptized membership. The future growth of the parishes, the spiritual vigor of the whole Church, as well as the mutual reinforcement of the internal and external mission of the Church, will significantly depend on the effective proclamation, as well as the actualization of the Gospel in the parish. At issue is nothing less than the evangelical nature of the Orthodox Church and the rediscovery of the Orthodox evangelical ethos.

THE URGENCY OF THE TASK

The twenty-first century is bound to be a century of continuing globalization, multi-culturalism and pluralism – all powerful currents undermining the sociological soil of the Christian faith and thereby people's connection to the local parishes. Dramatic changes have already occurred and will continue to occur in the way huge numbers of people in our society live, feel, think and act. We face the cultural phenomena of what have been called modernism and post-modernism – massive technological, social, economic and intellectual forces in both conflict and interaction with each other, and powerfully shaping our shrinking world. Some of the key factors which define the character our culture may be quickly mentioned: the growth of big cities; astonishing scientific and technological progress; the movement and mixture of peoples; the meeting of religions and subcultures in the neighborhood, school and place of work; the drive for individual freedom and acquisition of material goods; the pursuit of pleasure and entertainment; the explosion of communications through the printed and electronic media; the pernicious effects of war, economic disparity, and ecological neglect; the failure of systems of government, education, law and even religion; and the consequent loss of clear boundaries of community, identity, value, meaning, purpose, and direction.

The upshot of all the above is an enormous sociological dynamic which, though it does not impact everyone equally, influences all members of our society, including our fellow parishioners in both conscious and unconscious ways. A Christian author described the tectonic cultural changes of recent generations by saying: "The world has moved, but it neglected to send a change of address card."[4] What he meant was an address card to the Churches, since many Christians, both leaders and ordinary faithful, seem to be either unaware of or unmoved by the radical changes in our times. Nevertheless, we are all passengers on the same ship, and the impact is the greatest on the young. It is our youth who unavoidably breathe the air of post-modern popular philosophy: all religious faiths and values are relative, there is no certainty of truth, do your own thing, be tolerant of the choices and lifestyles of others, and have fun enjoying the ride into an uncertain future. The following words of a man interviewed in the streets of Boston may well express a diffused aspect of the post-modern consciousness often floating across the hearts and minds of people in our own parishes, especially the youth: "I don't know what I believe in. And if I believe – I believe there's some Higher Power, I think. But I don't know. . . But I'm open to everything. So I like to believe in everything, because I don't know what it is I truly believe in.[5]

This cultural crisis of faith is not something new. Church leaders and theologians have been talking about it for years. Among the Orthodox, the late Alexander Schmemann, Dean of Saint Vladimir's Theological Seminary, sounded a clarion call some forty years ago when he warned about the institutions of marriage, family, education, and work being understood in secular terms even by Orthodox Christians. He critiqued the inundation of worldly values into the membership of the Church, for example, reliance on success, ambition, affluence, status, profit, prestige, and the like.[6] He wrote: "It is this American secularism which an overwhelming majority of Orthodox wrongly and naively identify with *the* American way of life that is, in my opinion, the root of the deep spiritual crisis of Orthodoxy in America."[7] Unfortunately, his call was a voice in the wilderness, bearing little impact over against the influence of modern culture crashing upon us like a mighty tidal wave.

Archbishop Iakovos, former head of the Greek Orthodox Archdiocese of North and South America, issued a similar call for renewal in 1986[8] and soon established a theological commission to develop a comprehensive working agenda for the Church. The commission's final report in 1989 engaged issues of parish life, the changing composition of membership, the weakening of ethnic ties, as well as the cultural crisis of faith exemplified by the fact that our young people are more deeply influenced by society than the local parish.[9] Let it be noted that the crisis of faith is not a personal crisis, that is, a crisis of conscience in people who have grown up with a meaningful Christian commitment and come to question it. Rather, it is precisely a cultural crisis, that is, an absorption of a sociological loss of Christian commitment in a secular society where Christian faith is one of many options, an individual and personal choice often not seriously considered at all. The predictable results are drifting membership and perfunctory participation in the sacraments as, for example, in the case of couples who come to be married in the Church, even though they have been blissfully cohabitating for years, and then seem to be surprised by the Church's disapproval. To draw such couples into the life of the parish, speaking to them the truth with love and compassion, rather than with sternness and rejection, is a typical pastoral problem today of no small magnitude for the persons involved and for the parish itself.

In view of this crisis of faith in our culture, the above theological commission emphasized the crucial responsibility of the entire Church in stemming the tide of drifting membership and religious nominalism by means of planned and consistent action. The ecclesial and spiritual bonds of parishioners, if not supported and enhanced by purposeful and concerted efforts, will continue to diminish especially in view of the overwhelming percentage of interfaith marriages and the progressive weakening of ethnic ties. To quote the commission:

> In this free, pluralistic society *the Orthodox Church must take upon itself the* prime responsibility for maintaining and strengthening the Orthodox identity among its members both as an intrinsic goal as well as a presupposition for *effective mission in the world* (the emphasis is the commission's).

The significant implication is that the parish cannot be isolated from the larger Church and its institutions. To achieve its role and potential, the parish must be given the appropriate spiritual leadership, the basic presuppositions for effective ministries, and vigilant supervision and direction. The whole body of the Church, both leaders and faithful, need to work together as we confront the enormous tasks created by the influence of modernity and post-modernity on our people.

The most potent answer to the cultural crisis of faith, according to the theological commission, is nurturing a sense of living faith in the parish. The commission called for challenging and guiding our people beyond external formalism to an "internalization" of Orthodox truths and values, that is, an inward appropriation of the Orthodox way of life. In our parishes, we have the liturgical context of beautiful services, especially the treasure of the Liturgy, which itself cries out for greater actualization among all our the faithful. Our sacred tradition possesses the truths and practices to fortify the Church's identity as the Body of Christ. We have a rich spirituality to inspire the administrative structures and formational programs of the Church. Efforts are being made to enhance the socially supportive environment of the community as a parish family – social activities, conferences, camps, study groups, and philanthropic ministries.

The critical question is what will be the spark that gives birth to personal faith in Christ, strengthens that faith, energizes people spiritually, motivates them to action, and ties together all the aspects of parish life enhancing their particular functions. The commission pointed to prayer, clear teaching and the Gospel. According to the commission, living faith occurs in a parish context of "personal faith inspired by prayer, enlivened by a mystical sense of communion with the risen Christ, and communicated with an evangelical spirit as a heralding of the good news." These words sum up the essential ethos of Orthodoxy: the experience of union with Christ, nurtured by prayer and worship, and communicated with an evangelical spirit as good news of grace. All these key components, which are integrated and mutually supportive, are definitive and indispensable to the Orthodox way of life. Prayer and worship constitute long and rich traditions. But evangelism must receive far greater prominence as a way of reawakening the faithful to the treasures of prayer and worship themselves. Evangelism is preaching and teaching with conviction and the living voice, focusing on the centrality of Christ, and connecting all that we do in the parish with Christ, His saving work, and the blessings which flow from it. It is through evangelism that souls are particularly stirred, faith is awakened, commitment is strengthened, and an evangelical ethos is nurtured in an Orthodox context – an ethos centered on Christ, filled with prayer, and penetrating all parish activities in a vital and unifying way. To quote the theological commission once again:

> A true evangelical spirit keeps alive the horizon of living faith by which we apprehend that the risen Christ is present in the Church guiding us in our education, spiritual formation, liturgical life, moral and social concerns, youth programs, administration, and finances.

THE POWER OF THE GOSPEL

One of the most remarkable phenomena in history was the spread of Christianity in the Graeco-Roman world. Propelled by a transforming experience of the presence and power of God, the Christian movement triumphed in a society much like our own – a world of many gods and religions, of constant wars and migration of peoples, of diverse philosophies and lifestyles, of the breakdown of local boundaries and structures of meaning, and of a profound longing for personal security and protection from seen and unseen evil.

Within a few decades, the early Christians founded communities in virtually all the major centers of the Roman Empire, even Rome itself. In just over three centuries the Church established itself as the dominant religion of the Roman Empire, claiming the emperor himself as its most powerful convert and supporter.

Historians have long reflected on the reasons behind the amazing success of Christianity in the ancient world, reasons which are totally instructive for our own cultural situation. One factor was the cohesiveness of community and family life among Christians, transcending racial, social, economic, and generational boundaries. Despite conflicts and disagreements in the ancient Church, Christians possessed a strong sense of unity in Christ, bound by love for Him and for each other as brothers and sisters. Christians nurtured a consciousness of being an alternative society, distinct from and counter cultural to ancient paganism, a distinction enhanced by the experience of persecution. Another factor was their observable renewal of life. The Christian presence and witness touched and changed ordinary people. In contrast to pagan society, where anything was possible and everything permissible, the Christians had the disarming ability to point to their own way of life as concrete proof of what they proclaimed – God's love and forgiveness, holiness of conduct, honest business dealings, and unselfish service to others. Even pagan writers and opponents of Christianity, such as Lucian, publicly acknowledged that the Christians helped not only themselves but also pagans in need.

However, the greatest factor behind the astonishing triumph of early Christianity was its evangelical spirit: living, preaching, and teaching the good news. For the early Christians the proclamation of the Gospel was neither a matter of grand, abstract theology nor an issue of triumphant claims about the past. It was the announcement of a new way of life in Christ backed up by the transforming experience of the presence and power of God in the community. It was the sharing of the joyous conviction that Christ was alive, that the Holy Spirit energized the community of believers, that God was truly at work in their midst. Early Christianity was a spiritual movement, an explosion of spiritual dynamism, with an invincible sense of mission based on the assurance that Christians knew the true way of life to be shared with all. This powerful evangelical spirit can be seen not only among the Apostles but also among the Church Fathers such as Saint Justin Martyr, Saint Eirenaios, Saint Athanasios,

Saint John Chrysostom and many others. For example, in his work *On the Incarnation of the Word*, Saint Athanasios likens the spread of the gospel to a sunrise which is the work of the risen Christ Himself. He writes: "The Savior is working mightily among people; every day He is invisibly persuading numbers of people all over the world... Can anyone, in face of this, still doubt that He has risen and lives, or rather that He is Himself the Life?"[10]

But has not the Church preached and taught all these things for centuries? Do we not find all the above ideals not only in Holy Scripture but also in the writings of the Church Fathers? Does not the theology of the Church continue to expound and defend the essential truths of the Gospel, interpreting the mystery of the Trinity, the sacraments and Orthodox doctrine? Above all, does not our worship and hymnology gloriously celebrate the whole good news of salvation – the majesty and power of the Holy Trinity, the saving events of the life of Christ, and all the blessings flowing from the good news of salvation? Certainly, all these questions should be answered in the affirmative. The fullness of the gospel is enshrined in the total life of the Church, especially its rich tradition of worship.

And yet there is something seriously amiss. The deficiency is not in the tradition itself which is rich beyond comprehension, not in the abundance and beauty of liturgical services, not in the lack of theological treatises expounding Orthodox doctrine, not in the lack of catechetical material, not in the lack of books on spirituality. Rather, *the lack lies in the focus, the perception, the orientation, the living of the evangelical ethos in the community*. It is widely evident by the late arrival of many parishoners that the liturgical services are not celebrated with joy, but endured as a burden. Most theological writings are incomprehensibly abstract for the average person. The catechetical material and programs often bear too heavy a classroom orientation. The books and instructions on spirituality require motivated hearts to be of lasting benefit. Although individuals may be inspired and benefit by reason of their own initiatives, the parish as a whole seems to be rather unconscious and unmoved by the inherited treasures. All the received gifts of the Church, precious in themselves, are not adequately seen, communicated, heard, lived, and celebrated as good news by the majority of the faithful. The Gospel is enshrined in the total tradition but it is not adequately communicated with the living voice. In other words, the Gospel is not proclaimed and taught with sufficient focus and clarity *as* Gospel, and with ample faith and conviction, to create an atmosphere of purposeful awakening and a responsive stirring in which parish worship, teaching, and pastoral practice can come fully alive by the grace of God.

Indeed, if the Gospel resounded in the parish as in the case of the early Christians, similar results would follow. No Christian can say that God loved the ancient world more than He now loves us in the post-modern era. No Christian can assert that the gift of Christ, in terms of its beauty and truth, is less needed or less effective today. No Christian can allege that the power of the Holy Spirit has diminished over the centuries. No Christian can rightly suggest that the good news of salvation has lost either its relevance or potency in modern times. On the contrary, countless men and women today yearn for an authentic message of love and forgiveness in Christ. They long to be part of a caring and supportive community. They are ready to commit themselves to a way of life that is purposeful and helpful to others. If we see parishes faltering, their spiritual focus waning, their identity unclear, their worship feeble, their service orientation minimal, and their witness impotent to attract and hold their own baptized membership, then we know that something is out of kilter at the level of priorities and basic orientation. What is more, we do not have the luxury of escapism. We cannot blame the world, its pride and disobedience, its lust and moral decadence, its lostness and despair, since these were the very traits of the ancient pagan world in which Christianity originally triumphed.

Are we then to resort to self-criticism alone, blaming ourselves and our own people for lack of faith and commitment, for squandering our sacred treasures, and surrendering to the allurements of a world ruled by Satan? No, a response of this kind will not do either, because there is a better way. The better way is to center on Christ, to refocus on the good news, to start with the message with which Christ started, to repent and embrace the good news, and thus to recover the evangelical ethos of Christian life – all in the context of the treasures that we already possess and celebrate as Orthodox Christians.

Discovering the Orthodox Evangelical Ethos

Jesus began His ministry with the announcement of the good news of God's kingdom, saying: "The time is fulfilled, and the kingdom of God is at hand; repent, and believe in the Gospel" (Mk 1:14-

15). A formidable challenge that Jesus faced was how to break through "a wall of casual familiarity and complacency" in order to stir people's heart and minds, and thus convey His message in a personal and living way.[11] He lived among a religious people with a long tradition of worship and sacrifice, a people deeply aware of a rich heritage centered on the Mosaic Law and the Prophets, a people familiar with religious language and proud of their God-given privileged status among all the nations of the earth. The problem was that, as far as Jesus could see, it did not make much difference in their daily lives. It was as if the religious forms and ceremonies, the institution of religion, had taken the place of the living God. Jesus' answer was to confront them with the presence and power of God. He assured them that He "did not come to abolish but to fulfill the Law and the Prophets" (Mt. 5:17). His own focus was on the immediacy of God's presence as the source of renewal of human hearts and the inherited religion. That is what He meant by "kingdom of God" which He Himself made real through His presence, deeds and words.

The Orthodox preacher and teacher today confronts a similar reality in the parish. Orthodox Christians have a general familiarity with the form and language of the liturgical services. They have listened to the Bible, and particularly the Psalms recited many times. They have heard the frequent doxologies to the Holy Trinity and have chanted the triple *Kyrie Eleisons*. Parishioners know that Christ is God and Savior according to the Creed. He is the Leader of the Church, whose lordship is symbolized by the Pantokrator icons in the domes of our churches. They are aware and proud of the long and rich traditions of the Orthodox Church. But somehow the spiritual beauty and power of the banquet set before them do not penetrate very deeply into their hearts and minds. For the majority, religious life is a familiar routine partaken selectively, with little effect on daily life, while the burden of individual cares and the pull of modern culture seem overwhelming.

The most timely and effective answer to this reality of religious familiarity and complacency is internal mission by means of evangelization – preaching and teaching the Gospel. The following basic elements or aspects of preaching and teaching may serve as examples of how evangelization can be conducted in the parish in order to spark an evangelical spirit and nurture a broader evangelical ethos embracing the whole life of the community.[12]

The first and most important element is focus on the central message of salvation – the conviction that the Church has a saving message to proclaim, a *kerygma*, a heralding of good news. This message derives from its Holy Scriptures, its worship and theology, and the depths of its historical experience of God. Jesus began with the heralding of God's kingdom as a present reality. The Apostles began with the announcement that Jesus Himself was the agent of the kingdom, the risen Lord and Savior, the Victor over death and corruption, the Giver of light and life (Acts 2:22-36). The Church has the same apostolic message to proclaim about Christ and the kingdom today – a message of truth and grace, of love and forgiveness, of healing and reconciliation, of hope and joy – which must resound within the parish and beam out to the world as from a radio station never going off the air. To be agents of evangelization, bishops, priests, teachers, and other parish leaders must have first embraced the good news of Christ and the kingdom for themselves in word and deed. They must see themselves as heralds proclaiming the message with the conviction that it is ultimately dependent not on their wisdom and skill but on God's authority and power. It is a message that comes from God, it announces the work of God in Christ, it tells about God's blessings and demands, and it leads to God.

What must be emphasized in a particular way is that the evangelical quality of preaching and teaching arises from the conviction that the Gospel mediates God's presence and power here and now. The Gospel is not simply an abstract religious truth or an account of an important event in the past, but an announcement which carries with it the power of the risen Christ and the active presence of the Holy Spirit. When Saint Paul wrote to the Romans that "the Gospel is the power of God for everyone who believes" (Rom. 1:17), he meant it for the ongoing present. Day by day as he conducted his ministry the great Apostle was aflame with the evangelical spirit by which, as in the case of Jesus, he could announce the transformative grace of God breaking into people's lives: "Behold, now is the acceptable time; behold, now is the day of salvation" (2 Cor. 6:2)! Orthodox preachers and teachers must be convinced of the Gospel's spiritual power and convey the confidence that the faithful announcement of the good news ushers the same blessings today as in the days of the first Christians. When the name of Christ is mentioned and praised, when His gracious work of love and forgiveness is proclaimed and

taught in various ways, when His offer of new life and joy is celebrated, when His mercy and forgiveness are received, the same
gifts that are announced become realities in the present. In other
words, evangelical preaching and teaching is a spiritual event; it is
not merely the transmission of theological information or elucidation of it, but the imparting here and now of the life of new creation,
an ephiphany of God's grace transforming simultaneously the lives
of preachers and listeners.[13]

In practical terms, preachers and teachers do not have to be biblical scholars or great theologians, as if great learning would justify
or prove the validity of the gospel. Such a mentality is counter-pro-
ductive because it does not perceive, nor therefore allow, the living
God to do His work through the faithful proclamation of the good
news. They do not have to be eloquent speakers, although they must
be willing to put serious effort behind their work. Nor do they have
to raise their voices to high decibels, or thump on the pulpit, in order to add value or potency to the message. But they must be faithful to the message and receptive of God's grace. They must love
Christ, love the Scriptures, love the congregation, love to proclaim
the good news, and seek to connect the Gospel with every aspect of
the parish.

Is there a meeting of the Parish Council or the Ladies Society
tonight? Is there a pastoral visitation at a home or in the hospital
tomorrow? Is there a confession to be heard or a counseling meeting
scheduled the next day? Is there a meeting with the youth or an
adult recreational group on Saturday? Do not lose an opportunity
to recite with conviction a carefully chosen passage from Scripture,
presenting it as good news – affirming, rephrasing, celebrating, and
applying the passage to present circumstances. Let the whole range
of the imagery and language of the Gospel – which is the word of
God, the word of the Cross, the heralding of the new creation, the
announcement of grace, God's gift of love and forgiveness – resound
again and again in the life of the parish. Talk about Christ's encounter with Zacchaeus, or the blind man, or the Samaritan woman, or
the thief on the Cross as encounters which bear good news for today's
listeners. In many and various ways, not only in worship, but also
in meetings, educational sessions, recreational events. Seek this one
thing: to bring God into the lives of people and the people into the
presence of God. By unceasing focus on the message, as well as by
loving pastoral nurture, raise people's awareness that we are God's

co-workers and witnesses, that we are doing God's work, and that we are doing it with God's guidance and power. And let God do the rest. The result will be an awakening of the evangelical spirit, a Christ-centeredness, and a growing evangelical ethos in the parish.

A second important element in evangelization is an emphasis on the good news as a gift. The Gospel states that "God so loved the world that He *gave* His only Son, that whoever believes in Him should not perish but have eternal life" (Jn 3:16). When Jesus met the Samaritan woman, He said to her: "If you knew the *gift* of God, and who it is that is saying to you, 'Give me a drink,' you would have asked Him, and he would have *given* you living water" (Jn 4:10). In the Epistle to the Romans, Saint Paul asks: "He who did not spare His own Son but *gave* Him up for us all, will He not also *give* us all things with Him" (Rom. 9:32)? And again in Ephesians: "For by grace you have been saved through faith; and this is not you own doing, it is the *gift* of God" (Eph. 2:8). At the most sacred moment of the Divine Liturgy, when the priests offers the Eucharistic Gifts, he chants: "We offer to You these gifts from Your own gifts in all and for all." Orthodox theology teaches that Christ, the Gospel, the Church, the Holy Spirit, our families, our children, the life of each human being, all are gifts of God.

And yet the popular perception of Christian life and the Church itself is not in the perspective of a gift but that of an obligation. We often hear about fulfilling our religious duties and meeting our parish obligations. Christian life is often seen in moralistic categories. The prevailing view is that, to gain salvation and somehow obtain a ticket to heaven, one must accomplish so many good works and fulfill so many religious obligations, although these may be neither enjoyable nor very inspiring. Not infrequently and with all good intentions, priests and parish leaders reinforce this view of "obligatory Christianity" by harping on parishioners to come to Church more often, to give more of their time and money, and to be far better Christians than they are. Little or no attention is devoted to the very essence of Christianity as a gift, above all the personal gift of Christ Himself through whom we share the life of God the Father in the power of the Holy Spirit.

To be sure, the Gospel carries both gifts and tasks. It entails both blessings and demands. We need but to remember Christ's words about the straight and narrow; and to review with our mind's eye the Sermon on the Mount. The way of Christ is the way of the Cross.

But the Gospel as gift comes first. It forms the foundation from which we seek to fulfill our Christian duties. Before Christ delivered the demands of the Sermon on the Mount, He began with the Beatitudes: "Blessed are the humble... blessed are the meek... blessed are the merciful... blessed are the pure in heart... blessed are the peacemakers" (Mt. 5:3-9). This blessing was a present blessing as well. It was not intended only for the afterlife, but also for the daily lives of those who heard and welcome His message of the kingdom. By receiving the message, they were already blessed and were being transformed! Indeed, unless we first receive and are transformed by the gift and power of the kingdom, unless we are truly blessed by God's grace, the fulfillment of the kingdom's righteousness would be an exercise in futility. The gifts and graces of God always come first.

Preaching and teaching must reverse popular notions of "obligation Christianity" and develop an awareness of Christian life as a gift, a privilege, a joy. Preachers must avoid dwelling on what have been called "try-harder sermons," thus crushing the conscience of worshipers who are already burdened with myriad personal, family and work obligations. The One who said, "take up your cross and follow me" (Mt. 16:24), first said: "Come to me and I will give you rest" (Mt. 11:28). The blessings of Christ, His love and mercy, His forgiveness and healing, His strength and comfort, must receive primary attention because His demands can only be accomplished on the basis of His blessings. An essential aspect of evangelization is proclaiming the good news as a gift, creating a sense of gratitude and appreciation for God's blessings, and thus inspiring and empowering Christians to live a life worthy of the Gospel.

A third element of evangelization is leading people to a clear response to the Gospel. The very nature of the Gospel as a gift requires a response. The ministry of Jesus is marked by such questions as: "Do you believe?" "Do you want to be well?" "Do you want to enter into life?" Jesus taught that we must ask in order to receive and we must actively seek in order to find (Mt. 7:7-11). Christ came to the world and shed His precious blood on the Cross not merely to be observed and admired, but to be received and acknowledged as Redeemer and Lord.

The wall of the routine of the parish can gradually be broken by drawing attention to this element of response through appropriate, loving words. The response is the essence of the personal act of faith on the basis of free will. The response is not simply to this program or to that worship service, but to Christ Himself and to life with Him. Responding is like turning on the lights spiritually. Not all would want to turn on the switch of personal Christian commitment, but all should at least hear and know that such a crucial decision marks the serious beginning of the life in Christ.

While we do not have altar calls in the Orthodox Church, our worship services, and the readings from the Bible, as well as the teachings and examples of the saints, offer numerous lessons and opportunities to underscore the necessity of response to the Gospel – not only once but again and again. The response is essentially none other than that of faith, repentance, and obedience as an expression of authentic Christian life. Faith is the affirmation that Christ is true and reliable, both deserving and requiring our commitment. Repentance, a consequence of faith, is less a regret for past sins and more a matter of a new orientation, a changed world view, and a new way of life based on the Gospel. Obedience is primarily obedience to Christ Himself evidenced by a stable Christian life in service to Him and our neighbor. When the Gospel is preached and taught as both inviting and requiring a response, its power is released in the hearts of listeners by the grace of the Holy Spirit. It becomes evident in a sense of conversion and renewal in the hearts of individual believers. When the response reaches a certain critical mass, the atmosphere and character of the parish itself takes on an evangelical spirit and ethos.

A fourth element in evangelization is attention to the process of spiritual growth by means of prayer and holiness of conduct. The Gospel looks to create a sense of permanent relationship, an abiding sense of communion with Christ, the risen and living Lord, who is constantly with us and who guides us in our daily walk. In the Gospel of John, Christ compares His relationship with His followers to that of a vine and its branches: "I am the vine, you are the branches. Whoever abides in me, and I in him, he it is who bears much fruit" (Jn 15:4-5). Jesus taught the disciples not only to abide in His love and in His word, but truly in Him by means of a mutual indwelling, a mystical union: "If anyone loves me, he will keep my word, and my Father will love him, and we will come to him and make our home with him" (Jn 14:23). The same sense of mystical union with Christ is found in Saint Paul who wrote: "For me to live is Christ" (Phil. 1:21). And again: "I have been crucified with Christ; it is no longer I who live, but Christ who lives in me; and the life I now live in the flesh I live by faith in the Son of God, who loved me and gave Himself for me" (Gal. 2:20). This consciousness of personal connection and communion with Christ can arise only from a disciplined life of prayer and a sense of Christian integrity in all our daily affairs. The deepest aspects of Orthodox spirituality, theology and worship – the whole understanding of salvation as participation in the life of God (*theosis*) – are anchored on this evangelical teaching of the mystical union with Christ, the source of the greatest spiritual power and renewal in the parish.

Such biblical passages and spiritual principles must be attended to and taught to our people, especially the principle of Christ-centeredness. The treasure is not tapped if preaching and teaching concentrate on explaining Christian virtues in the abstract and giving practical advice without connecting the discourse specifically with Christ. Often one hears valuable sermons on love, humility, sacrifice, forgiveness, and generosity in which the name of Christ is hardly mentioned. Little is heard about Christ Himself – His own love, humility, sacrifice, forgiveness, and generosity as exemplified in His ministry. And yet it is an easy matter to lift up an event or teaching from the Gospels expressing these qualities. In fact it makes the task of preaching more concrete, clear and effective. In similar fashion, teaching sessions in the classroom or church hall offer valuable instruction on fasting, icons, the lives of saints, traditional customs, and important events in Church history. The opportunity need not be lost to connect these treasures with Christ, to remind participants of the centrality of Christ, and to celebrate the gift of His holy presence in our midst. Evangelical preaching and teaching, while affirming all the treasures of the Orthodox tradition, seeks to bring Christ into the center of things where He truly belongs and thus to create the conscious awareness that the Christ of the Pantokrator icon in the domes of our sanctuaries is truly the Lord of the parish and the Lord of our personal lives as well.

A final element in evangelization is witness. Jesus used the metaphors of salt and light to describe the disciples' role of witness and mission in the world. When Christ dwells in the hearts of believers, when the local parish is Christ-centered in its mindset and activities, then all who bear the name Christian will spontaneously function as salt and light wherever they may be in the world. In the early chapters of 2 Corinthians, Saint Paul uses other striking imagery to describe his missionary work which he connects with the proclamation of the Gospel, as well as the light of the new creation that the Gospel imparts to receptive hearts. Saint Paul speaks of his apostolic ministry as the sharing of "the fragrance of the knowledge of God" and "the aroma of Christ to God" (2 Cor. 2:14-15). This aromatic fragrance of Christian witness, according to Saint Paul, is not some external additive but an intrinsic quality arising out of "the light of the gospel of the glory of Christ" shining in the hearts of those who gladly hear and receive the good news. The Apostle uses the imagery of the act of creation to describe the mystery of how God Himself lights up the light of His grace by means of the Gospel:

> For what we preach is not ourselves but Jesus Christ as Lord, with ourselves as your servants for Jesus' sake. For it is the God who said, 'Let light shine out of darkness,' who has shone in our hearts to give the light of the knowledge of the glory of God in the face of Christ (2 Cor. 4:5-6).

Saint Paul goes on to say that this act of creation in the soul, which is the source of witness and mission, is also "the treasure in earthen vessels," the transcendent power of God in us which upholds us in times of suffering so that, afflicted we are not crushed, perplexed we are not driven to despair, struck down we are not destroyed, so that the life of Jesus may be manifest in our mortal humanity (2 Cor. 4:7-10).

Evangelization, the preaching of the Gospel, is not the only ministry in the Church. There is also worship, catechesis, pastoral guidance, philanthropy, and mission. However, all ministries of the Church, to function properly and in full power, must be penetrated with an evangelical spirit – the love of Christ, the zeal to proclaim the good news, the joy to see people coming to Christ and growing in Christ, the commitment to pray and work for the cause of the kingdom and its righteousness. The evangelical spirit is none other than the burning faith that the risen Christ in His great love and mercy is in our midst doing His gracious work in us and through us. In this perspective of living faith, all believers have the possibility of becoming the "aroma of Christ," "the fragrance of the knowledge of God," wherever God has placed us. When a sufficient number of believers shine with the light of Christ, then the local parish itself, by the grace of God, becomes a burning bush of God's presence for all to see, rejoice, and respond.

NOTES

[1] Anastasios Yannoulatos, "Discovering the Orthodox Missionary Ethos," *Martyria/Mission: The Witness of the Orthodox Churches Today*, edited by Ion Bria (Geneva: World Council of Churches, 1980), pp. 20-29.

[2] *Ibid.*, p. 20.

[3] Peter E. Gillquist, *Becoming Orthodox: A Journey to the Ancient Christian Faith* (Ben Lomond: Conciliar Press, 1992) and the abundance of literature published by Conciliar Press. A similar evangelical stirring through incoming coverts is occurring in England. See Michael Harper, *A Faith Fulfilled: Why Are Christians Across Great Britain Embracing Orthodoxy?* (Ben Lomond: Conciliar Press, 1999).

[4] David W. Henderson, *Culture Shift: Communicating God's Truth to Our Changing World* (Grand Rapids: Baker Books, 1998), p. 16. See also Stanley J. Grenz, *A Primer on Postmodernism* (Grand Rapids: Eerdmans, 1996) and Nancey Murphy, *Anglo-American Postmodernity: Philosophical Perspectives on Science, Religion, and Ethics* (Boulder: Westview Press, 1997).

[5] Henderson, p. 183.

[6] Alexander Schmemann, "Problems of Orthodoxy in America: The Spiritual Problem," *Saint Vladimir's Theological Quarterly* 9 (4, 1965), pp. 171-193.

[7] *Ibid.*, p. 174.

[8] In his keynote address to the Clergy-Laity Congress in Dallas, Texas, entitled "Rekindling an Orthodox Awareness."

[9] Commission on the Archdiocesan Theological Agenda, "Report to His Eminence Archbishop Iakovos," *The Greek Orthodox Theological Review* 34 (1989), pp. 283-306. This report, dealing with issues of faith, leadership, the parish, and social realities facing the Church, and including a modern Greek translation, was republished in a separate small volume and distributed to all the delegates of the Clergy-Laity Congress in Washington, D.C. (1990) under the title: *Report to His Eminence Archbishop Iakovos Concerning the Future Theological Agenda of the Greek Orthodox Archdiocese* (Brookline: Holy Cross Orthodox Press, 1990). It is still highly instructive today.

[10] Saint Athanasios, *On the Incarnation of the Word*, trans. and ed. by a Religious of C.S.M.V. with an Introduction by C. S. Lewis (London: Mowbray, 1953), p. 61.

[11] This idea and language is taken from W. A. Elwell and R. W. Yarbrough, *Encountering the New Testament* (Grand Rapids: Baker Books, 1998), p. 138.

[12] See further Theodore Stylianopoulos, *The Good News of Christ: Essays on the Gospel, Sacraments and Spirit* (Brookline: Holy Cross Orthodox Press, 1991), pp. 1-29.

[13] Anthony Coniaris, *Preaching the Word of God* (Brookline: Holy Cross Orthodox Press, 1983), pp. 8-9.

CHAPTER FOUR

HOLY TRINITY, HOLY COMMUNITY AND EVANGELISM

My task in this chapter is to reflect on the broader theological presuppositions of the proclamation of the Gospel. In the Orthodox perspective evangelism is not only the act of the announcement of the good news as God's message of salvation but also an invitation to join the living community of faith, the Church, in which the blessings of the Gospel are actualized. Church and Gospel are inseparable elements of Christian existence. While the message of salvation, the good news of God's saving work through Christ and in the Holy Spirit, is the empowering focus of the identity and mission of the Church, there would be no Gospel to preach apart from the historical birth of the Church as the concrete community of faith entrusted with the Gospel. In turn, the Church itself comes into existence by the action of God, and specifically through the ministry of Christ and the gift of the Spirit on Pentecost. God, Church and Gospel are intimately connected. In its fullness the Gospel message is none other than the momentous news of the self-disclosure and saving activity of God – Father, Son and Holy Spirit – lived and testified by the Church as God's people, and proclaimed to all as universal good news.

A key passage in the Gospel of Saint Matthew integrates the three elements of our topic, "Holy Trinity, Holy Community and Evangelism." I have in mind the great commission of Mt. 28:16-20 in which the risen Christ, speaking as a transcendent Revealer in the setting of a mountain, addresses the disciples with the following words:

> All authority in heaven and on earth has been given to me. Go therefore and make disciples of all nations, baptizing them in the name of the Father and of the Son and of the Holy Spirit, teaching them to observe all that I have commanded you; and behold, I am with you always, to the close of the age (Mt. 28:18-20).

71

In the Orthodox Churches, this magnificent text is recited at the celebrations of the mystery of Baptism. The sacred text functions both as a crowning conclusion to the Gospel of Matthew, summing up central themes of the Gospel, as well as a permanent agenda for the life and mission of the Church until the coming of the Lord. Let us keep it in view as we explore the three related parts of our topic.

HOLY TRINITY

In the tradition of Eastern Christianity the Holy Trinity is the mystery of the living God encountered in personal prayer, worship and daily life. In speaking about the Holy Trinity, we must not regard the matter primarily as an intellectual challenge, as if we were to analyze a complex theological doctrine or paradigm, but rather as a profound mystery revealed and celebrated in the life of the community of faith. The mystery is none other than the personal disclosure of the plentitude of the living God as Father, Son and Spirit, a mystery both transcendent and immanent, which is the ground of the good news of salvation and the source of all blessings. And the key to that mystery is the person of Christ in whom the Father is revealed by the power of the Holy Spirit.

The above text of the great commission emphasizes the status of Jesus as the risen Lord who declares: "All authority in heaven and on earth has been given to me" (Mt. 28:18). Who has given all authority to the risen Christ? It is God the Father in whom all authority in heaven and on earth resides. The words concerning the authority of Jesus sum up the christology of Saint Matthew evidenced in significant passages throughout the Gospel. Chief among them are the account of the birth of Jesus as Emmanuel/"God with us" (Mt. 1:23), the texts of the baptism and transfiguration of Jesus where He is manifested as the Father's "beloved Son" (Mt. 3:17; 17:5), and the majestic prayer of Jesus in Mt. 11:25-27:

> I thank thee, Father, Lord of heaven and earth, that you have hidden these things from the wise and understanding and revealed them to babes ... All things have been delivered to me by my Father; and no one knows the Son except the Father, and no one knows the Father except the Son and any one to whom the Son chooses to reveal him.

Full divine authority radiates from the risen Christ. In His presence, the disciples prostrate themselves in an act of worship. By this divine authority, which Jesus as risen Lord and unique Son of God possesses, He commissions His followers to make disciples of all nations. One part of the commission is to baptize "in the name of the Father and of the Son and of the Holy Spirit" (Mt. 28:19), a most ancient trinitarian formula no doubt known and used by the community of the Evangelist Matthew as a baptismal confession. Because the risen Jesus, by His manifested status as Lord and Son of God, possesses full divine authority, He can be placed on the same level and in the same sequence along with the Father and God's Spirit. Christian faith and worship express a momentous understanding of God as Trinity. Of course, to draw a nuanced distinction, we must say that the reference is not quite trinitarian in the sense of presupposing the developed trinitarian problematic and doctrine of the fourth century, but rather "triadic" in that it gives prototheological expression to the early Christian experience and belief in God as Father, Son and Spirit.

There are other triadic texts in the New Testament that, directly or indirectly, bear decisive trinitarian implications. For example, the account of the baptism of Jesus highlights the divine sonship of Christ, who is identified as the "beloved Son" by the voice of the Father, and upon whom the fullness of the Spirit descends (Mt. 3:16-17). In 2 Cor. 13:13 Saint Paul ends with the blessing, "The grace of the Lord Jesus Christ and the love of God and the communion of the Holy Spirit be with all of you," a familiar benediction in the Liturgy of Saint John Chrysostom. In Eph. 4:4-6 we find another direct triadic text having the marks of an early Christian confessional formula: "There is one body and one Spirit, just as you were called to the one hope that belongs to your call, one Lord, one faith, one baptism, one God and Father of us all, who is above all and through all and in all." Many more New Testament texts and even entire chapters, can be cited which, implicitly or explicitly, presuppose and reflect the rich early Christian understanding of God as Trinity (e.g., Acts 1:1-5; 1 Cor. 12:1-6; 2 Cor. 3; Rom. 1:1-6; 5:1-5; 8:1-17; Eph. 5:18-20; Jn 4:10-14; 14:15-24; Rev. 1:4-6). All these texts originate not from one author or one congregation but from the entire life of the early Church to which they bear testimony. In other words, the Christian understanding of God as Trinity arises from primary revelatory ground, the corporate religious experience of the early Christians in response to the ministry of Christ and the gift of the Spirit. Knowledge of the Holy Trinity expresses the heart of Christian faith, piety and worship.

Despite this evidence from the New Testament, two objections have often been raised against the view of God as Trinity. One objection is at the popular level and the other at a sophisticated one, but both are comparably superficial, equally false and correspondingly dangerous. The popular one holds that the gods of all religions are basically the same. All religious people, it is said, seek to climb to the same mountain but from different sides. In ancient times, a similar idea was expressed that there were many gods bearing many names, Zeus, Apollo, Baal, Serapis, and numerous others, but all referred to the same reality. In biblical perspective, nothing could be further from the truth. This sort of syncretistic view of God is diametrically opposed to the Jewish and Christian view of God as the living God of Abraham, Jacob and Isaac. It is against the polytheism of the times that the Hebrew Prophets raised their voices and proclaimed the God of Israel as the only true and living God. The biblical teaching about God developed precisely in polemical rejection of idolatry, that is, the rejection of the many gods of paganism seen as false gods and humanly devised idols. We read in Dt. 6:4-5, "Hear, O Israel: The Lord our God is one Lord; and you shall love the Lord your God with all your heart, with all your soul, and with all your might." This core Old Testament confession of faith, while affirming loyalty to the true and living God of Israel, intends to reject and exclude the worship of pagan deities, for example, Baal the fertility god of Canaan, or Moloch to whom children were offered as sacrifice. Heaven forbid that the name of the Holy One of Israel, the Father of Jesus Christ, should be mentioned in the same breath with such gods!

A community's beliefs about God and its worship of God directly impact on the community's life and values. It is for this reason that Saint Paul was extremely concerned about the eating of idol meats by Christians in Corinth, a custom bound up with the celebration of pagan feasts and the worship of pagan deities. It was an issue to which the Apostle Paul devoted concentrated attention in his First Epistle to the Corinthians (chaps. 8-10). He did not necessarily deny the existence of false deities but he utterly rejected their standing. He writes: "Indeed there are many 'gods' and many 'lords' – yet for us there is one God, the Father ... and one Lord, Jesus Christ" (1 Cor. 8:5-6). At the end of his pastoral admonitions Saint Paul uses stronger language:

What do I imply then? That food offered to idols is anything, or that an idol is anything? No, I imply that what pagans sacrifice they offer to demons and not to God. I do not want you to be partners with demons. You cannot drink the cup of the Lord and the cup of demons. You cannot partake of the table of the Lord and the table of demons (1 Cor. 10:19-21).

The second, modern and more sophisticated objection to the trinitarian view of God may be traced back to German theologians in the late nineteenth and early twentieth centuries. Perhaps the greatest exponent of this position was Adolf von Harnack (1851-1930) who argued that the development of dogma was part and parcel of the "hellenization" of Christianity. According to this view, the trinitarian doctrine was fatally influenced by Greek philosophical thought and was not derived from the witness of Scripture. The Bible speaks of the saving activities of God, so it was claimed, not the metaphysical nature of God. Church dogma allegedly developed on the basis of philosophical principles and abstractions, not the living faith of the Bible. The Church Fathers were presumably lured into the realm of pagan thought, dangerously leaning toward tritheism, and thus departed from the good ground of Jewish monotheism.

That argument about the hellenization of Christianity has now grown stale. One reason is the fact that ancient cultures and religions were not sealed off from one another. The impact of Hellenic language and culture was already felt by the Jews in Alexandria, Palestine and elsewhere, beginning with Alexander the Great, several centuries prior to the rise of Christianity. More importantly, biblical scholarship during the last half century has emphasized the Jewish background of the New Testament, including the Gospel of John, the Pauline Epistles and the Book of Revelation, documents which contain primary christological and triadic texts. It can be further argued, as many biblical scholars do, that the whole stream of the biblical tradition, including the Old Testament, is to speak of God not as an isolated singularity or exclusive monad. God existed and acted by means of His personified Wisdom or Logos and by the power of his Spirit. In this perspective, the Jewish heritage already bears intimations of the plentitude of God – Yahweh existing and revealing Himself through His Wisdom and Spirit, the two "hands" of God according to Saint Eirenaios, in relational and reciprocal terms.

Nevertheless, the decisive step to the experiential understanding of God as Holy Trinity is taken in the New Testament. This understanding is centered on the person and saving work of Christ whom the early Christians came to exalt and worship as Lord and Savior. This crucial step was not at all a denial of monotheism but a movement to a richer, more expansive understanding of monotheism based on Jesus' ministry, particularly His death and resurrection. The Apostle Paul, "a Hebrew of Hebrews" (Phil. 3:5), shows not the slightest concern that he is compromising the Jewish legacy of monotheism when he proclaims the risen Christ as Lord, the One who bears the Name above every name (Phil. 2:9-11). With startling and disarming ease he is able to appeal to God and to Christ in the same breath, attributing to them equal divine prerogatives. For example, he writes in 1 Cor. 8:6: "For us there is one God, the Father, from whom are all things and for whom we exist, and one Lord, Jesus Christ, through whom are all things and through whom we exist." Similarly the Evangelist John draws from the Old Testament the concept of personified Wisdom to proclaim the pre-existence of the Divine Logos or Word, whom he names as eternal God, the Only Son and Revealer of the Father (Jn 1:1, 18; cf. 20:28). According to the Evangelist John, Jesus of Nazareth is the incarnate God, not the Father but the Son, distinct from the Father yet united with him, the One who fully shares the Name and deep being of God, and therefore who shares all the divine prerogatives of life and judgment, including the sending forth of the Spirit who proceeds from the Father (Jn 1:14; 8:24,28,58; 10:30; 14:9-11; 15:26). Presenting Jesus' ministry against the background of Jewish life and thought – Temple, Jewish festivals, Old Testament events and concepts – the Gospel of Saint John provides the single richest resource of the Christian understanding of God as Trinity.

Let me add a personal note with regard to the argument that the idea of God as Holy Trinity is a metaphysical abstraction, a result of philosophical speculation by the Church Fathers. Growing up in the Church, I recited the Creed as I recited the Lord's Prayer. I never thought of the Creed as something abstract or distant. I took for granted that all others in the Church did the same and thought in the same way. Just as we prayed, "Our Father, who art in heaven," so also we prayed, "I believe in one God, Father Almighty... and in one Lord, Jesus Christ... and in the Holy Spirit..." I still do and so does my congregation. The Creed is a confession of faith summarizing what the Scriptures proclaim. It helps us to recall and praise the name and saving work of God – Father, Son and Holy Spirit – in salvation history. The Creed in essence is liturgically rooted and has become an integral part of liturgy. It grew out of the life experience and the prayers of the Church. It still functions as a prayer, a hymn, a song of faith, proclaims the good news of salvation in confessional and doctrinal language.

As a theological student and later professor of theology, I have spent considerable time reading the Church Fathers, such as Saint Ignatios of Antioch, Saint Justin the Martyr, Saint Athanasios, the three Cappadocians, and others. While doing so, I have always wondered whether the detractors of the trinitarian understanding of God had read the same Church Fathers I was reading. It was obvious to me that the Church Fathers were primarily students of the Bible. Having in view the whole history of salvation, they focused on Christ, His teaching and healing ministry, and the central events of salvation – incarnation, death and resurrection, and the gift of the Spirit. They thought and argued issues as intellectuals of their time, and in the process used a few key philosophical terms, such as *ousia* (essence or substance), *hypostasis* (subsistence, person) and *homoousios* (of the same essence or substance), in order to defend and secure the right teaching about what they considered to be primarily an ineffable mystery as expressed in the Bible. However, their dominant terminology, basic categories and focal attention was thoroughly biblical.

For example, Saint Athanasios in his *Letters to Serapion* mainly intends to demonstrate the divinity of the Son, whereas Saint Basil in his work *On the Holy Spirit* is concerned to do the same with regard to the Spirit. But both rely on Scripture and arguments drawn from Scripture. And the chief argument in both cases, supported by numerous biblical texts, is utterly clear and overpowering: if Scripture attributes to the Son and the Spirit titles, prerogatives, powers and activities which belong to God the Father, then the conclusion is inescapable that the Son and the Spirit belong to the same uncreated realm of the being and life of God. It was such thoroughly biblical considerations that guided the Church Fathers to formulate a full trinitarian doctrine as reflection on Scripture and the data of Christian worship since apostolic times.

I conclude the first part of this study with a brief description of my understanding of God as Trinity, the central mystery of faith, as I see it in Scripture and the Church Fathers, a perspective which I find utterly coherent and compelling. God is primarily God the Father, the source of deity and of all life. As Scripture abundantly attests, the Father is the primary cause and actor behind creation, revelation and redemption. But the Father is not alone, an isolated, solitary deity. He acts and reveals Himself, again according to Scripture, through His Son and by the power of His Spirit.

The trinitarian theology of the Church Fathers, reflecting on this mystery, helps us to understand that the Son and the Spirit are not separate deities but exist in eternal communion and union with the Father. The Father gives all that He is to the Son, except Fatherhood (the attribute of being Father), because the Son is the Son and not the Father, and it was the Son who assumed human flesh, died on the Cross and was resurrected on the third day for our salvation. The Father equally gives all that He is to the Spirit, except Fatherhood and Sonship, because the Spirit is not the Father, nor the Son, and it was the Spirit who was revealed on the day of Pentecost. Thus the Trinity is one God, Father, Son and Spirit, sharing all things – existence, essence, sovereignty, kingdom, will and activities in creation and the work of salvation.

The patristic principle that in God as Trinity all things are shared safeguards monotheism, while the principle that the attributes of being Father, Son and Spirit are not shared requires and safeguards Trinity. How do we know this? We know it not from purely rational analysis or philosophical speculation but from historical revelation enshrined in the witness of Scripture. We know it from the fact that, according to Scripture, it is the Father who sends the Son to the world and not the reverse. It is the Son who becomes incarnate, neither the Father nor the Spirit. And it is the Spirit who was revealed on Pentecost. Accordingly we affirm the full unity of the one true God disclosed in three distinct persons, dwelling in one another and sharing all things, yet being truly distinct persons without losing their unity. Such in brief terms is the trinitarian teaching of Holy Scripture and the Church Fathers.

HOLY COMMUNITY

The Gospel of Saint Matthew is known as the ecclesiastical Gospel. It was the most popular Gospel in the ancient Church because of its usefulness, particularly its systematic arrangement of Jesus' teaching in several long discourses such as the Sermon on the Mount (chaps. 5-7). It is also the Gospel which explicitly uses the word *ekklesia* – Church (Mt. 16:18; 18:17). The great commission (Mt. 28:18-

20), with which we began, itself testifies to the ecclesiastical character and consciousness of the Evangelist Matthew. For Matthew's community, Christ's commission to make disciples of all nations certainly implies that the new converts were to join the Church of Christ about which the Lord had said the "gates of hell" would not "prevail against it' (Mt. 16:18). The manner of making disciples – baptizing them in the name of the Father and the Son and the Holy Spirit, as well as teaching them all that the Lord had commanded in the Gospel – underscores the reality of the Church and its task of evangelism. The disciples are not merely to announce the Gospel and move on, but to baptize and teach in order to form and build up the Church of Christ. The great commission connects Trinity, Church and evangelism. And the connection is not only ethical, a matter of ethical obedience to Jesus' teaching, but also sacramental, a matter of a new life transformed and sanctified through Baptism, a life of holiness appropriate to the new creation in Christ. Holy Trinity and holy community are intimately connected and serve as closely related sources evangelism.

The relationship of the Holy One of Israel with His people, defined by mutual love, fidelity and holiness, has deep roots in the Old Testament. The idea of biblical revelation as such carries with it the presupposition of the creation of a faith community that receives its identity and vocation from the gift of its knowledge of and relationship with the holy God. God's call of Abraham created not only a relationship with Abraham and his immediate clan, but formed a permanent covenant commitment with Abraham's descendants according to the God's promise: "I will make of you a great nation and I will bless you" (Gen. 12:2). And again: "I will maintain my covenant with you and your descendants after you throughout the ages as an everlasting pact, to be your God and the God of your descendants after you" (Gen. 17:7). God's personal self-disclosure established a deep and personal relationship with Abraham and the people of God, a relationship by God's free and elective grace, based on divine love. And God's purpose was universal: that God's people would be a light and a blessing to all nations. The story of Moses and the liberation of Israel from Egypt recapitulates God's purposeful will to liberate his people in order that they may serve him, the Holy One, as a holy people. We read in Dt. 7:6-8:

> For you are a people holy to the Lord your God; the Lord your God has chosen you to be a people for his own possession, out of all the

peoples that are on the face of the earth ... because the Lord loves you, and is keeping the oath which he swore to your fathers, that the Lord has brought you out with a mighty hand, and redeemed you from the house of bondage.

The Old Testament prophets were severe critics of Israel's violation of the covenant of mutual love and fidelity, a violation which reached its profane zenith in both idolatry and flagrant injustice among God's own people. The result was divine judgment and national catastrophe with the destruction of the Temple and the exile to Babylon. In those days, the Prophet Ezekiel proclaimed a dramatic vision of God's holy presence, the *shekinah*, departing from the Temple and leaving the people unprotected. Yet Ezekiel, as much as the Prophet Jeremiah (Jer. 31:31-34), envisioned not the obliteration of the covenant but its renewal in God's time. In the words of Ezekiel speaking as the mouthpiece of God:

> I will vindicate the holiness of my great name, which has been profaned among the nations, and which you have profaned among them; and the nations will know that I am the Lord, says the Lord God, when through you I vindicate my holiness before their eyes ... A new heart I will give you, and a new spirit ... and cause you to walk in my statutes and be careful to observe my ordinances (Ez. 36:23,26-27).

The concept of holiness includes not only the element of distinctiveness and separation from all other nations by means of God's election, but also the element of sanctification, being blessed and guided by the numinous presence and power of a holy God who demands covenant fidelity and loving obedience to his laws.

The saving work of Christ, His life, death and resurrection, is to be understood in the same context of covenant, liberation and holiness. On the night of his sacred passion Jesus, while at table with His disciples, looked back to the prophecies of Jeremiah and Ezekiel and fulfilled them. With certain solemn words and actions He inaugurated the renewal of the covenant. He said: "This is my body ... This is my blood of the covenant which is poured out for many" (Mk 14:22-24). The tradition of the Last Supper serves as the sacramental basis for the renewal and deepening of the covenant between God and his people. We have now a new Moses, a new Exodus, a new covenant, a new people reconstituted around the person and the saving work of the Son of God. Saint Paul's account of the Lord's Supper in 1 Cor. 11 shows that it was already a firmly established institution traced back to the Lord himself: "I received from the Lord what I handed to you, that the Lord Jesus on the night when He was betrayed took bread..." and so on (1 Cor. 11:23). The Lord's Supper as the corporate sacramental basis of the new people of God is also clearly evident in 1 Cor. 10:14-22 where Saint Paul compares the sacred meal of the Christians to those of the Jews and pagans. He writes in part: "The cup of blessing which we bless, is it not a participation in the blood of Christ? The bread which we break, is it not a participation in the body of Christ? Because there is one bread, we who are many are one body, for we all partake of the one bread" (1 Cor. 10:16-17).

Similar sacramental aspects of participation in the death and resurrection of Christ, and therefore of renewal and a life of holiness through freedom from the powers of sin and death, resonate in what Saint Paul has to say about Baptism in Rom. 6. By being baptized the Christian participates in the death and resurrection of Christ as saving events. The Christian thereby dies to the old nature under the power of sin and rises to a new life of righteousness empowered by the Spirit. Saint Paul's whole theology of the Church as the mystical body of Christ, in which there is no Jew or Gentile, no slave or free, no male or female, is sacramentally rooted in Baptism and Eucharist, the communal liturgical acts which incorporate and transform believers into Christ's holy body.

However, the holiness of the community should not be narrowly conceived as dependent on the sacramental acts alone. For in fact and by virtue of the gift of the Spirit, the entire community, whether in the context of worship or not, is the temple of the Holy Spirit and should function by the leading of the Spirit in all aspects of ecclesial life. The Apostle Paul viewed his missionary work as a ministry of "a new covenant, not in a written code but in the Spirit" (2 Cor. 3:6). The reality of new creation in Christ took hold among men and women of faith in such a way that they themselves, in the words of Saint Paul, became a living "letter from Christ ... written not with ink but with the Spirit of the living God, not on tablets of stone but on tablets of human hearts" (2 Cor. 3:3). In other words, the return of the *shekinah* of God, the outpouring of the Spirit on the day of Pentecost, was not a return to the physical Temple of Jerusalem but to the community of God's people who now formed the new, living temple of the Lord. Saint Paul asks: "Do you not know that you are God's temple and that God's Spirit dwells in you? ... For God's temple is holy, and that temple you are" (1 Cor. 3:16-17). It is this awareness of the abiding presence of the Holy Spirit in the community, the source of its holiness, which motivates Saint Paul to call time and again for appropriate holiness of life among Christians, whether in matters of sexual purity (1 Cor. 5:1, 6-8; 6:18-20), or disputes among Christians who file lawsuits before secular courts (1 Cor. 6:1-11), or manifold other aspects of daily conduct (Rom. 14:13-17; 1 Thess. 4:3-8).

In this context, I would be remiss not to mention the First Letter of Peter and its vision of holiness associated with baptism as new birth. The Letter of Peter combines the baptismal base of newness of life as well as the wider call for holiness of life. Both aspects are closely connected to the eternal election and saving action of God expressed in trinitarian language. The Christians are "chosen and destined by God the Father and sanctified by the Spirit for obedience to Jesus Christ and for sprinkling with his blood" (1 Pt. 1:2). The imperishable gift of new birth, achieved through the death and resurrection of Christ, is received through the living word of God, the Gospel, as well as Baptism (1 Pt. 1:3, 23; 2:2; 3:21). The essence of pastoral exhortation is to live out God's gift in holiness of conduct. "As He who called you is holy, be holy yourselves in all your conduct; since it is written, 'You shall be holy, for I am holy'" (1 Pt. 1:15-16/Lev. 11:44-45). Having tasted the kindness of the Lord, and having been cleansed and sanctified by the Spirit, Christians are to come "to that living stone... and like living stones be yourselves built into a spiritual house, to be a holy priesthood, to offer spiritual sacrifices acceptable to God through Jesus Christ" (1 Pt. 2:4-5).

In a magisterial work on biblical prayer entitled, *They Cried to the Lord: The Form and Theology of Biblical Prayer* (1994), Patrick D. Miller includes a section on "The Trinitarian Character of Christian Prayer" (pp. 314-321). Miller defines the specific character of Christian prayer, and for that matter the nature of all Christian existence, by reference to the Trinity as the center of Christian life. The key to the new Christian identity and self-understanding is Christ Himself in His status and saving function. According to Miller, Jesus' ministry is summed up by the filial relationship of Jesus with the God of Israel. While the God of Israel remains the same central subject of prayer and life, it is the unique Son who addresses God as Father and also teaches the disciples to do the same (Mt. 6: 9-15; 11:25-30). By virtue of their faith and union with Christ, Christians are made children of God, brothers and sisters of Christ, and joint heirs of God with him. Thus the Christian community has its being in relation to Jesus Christ and shares with him the filial relation to God. Every facet of our relation to God, every blessing and every benefit, happens through Jesus Christ who lived and died as God's presence among us mediating every dimension of our life and death with God. But the filial relation is made effective through the power of the Holy Spirit who sanctifies all aspects of existence. "When we cry, 'Abba! Father!' it is the Spirit Himself bearing witness with our spirit that we are children of God" (Rom. 8:15-16). It is the Spirit who actualizes the gift of adoption, our participation in Christ's filial relation to the Father, and therefore our family status in the faith community as the people of God. Accordingly, all aspects and dimensions of Christian life are related to God as Trinity. Just as all blessings come from the Father, through the Son and in the power of the Holy Spirit, so also every human word or action is offered to God the Father through the Son and in the Spirit. In Christian life and thought, Holy Trinity and holy community belong together.

EVANGELISM

The third major element in the great commission is evangelism. While neither the term Gospel (*euangelion*), nor the verb "to evangelize" (*euangelizesthai*), occur in this particular text, nevertheless its evangelistic character is most prominent, indeed stronger and more explicit than the other two related elements of Trinity and community. For the whole exegetical thrust of the passage is precisely the missionary charge of the risen Lord: "Go therefore and make disciples of all nations" (Mt. 28:18). The main verb and pivot of the text is *matheteusate*, i.e., make disciples, whereas "going forth," "baptizing" and "teaching" are all participles in the original Greek. The noun *mathetes* means literally a learner or pupil, implying an activity which involves disciplined effort and training in a communal setting. Typically Matthean, the verb undoubtedly reflects the systematic evangelistic and catechetical interests behind the composition of Matthew, the most clearly organized document among the Gospels. The same verb occurs in what has been called the "signature" of the author of the Gospel in Mt. 13:52: "Therefore every scribe who *has been trained* (*matheteutheis*) in the kingdom of heaven is like a householder who brings out of his treasure what is new and what is old."

The work of evangelism is not merely announcing the gospel but also "making disciples," presupposing training and nurturing in the community of faith to which Lord has promised: "I am with you always, to the close of the age" (Mt. 28:20). The work of evangelism is a corporate ministry of the Church. Missiology and ecclesiology are integrally connected.

Jesus began his ministry with a distinct message: "The time is fulfilled, and the kingdom of God is at hand; repent, and believe in the Gospel" (Mk. 1:14-15). After His death and resurrection, the apostles included in their message the announcement that Jesus himself was the inaugurator of the kingdom, the risen Lord and Savior, the Victor over the forces of death and corruption, and the Giver of life (Acts 2:22-36).

One of the most characteristic aspects of the Christian movement, anchored on Jesus and the apostles, was its sense of evangelism and mission. Energized by the pentecostal experience of the presence and power of God, the early Christians were driven by the conviction that they had a divine message to proclaim, and not only a message, but also a gift of new life from God, intended for all people without regard to race, gender, wealth, education and the like. One of the reasons behind the success of Christianity was the unity and cohesiveness of the Christian community which new converts were expected to join as a matter of course. To be a Christian was to be a member of the Church. Despite significant internal disputes, the ancient Church fostered a sense of unity in Christ. The diversity of membership of men and women, Jews and Greeks, slaves and free, was bound by its love for Christ and for each other as brothers and sisters. The Church was marked by the consciousness of being an alternative to pagan society; a community with a remarkable ability to point to its own observable renewal of life and holiness of conduct, including honest business dealings and selfless service to others. Pagan authors and opponents of Christianity themselves acknowledged the virtues of those who were called by the name of Christian. To be effective, evangelism requires the evidence of the living community of faith both as concrete testimony of the life of the Gospel as well as the communal setting for the making of disciples.

What is the content of the Gospel which is proclaimed as good news? The heart of the Gospel is the message about the death and resurrection of Christ as events of redemption. Saint Paul writes to the Corinthians about "the Gospel, which you received, in which you stand, by which you are saved, if you hold it fast... that Christ died for our sins in accordance with the scriptures, that he was buried, that he was raised on the third day in accordance with the scriptures" (1 Cor. 15:1-3). The cross and resurrection of Christ are the decisive events of salvation by which the forces of sin, death and Satan are defeated, God's blessings of love and forgiveness are poured out to sinful humanity, and the life of new creation is inaugurated. But the Gospel includes the entire ministry of Christ – incarnation, teaching, healing, death, resurrection and ascension – as the disclosure of the saving work of God. The Evangelists Matthew and Luke present the birth of Jesus as the good news of the coming of the Savior and Emmanuel – God with us (Mt. 1:21-23; Lk. 2:10-11). The Evangelist Mark views Jesus' entire adult ministry as good news when he begins his Gospel with the words: "The beginning of the Gospel of Jesus Christ, the Son of God" (Mk. 1:1). And the Evangelist John proclaims the mystery of the incarnation in which the eternal Word or Logos of God "became flesh and dwelt among us, full of grace and truth" (Jn 1:14). Ultimately the gospel is the person of Christ himself, what God accomplished through him, and the blessings that flow from the crucified and risen Christ.

The Gospel is preached and taught with the aim of evoking and strengthening faith in Christ, of bringing people under His lordship, of drawing men and women more deeply into the life of the Church, and of building up their lives in the new life in Christ. Worship is a celebration of the Gospel through liturgical and sacramental action. In Baptism the believer shares in the death and resurrection of Christ, is united with him, and becomes a new creation. In the Eucharist we recount and celebrate the crucified and risen Christ whom we receive through the eucharistic gifts being renewed as his mystical Body. Seen in this perspective, the Gospel is the foundation of the Church, the core of theology and teaching, the basis of all that we are and do as Christians.

Evangelism is integrally related not only to holy community but also to Trinity. Of course the focus of the good news is Christ and his redeeming work. It is for this reason that Saint Paul most often refers to the Gospel as "the Gospel of Christ" (Rom. 15:19; 1 Cor. 9:12; 2 Cor. 2:12; 9:13; 10:14; Gal. 1:7, etc.). However, the good news is also called "the Gospel of God" (Mk. 1:14; Rom. 1:1; 15:16; 1 Thess. 2:2,9). It is God the Father who is the main actor behind the work of redemption through his Son. The proclaimed Gospel is the active power of God as a transforming reality revealing here and now the saving righteousness of God to all who believe (Rom. 1:16-17). Bearing in mind the mystery of the incarnation, and that Christ is the fullness of the presence of God, Saint Paul could say: "All is from God... that is, God was in Christ reconciling the world to Himself" (*Theos en Christo kosmon katalasson*, 2 Cor. 5:19).

Moreover, God's saving work in Christ, and the blessings that flow from the good news, are communicated through the Holy Spirit. The Spirit is the effective power behind all the ministries of the faith community, preaching, teaching, healing, prophecy and every other ministry (1 Cor. 12:7-11). Similarly the spiritual qualities evidenced among believers are the fruit of the Spirit, love, joy, peace, patience, kindness, goodness, and all the other personal charisms (Gal. 5:22-23). Accordingly, the Holy Trinity as one, true and living God is fully involved in the total work of redemption, sanctification and glorification – God the Father working through His Son and in the power of His Spirit. From this perspective, evangelism entails the announcement not merely of an abstract truth but of the active and transforming presence of God as Trinity. Proclaiming and receiving the good news about Christ and new life in Him is truly participating in the life of the Holy Trinity – the plentitude of life, light and love. The paschal promise of Jesus is: "In that day you will know that I am in my Father, and you in me, and I in you" (Jn 14:20). Where Christ finds love and obedience, He comes to dwell in the Christian believers, together with His Father and the holy fire of the Spirit (Jn 14:23-26). Wherever this precious gift is effectively proclaimed and faithfully received, Holy Trinity, holy community and evangelism are united in one seamless spiritual reality evidenced by a vibrant Church, a radiant witness of mercy and glory, God's holy people declaring "the wonderful deeds of Him who called you out of darkness into His marvelous light" (1 Pt. 2:9).

PART TWO

SPIRITUAL LIFE

CHAPTER FIVE

PRAYER IN SCRIPTURE AND TRADITION

Prayer is both a "holy art" and "holy work" – a gift and a task. As a gift, prayer is the power of God's grace raising us to the realm of God's life. As a task, prayer is unceasing struggle to walk Christ's straight and narrow path, to bring our whole life under His lordship, to let Him change us and our ways that we may be worthy of God's blessings. The "Liturgy," the abiding spiritual center of our life in Christ, etymologically means the "work of the people." We come to the Liturgy to labor in prayer committing "ourselves and one another and our whole life to Christ our God." We also "lift up our hearts" in prayer to experience the grace and joy of God's kingdom. It is said that prayer is the very soul of Orthodoxy, the breath of the Church, the light of each Christian's conscience.

If prayer is the soul of Orthodoxy, as it is, why are so many of our faithful habitually late for worship? If the Liturgy is the center of spiritual life and renewal, as it is, why are we not more empowered to draw others to the Liturgy and the life of the Church through love, joy, goodness, faithfulness and the other fruits of the Spirit? If the lives of the saints are filled with prayer and prayerfulness, as they are, how do we explain the phenomenon of prayerlessness in our own lives? If we have beautiful churches, as we do, should not our hearts also be beautiful chapels, making melody to the Lord with hymns and prayers (Eph. 5:19), and thus be "true worshipers" praising and adoring our God "in spirit and truth" (Jn 4:23-24)?

These are discomforting questions but need to be asked. Writing and reading about prayer may be inspirational, but they can soon be forgotten. Only the actual "work" of prayer, both private and corporate, and connected with the whole course of life, can become the "gift" of prayer releasing the grace and power of God. Christ taught us to pray: "Thy kingdom come, Thy will be done." He also admonished us to be doers, not only hearers, of His words. Because we are His hands and feet, the Lord's will and kingdom cannot be actualized apart from our own faithful consent and eager efforts through prayer in the context of our personal and communal lives.

EXAMPLES OF PRAYER

The primary example of prayer is Jesus Himself. Jesus grew up in an extended family of devout Jews and in a religion of prayer. The Gospel of Luke (chaps. 1-2) tells about Zechariah the priest, Elizabeth, Mary, Symeon the elder, and Anna the prophetess, whose lives were filled with prayer. When Mary visited her cousin Elizabeth, Elizabeth was inspired with the Holy Spirit and cried out to Mary: "Blessed are you among women, and blessed is the fruit of your womb!" And Mary replied: "My soul magnifies the Lord, and my spirit rejoices in God my Savior" (Lk. 1:41-47). Pious Jews prayed three times a day. A key prayer was the biblical creed of faith from Deut. 6:4-5, "Hear, O Israel: The Lord is our God, the Lord alone; and you shall love the Lord your God with all your heart, and with all your soul, and with all your might."

Like all devout Jews, Jesus was a man of prayer. He regularly prayed at meals and observed the traditional Jewish festivals. He frequented the centers of Jewish religious life, the Temple and the synagogues. When He cast out the money changers from the Temple area, He did so in order to cleanse its sacred precincts from commercialism. His holy zeal was to restore the Temple from a "den of robbers" to a "house of prayer for all the nations" (Mk 12:17).

In particular the Gospels emphasize that Christ practiced solitary prayer away from the crowds and sometimes away from the disciples as well. We read: "In the morning, long before daylight, He rose and went out to a lonely place and there He prayed" (Mk 1:35). After teaching and dismissing the crowds, "He went up into the hills to pray" (Mt. 15:23). Prior to the selection of His disciples, He withdrew into the wilderness to pray and "all night He continued in prayer to God" (Lk. 6:12). On one occasion, when the people wanted to acclaim Him king, Jesus left both them and the disciples, and "withdrew again to the mountain by Himself" (Jn 6:15).

At Gethsemane, Christ was sorrowful and distraught. He asked the disciples to pray with Him, looking to them for support. He went a little farther to be by Himself, fell to the ground, and prayed: "Abba, Father, all things are possible with You; remove this cup from me; yet not what I will, but what You will." Returning, He admonished the sleepy disciples: "Watch and pray that you may not enter into temptation; the spirit indeed is willing, but the flesh is weak" (Mk 14:36-38). His last breath on the Cross was a prayer: "Father, to Your hands I commit my spirit" (Lk. 23:46).

Christ was fully God, one with the Father and the Spirit, sharing the essence and attributes of the Triune God. But He was also fully human, sharing all the attributes and frailties of human nature, except sin. He experienced the whole range of human emotions from birth to death. He was not "acting" when he was joyful or indignant, when He needed to eat and drink, when He became tired and needed to rest, when He felt agony and pain. Nor was His devotion to prayer merely for pedagogical reasons, simply to instruct His disciples and us about prayer. He both needed and rejoiced in prayer. He found prayer a source of comfort, refreshment and strength to fulfil His mission. Prayer was a way He affirmed and renewed his closeness to the Father, the hallmark of Christ's life and mission. The mystery of the Incarnation assures us that Christ's life of prayer was as real as it was powerful. His example serves as the archetype of deep, personal prayer.

Another example of prayer is the Apostle Paul, the most successful missionary of the apostolic Church. A man of action, Saint Paul preached the Gospel and established churches throughout the eastern Mediterranean and then planned to go to Rome and even as far as Spain (Rom. 15:17-29). He candidly mentions the enormous work that Christ accomplished through him (Rom. 15:17-29) as well as the many trials he suffered (2 Cor. 11:23-29). He was a warrior of Christ ready to fight for the truth of the Gospel before Jews, Gentiles, and even fellow Christians (Gal. 2:6-14). Nevertheless, Saint Paul was also a man of prayer, indeed a mystic of Christ privileged with heavenly visions. His conversion on the road to Damascus led him to a singular focus on Christ and life in union with Him. In one of his mystical experiences, he was lifted up to the "third heaven" where he beheld "visions and revelations of the Lord" and "heard things that cannot be told" (2 Cor. 12:1-4). At the core of Saint Paul's spirituality was a conscious communion with the risen Lord to the extent that he could say: "For me to live is Christ" (Phil. 1:21) and again: "It is no longer I who live, but Christ who lives in me; and the life I now live in the flesh I live by faith in the Son of God, who loved me and gave Himself for me" (Gal. 2:20).

When we read the Epistles of Saint Paul, we see that his life and thought were filled with prayer and prayerfulness. Large sections of his Epistles read like prayers in which he spontaneously referred all his joys and trials to God. They also abound with specific pastoral exhortations to pray. He tells the Christians in Rome, "I remember you always in my prayers" (Rom. 1:10), and appeals to them, "strive with me in prayer to God" (Rom. 15:30). To the Thessalonians, he writes: "Rejoice always, pray constantly, and give thanks in all circumstances, for this is the will of God in Christ for you" and again asks, "pray for us" (1 Thess. 5:16-18,25). Joy and thanksgiving, even in the midst of trials and persecutions, are the distinctive elements of Saint Paul's prayers. The Epistle to the Philippians was written from prison, a place of cruelty and inhumanity especially in the ancient world. Yet not the slightest hint of personal complaint or self-pity is found in it. Rather, Saint Paul is eager to encourage the Philippians with these words:

> Rejoice in the Lord always; again I say, rejoice. Let all know your forbearance. The Lord is at hand. Have no anxiety about anything, but in everything by prayer and supplication with thanksgiving, let your requests be made known to God. And the peace of God, which passes all understanding, will keep your hearts and your minds in Christ Jesus (Phil. 4:4-7).

The following three examples of prayer are drawn from the Church Fathers. One was fully engaged with the Church's work in the world. Another was a monastic throughout his life. The third was involved in both.

The first is Saint John Chrysostom, a lover of the Gospel of Christ and a great admirer of Saint Paul. He, too, was a man of action and prayer. Endowed with exceptional gifts of intelligence and eloquence, he nevertheless put aside a promising career as a lawyer to concentrate on spiritual life. As a zealous young Christian in his twenties, he spent several years in a cave praying and reading one book, the Bible, until bad health forced him back to the city. In Antioch, where he served as deacon and priest, he devoted himself to evangelical preaching and philanthropic activities. He became the "golden mouth" (*Chrysostomos*) of Christ and the applied Gospel. Later, as Archbishop of Constantinople, he led a life of strict fasting and private prayer, while his public witness was a bustle of evangelical activities through preaching, philanthropy and missionary work. His zeal and uncompromising spirit brought him into conflict with emperors and bishops. Condemned by an ecclesiastical court and forced out of office by the emperor, Saint John Chrysostom mightily resisted his persecutors until finally soldiers drew their swords against the crowd protecting him, and the Church of Saint Sophia began to burn. He was exiled and died in Armenia while suffering terrible physical hardships. But he endured all with amazing spiritual strength derived from his deep faith and the life of prayer. The man with the golden words counted prayer as his great inspiration. His principle was: "First comes prayer and then words" (*Proteron euche kai tote logos*). His last words were in fact a prayer: "Glory be to God for all things" (*Doxa Theo panton eneken*).

The second Church Father, also named John, was a monastic. He spent forty years in solitude on Mount Sinai, and afterwards, until death, served as abbot of Saint Catherine's monastery located at the foot of the mountain. He is known as Saint John of the Ladder because he wrote what in later centuries became the most famous book of Orthodox spirituality, *The Ladder of Divine Ascent*. It is a stern and yet compassionate book. Beyond ascetic strictures and toils, Saint John was a seeker of God's love and of how to enliven the heart with God's holy presence. Cardiologists tell us that a baby's heart begins to beat when some electrical charge flashes through its nerve system while the infant is developing in the mother's womb, a unique, wondrous event! For Saint John, prayer fulfils a similar spiritual function. Prayer draws the "electrical" charge of God's grace and gives the soul its spiritual beat, the basis of all spiritual life. He wrote in *The Ladder of Divine Ascent*: "The first ray of light is lit by prayer. Prayer gives the first hint of what we are seeking and prayer awakens more fervently the mind and heart to God. Prayer is the beginning and basis of all striving toward God."

The third example from the Church Fathers is a Russian saint of the nineteenth century, Saint Theophan the Recluse. Saint Theophan grew up in a pious home and later excelled in seminary studies. For many years he served the Church with exceeding devotion and wisdom as priest and bishop. However, drawn to the life of stillness (*hesychia*), he retired to a monastery and embraced total solitude even among the monastics, which earned him the title "the Recluse." But he never cut contacts with people whom he advised through countless letters. Saint Theophan's special gift was to combine prayer and study. He was a man of wide learning and profound spirituality. His life's harvest include many books on the spiritual life written with penetrating insight and clarity, as if he lived and wrote in our own days. A summary of his teachings on prayer may be found in a valuable anthology entitled *The Art of Prayer*. His chief aim was to show people how to transform Christian existence into a conscious sacrament of grace through deliberate and systematic spiritual growth. The key was heartfelt prayer and a disciplined life of prayer. By prayer, believers truly attain to inward communion with God and possessed the power of a "battle-ax" against the devil and his works. For Saint Theophan, prayer summed up the essence of the inner life with God which begins with a spark, fans into a flame, and kindles one's whole being with the fire of divine love. Prayer is the basis, criterion and guide behind all spiritual endeavors. He writes in *The Art of Prayer:*

> What is prayer? Prayer is the test of everything; it is the source of everything, the driving force of everything, and the director of every-thing. If prayer is right, everything is right. Prayer will not allow anything to go wrong. If you are not successful in your prayer, do not expect success in anything. It is the root of all.

PRAYER AS INVOCATION

Prayer is defined by a variety of forms such as petition, confession, intercession, thanksgiving, and doxology. Like the Psalms, most prayers combine several of these forms. A prayer may begin with the praise of God, then make an entreaty of petitions, and end with additional words of praise to God. Or a prayer may begin with thanksgiving, offer confession of sins, and finish with the praise of God. However, the meaning of prayer is defined not only by the various forms of prayer but also by the very nature of prayer as an act of personal of faith and communication with God. All prayers, whatever their forms, share basic elements or aspects which can be said to define the essence of prayer. Three such elements disclose the essential meaning, or what we may call the theology of prayer: invocation, relationship and communion.

What is prayer as invocation? To pray is to "invoke" or call upon the name of God. The highest moment of invocation is the *epiklesis* ("invocation") at the consecration of the eucharistic gifts in the Divine Liturgy. The bishop or priest prays to God the Father: "We ask, pray, and entreat You: Send down Your Holy Spirit upon us and upon these gifts here presented. And make this bread the precious Body of Your Christ. And that which is in this cup the precious Blood of Your Christ." All prayers, whether petitionary, confessional, intercessory, or doxological, are defined by this element of invocation.

The act of invocation, often underscored by the explicit use of verbs of invocation such as "ask" (*aito*), "entreat" (*iketeuo*), "cry" (*krazo*), and "invoke" or "call upon" (*epikaloumai*), is significant in itself because it tells something about God, something about those who pray, and something about the nature of prayer itself.

Concerning God, the act of invocation tells us that the One we turn to and address in prayer is accessible and approachable. God is a personal and loving God who not only makes Himself available but also takes the initiative to seek us out. In a great moment of salvation history, God spoke to Moses from the burning bush and charged him to lead the people out of Egypt. Because Moses expressed grave fears about the immensity of the task, God promised him: "I will be with you" (Ex. 3:12). When Moses asked for God's name, God revealed His sacred name, YAHWEH, which means "I AM WHO I AM." He told Moses: "Say to the people of Israel, I AM has sent me to you'" (Ex. 3:14). God's sacred name intimates the mystery of God's being and character – the One who, although a great mystery, eternally exists and is always there for us. We can approach Him in prayer because He is accessible. By His very name God assures us: "I am here. I am with you. I am here for you!"

Orthodoxy iconography features many icons of Christ painted in various styles. In all of the icons the halo or crown of Christ is inscribed with the letters "*O ΩN*," meaning "HE WHO EXISTS" or "HE WHO IS." According to the Church Fathers, Christ was the "hidden" Revealer of God in the Old Testament. It was Christ, the eternal Logos of God, who spoke to Moses from the burning bush. What was hidden in the Old Testament became clear in the New. In the New Testament Christ is revealed as Emmanuel – "God-with-us" (Mt. 1:23). During His ministry Christ said to those who listened to Him: "If anyone thirst, let him come to me and drink" (Jn 8:37), and again: "Where two or three are gathered in my name, there am I in the midst of them" (Mt. 18:20). After the resurrection, when He commissioned the disciples to evangelize the world, He promised: "I am with you always, to the close of the age" (Mt. 28:20). Christ's words are trustworthy. Because He is accessible and approachable, we can invoke His name in prayer knowing that He is always with us. He has promised His followers: "Ask and it will be given to you; seek and you will find; knock and it will be opened to you" (Mt. 7:7). And again: "Come to me, all who labor and are heavy laden, and I will give you rest" (Mt. 11:28).

The act of invocation also tells something about ourselves. When we pray, we come to God as supplicants. We approach God as those who have been given the privilege and charge to call upon God as Father. As often as we pray, whether alone or together, we seek to affirm and actualize our status as sons and daughters of the Almighty. Moreover, because God deigns to be at our disposal, to call upon God is to activate His immense reservoir of grace and power. Through invocation, we connect with the Lord of the universe and can release His infinite love for forgiveness, healing, renewal and salvation. Saint Paul, who described Christians as "those who call upon the name of Jesus Christ" (*oi epikaloumenoi to onoma tou Iesou Christou*, 1 Cor. 1:2), equates invocation with the process of salvation. Emphasizing the importance of personal faith and the nearness of the risen Lord, Saint Paul writes: "If you confess that Jesus is Lord and believe in your heart that God raised Him from the dead, you will be saved... For everyone who calls upon the name of the Lord will be saved" (Rom. 10:9,13). Our private and corporate prayers are replete with invocations to the Father, the Son and the Holy Spirit. By invoking the name of God we engage the holy and mighty God, Creator and Lord of life. Calling upon God's name is not the only criterion of salvation. But it is the foundation of the whole process of salvation.

The act of invocation tells us, as well, something about the nature of prayer itself. To call upon the Lord of the universe is a daring and awesome act. God is holy and burning fire consuming what is unclean. When Moses approached the burning bush, God said to Him: "Take off your shoes, because the place on which you stand is holy ground" (Ex. 3:5). Moses' shoes were likely made of leather. Some Church Fathers interpret leather as signifying hardness of heart or insensibility of soul which must be put off before approaching God's holy presence.

In a parallel vision, when the Prophet Isaiah saw God enthroned in glory (Is. 6:1-9), the angels covered their faces with their wings as they hovered around God's throne and sang: "Holy, holy, holy is the Lord of hosts; the whole earth is full of His glory." The prophet's spontaneous reaction was to say: "Woe is me! For I am lost; for I am a man of unclean lips, and I dwell in the midst of a people of unclean lips; for my eyes have seen the King, the Lord of hosts!" In a dramatic gesture, one of the angels took a burning coal from the altar of the Temple and touched the prophet's mouth, saying: "Behold, this has touched your lips; your guilt is taken away, and your sin is forgiven." The angel's statement to Isaiah is now recited by the priest in the Liturgy after his reception of Holy Communion. With regard to the Prophet Isaiah, once cleansed and empowered, he eagerly accepted his call ("Here I am! Send me!") and fulfilled his mission as one of the greatest prophets in the Old Testament.

The invocation of God is awesome to contemplate. To call upon God means to come before God's holy presence. The immediate experience of God evokes powerful attraction and equal fear because of God's majesty and holiness. The fear arises from the sense of human sinfulness in the presence of the holy, the sense of being like dry grass before the divine fire. Many avoid prayer because of the discomfort of being judged by a righteous God who desires reformation of life in alignment with His will and purpose. The attraction comes from the beauty and power of God's love, from the inward yearning to share in the light and holiness of God. Those who are responsive to God's beauty and love, and desire to be cleansed and transformed, are drawn to prayer. The saints counsel that we must approach prayer not routinely and formally, but with spiritual awareness and receptivity. In the Divine Liturgy we symbolize the Cherubim in Isaiah's vision singing the Trisag
ion: "Holy, holy, holy, Lord Sabaoth, heaven and earth are filled with Your glory." When Holy Communion is presented to the faithful, the priest proclaims: "With the fear of God, faith and love, draw near!" When we celebrate the Divine Liturgy or pray privately, we should do so with awesome awareness that we are in the presence of the living God. Prayer as invocation brings us before the throne of God, calling upon Him, seeking to connect with Him, to be judged and cleansed, to receive from Him light and life.

Prayer as Relationship

A second essential element of prayer is relationship. Prayer as relationship reveals a deeper level of meaning and power in the mystery of prayer. Most of us pray in time of need. We invoke God when urgencies or dangers arise without developing an abiding relationship with God. Saint Symeon the New Theologian tells how as a young man he began fervently to invoke God like the blind man who called out to Christ "Son of David, have mercy me!" Soon afterwards he was blessed with a sublime vision of Christ radiant with the uncreated light of divinity. However, Saint Symeon completely lost this spiritual treasure and turned to worse wickedness because of immaturity, carelessness and lack of a stable relationship with God. When we call upon God with consistency, spend more time with Him in prayer and look after our Christian lives with care, prayer can lead us into deeper knowledge of God and thus to an abiding relationship with Christ.

How do we come to know another human being as a person? Is it by knowing anatomy, psychology or history? Although all knowledge is helpful, the best way to know another as a unique person is directly and specifically: by looking into that person's face and eyes, by talking and spending time with her or him, by sharing hopes and fears. Most human relationships are rather casual and often marked by a certain distance and remoteness. Sometimes even spouses and family members, living in immediate physical proximity, nevertheless experience a sense of distance. How can the distance be eliminated and a true connection of hearts and minds be established? The key is the willingness to enter into relationship through honest dialogue and the desire to share life, thoughts and activities.

Prayer is a way of looking into God's face and allowing Him to look into our own. Prayer is a way of talking and spending time with God, a way of bridging the gap and establishing a personal relationship with Him. Not infrequently Christians confess that they do not feel close to God. Despite their good works and participation in worship services, God seems remote and distant. He is a kind of impersonal "force" throughout the universe rather than a loving Father who embraces our whole life and abides in our hearts. The key to bridging the distance and removing the sense of remoteness is the willingness to enter into relationship through honest dialogue and the desire to live in nearness to God. Developing such a relationship with God, just as with other people, requires a free, conscious choice to know God through personal encounter. The most direct and personal way of doing that is through regular times of prayer. Working for such a relationship seems risky to most of us because it may entail significant changes in our lives. The saints assure us, however, that experiential knowledge of God is an adventure in divine love which is both judging and healing, forgiving and illuminating, cleansing and transfiguring. Prayer does not diminish us; rather it enhances our lives with the grace and beauty of God.

A number of images in the Bible and tradition exemplify prayer as relationship. To pray is to speak with God. Prayer as dialogue suggests a continuous relationship with God in which prayer is not only talking with but also listening to God as we seek to grow in our relationship with Him. Saint John of the Ladder uses the striking image of prayer as a mirror, or the light of the mind which shows where we stand spiritually. Prayer as true dialogue is a conversational journey of give and take, including ups and downs. However, the dialogue must be deeply personal and completely honest because formal prayer and ritual can sometimes be a way of avoiding God and evading the personal encounter with Him while being satisfied about fulfilling our duty to Him.

Another image is that of prayer as food for the soul. Prayer provides needed daily spiritual sustenance. We pray, "Give us this day our daily bread," but the most important Bread is Christ Himself who said not to labor for the food that perishes but for the food of eternal life, His grace. Our physical energies would be quickly depleted without regular material sustenance. To attain to its proper strength and vigor, the soul needs the constant food of daily prayer.

Saint John of Kronstadt uses additional striking images. Prayer is spiritual breathing. Our lungs breathe in oxygen and breathe out carbon dioxide, eliminating toxicity and receiving renewing power. Prayer is the ongoing spiritual breathing of the soul – we breathe in the grace of the Spirit and we breathe out sin.

Prayer, according to Saint John of Kronstadt, is also gardening. Gardening involves planting and weeding. Left unattended, a field grows weeds and becomes wild. Attentive, persevering prayer plants spiritual flowers but also takes out the weeds, the unhelpful attitudes and destructive habits, from our lives and the life of the Church so that both can truly be a beautiful garden testifying to God's presence and glory. To quote a theological student: "Prayer for the Christian is like water for a plant. If the plant is watered, it lives and thrives. If it is neglected, it dries out and eventually dies."

Prayer as relationship is anchored on the biblical truth of covenant – *diatheke* – a word that in its more traditional rendering of "testament" names the Scriptures of the Old and New Testament. Covenant defines the entire history of salvation as a dialogical relationship, reciprocity, partnership, synergy and mutual loyalty between God, the main actor, and His people, the recipients of His blessings. The Mosaic Law and the Temple were given so that the

Israelites could live as the holy people of the holy God. Saint Paul draws from this covenant imagery of the Old Testament when he tells the Corinthians that the Christians themselves are now the living Temple of God and that they were to lead holy lives in spiritual separation from the world. "For we are the temple of God; as God said: 'I will live in them and move among them, and I will be their God, and they shall be my people . . . I will be a father to you and you shall be my sons and daughters, says the Lord Almighty'" (2 Cor. 6:16-18). Accordingly, our relationship to God is not merely one of isolated partnership but of family relationships, a covenant of love and faithfulness lived and celebrated in community – God's holy people.

Prayer as relationship entails freedom on both sides as it is appropriate to God and to His people who are His sons and daughters. God neither forces nor intimidates human beings to respond and obey Him. On our part, we can neither control nor manipulate God to accomplish selfish designs. Prayer is a dynamic, free-flowing relationship of ups and downs in which, just as in the case of parents and children, we are allowed to express not only our thanks and requests to God but also our honest questions and even complaints.

The great Moses never made it to the Promised Land. Jacob tried manipulation but ended wrestling with the heavenly Stranger before being blessed and re-named "Israel," meaning "one who strives with God." He called the place of his struggle "Peniel," meaning "the face of God" and said: "I have seen God face to face, and yet my life is preserved" (Gen. 32:24-30). Jonah unsuccessfully tried to escape his task of pronouncing doom, knowing that a merciful God would not follow through with destruction. When the Ninevites repented and were forgiven, a humiliated Jonah complained bitterly to God. "Are you angry?" God asked. Jonah replied: "I am angry unto death." Recall also Peter, the leader of the apostles. He whom Christ called "Rock," nevertheless nearly sunk in the water and later denied Christ three times. Are not these images reflections of our own open-ended relationship with God, our waverings between faith and doubt, trust and uncertainty, hope and despair as we seek God's hand in life?

A difficult question is that of "unanswered prayer." A story tells of a man who fell off a cliff and managed to grasp a bush on the way down. "Help, help!" he yelled. From above, a voice answered:

"Pray!" The man hesitated a moment, and then said: "Is there any-one else up there?" Beyond the humor of it, there is a serious aspect to this tale. Our relationship with God includes times of pain and testing. I do not refer only to people with a superficial view of God as Santa Claus who quit spiritually because they, according to their false perceptions, do not get immediate satisfaction of their desires. There are cases of long-standing Christians who have turned away from God because of immense suffering and no apparent help.

We have no easy answers to "unanswered prayer." As believers, we point to Saint Paul who suffered from "a thorn in the flesh," probably a periodic, debilitating ailment. Saint Paul asked the Lord three times to take it away. The Lord said: "My grace is sufficient for you, for my power is made perfect in weakness" (2 Cor. 12:7). While the answer to the specific plea was "no," Saint Paul perceived a larger "yes" of affirmation by God. He understood the negation of his re-quest as a check against spiritual pride on account of the abundance of revelations. Saint Paul broke out into a triumphant cry: "I will all the more gladly boast of my weaknesses, that the power of God may rest upon me. For the sake of Christ, then, I am content with weaknesses, insults, hardships, persecutions, and calamities; for when I am weak, then I am strong" (2 Cor. 12:10).

We can also point to the dramatic scene of Christ at Gethsemane. He prayed three times to be delivered from death by crucifixion. He prayed with tears and cries to the Father: "Remove this cup from me; nevertheless not my own will, but thine, be done" (Lk. 22:42-44; Heb. 5:7-8). The Gospels do not report an explicit answer to Christ's agonizing plea. Events showed that the answer was "no." However, we can be sure that Christ knew inwardly that He had to drink the bitter cup of suffering for the life of the world. He recommitted Him-self to this act of love, death on the Cross, to rescue us from the powers of sin and corruption. The experience of prayer gave Him, just as it did Saint Paul, a larger, more inclusive "yes" about His identity with the Father and the Father's purposes about the salva-tion of the world. Thus Christ came out of the Gethsemane prayer with new assurance and strengthened courage to face His holy pas-sion according to God's will.

Unanswered prayer? I do not believe there is such thing. God answers our prayers in various ways, whether directly or indirectly. His answer can be "yes," "no," "wait," or something different than what was requested. When we do not receive the answer we want, or the wait is long, we must allow God to act according to His freedom and wisdom. We must be patient and open to understanding why it had to be "no" or "wait" or a different answer altogether. We believe in God's love and goodness. We trust in His redeeming purposes. We humbly accept His providential will over us knowing that "in everything God works for good with those who love Him, who are called according to His purpose" (Rom. 8:28).

PRAYER AS COMMUNION

Prayer as communion is the highest level of the experience of God. The element of communion is already present in invocation and becomes more conscious in a vital relationship with God. However, when communion becomes predominant, the Christian attains to a fulness of spiritual maturity imaging "the measure of the stature of the fulness of Christ" (Eph. 4:13). Interesting to note as a theological reflection is that covenantal relationship with God, based on the Law and the Temple cult, defined the essence of salvation in the Old Testament, whereas incarnation and communion defined salvation in the New. The Prophet Jeremiah foresaw a time when God would make a "new covenant" in which He would write His Law in the hearts of His people (Jer. 31:31-33). The new covenant was fulfilled in Christ who embraced human nature in His incarnation and promised to dwell among and within His followers by the power of the Holy Spirit. According to the Apostle Paul, the new covenant in Christ is "written not with ink but with the Spirit of the living God, not on tablets of stone but on tablets of human hearts" (2 Cor. 3:3,6). These theological considerations indicate that prayer as communion reveals the most profound dimensions of the knowledge and experience of God.

The language of communion and union predominates in the Gospel of John, especially in what is called the Farewell Discourse (John, chaps. 13-17). As Christ anticipated His departure from the world, He assured His disciples that, if they practice love and obedience, He will always abide in them and they in Him in a union as intimate as that of a vine and its branches (Jn 15:1-11). "As the Father has loved me, so have I loved you; abide in my love" (Jn 15:9). And again: "If a man loves me, he will keep my word, and my Father will love him, and we will come to him and make our home with him" (Jn 14:23). Christ told the disciples that the seal and perfection of this "mystical union" with Him is the resurrection experience: "Because I live, you will live also. In that day you will know that I am in my Father, and you in me, and I in you" (Jn 14:19-20). The life of the Christian is a paschal festival in union with the risen Lord. We are united with Christ in many ways: faith, love, obedience, witness, and above all Holy Communion. However, the paschal experience of new creation becomes a conscious, transforming reality through prayer above all because prayer is the most direct and personal encounter with the risen Lord.

The first to reflect theologically on prayer as communion was Origen, perhaps the greatest Christian thinker of all time. In his work *On Prayer* Origen conceived of the highest purpose of prayer as participation in the life of God. Prayer was neither to inform God about our material needs nor to change His providential purposes in our lives, but rather to lift up our hearts and minds to heaven in order to gaze at the divine glory and be illuminated with the radiance of God. In prayer the believer is "mingled" (*anakrathenai*) with the Spirit of the Lord whose glory fills heaven and earth. The praying believer is purified and changed into a new creation and the whole of life becomes "a single great prayer." In the same line of thought Evagrios, a student of Origen, defined prayer as the highest spiritual activity which he identified as true knowledge of God. In his own work *On Prayer* published in *The Philokalia*, Evagrios has contributed to the Christian tradition the classic definition of prayer as true theology, that is knowledge of God: "If you are a theologian, you will pray truly, and if you pray truly, you are a theologian."

The element of communion shows that prayer is not merely a means to an end but an end in itself. Through prayer we seek not merely the gifts of God but God Himself, that is, to be with Him, live in Him, and delight in His presence. Saint Isaac the Syrian says that the primary purpose of prayer is to attain divine love. Other saints have referred to prayer as "heaven in the heart," "inner worship," and "worshiping in spirit and truth." They have spoken of various depths of prayer – prayer of the mind, the heart, and ecstasy of the spirit in which one does not know whether one is in heaven or on earth. In *The Way of the Pilgrim*, through the life of prayer the pilgrim came to know that the "mystery of prayer is a foretaste on earth of the bliss of heaven." Through the practice of the Jesus Prayer, the pilgrim was astonished to discover the wondrous changes occurring within him as he attained to self-acting prayer of the heart. Inexpressible peace and sweetness filled his soul.

Strangers appeared to him as if they were his own brothers and sisters. His lonely hut seemed like a splendid palace. All of creation shone with the light of God's glory. The pilgrim writes:

> When ... I prayed with my heart, everything around me seemed delightful and marvelous. The trees, the grass, the birds, the earth, the air, the light seemed to be telling me that they existed for man's sake, that they witnessed to the love of God for man, that everything proved the love of God for man, that all things prayed to God and sang His praise.

The sentiments of the Russian pilgrim express what the Church Fathers call the mystery of *theosis*. *Theosis* is usually translated as deification or divinization. The biblical word for it is glorification, that is, a radiant transformation by participation in the uncreated grace of God. It is the new creation taking concrete form through the indwelling of the Holy Spirit and in union with the risen Christ. Saint Paul refers to it as "the light of the knowledge of the glory of God in the face of Christ" which God shines in our hearts (2 Cor. 4:6). According to Saint Paul, by gazing inwardly at this light, the Christian beholds the glory of the Lord and is changed into the likeness of Christ from one degree of glory to another (2 Cor. 3:18). *Theosis* is involved in the whole process of spiritual growth marked by various stages from repentance to perfection.

Prayer is the existential, energizing context of *theosis*. We invoke God to connect with Him. As we develop an enduring relationship with Him through prayer, we become conscious of His personal presence and power. The goal of prayer is full mystical union and communion with God, a true image of our eternal glorification with Him which is rarely achieved on earth. The elements of prayer as invocation, relationship and communion parallel the three main stages of spiritual life: purification, illumination, and perfection. These elements, just as the stages of spiritual life, are closely related and coexist in the dynamics of Christian existence, and yet they are also qualitatively distinct by the depth of participation in the life of God. Properly speaking, *theosis* involves the highest levels of prayer as communion and belongs to the final stages of spiritual growth.

The transfiguration of Christ, when His human nature was transformed into light by the radiance of divine glory, expresses actual *theosis*. Christ's transformation in glory occurred in the context of prayer. The Evangelist Luke notes that Jesus "went up to the mountain to pray. And as He was praying, the appearance of His countenance was altered, and His raiment became dazzling white" (Lk. 9:28-29). Saint Symeon the New Theologian reports in his *Discourses* that his first experience of *theosis* occurred when he devoted entire nights to fervent prayer for the forgiveness of his sins. While in prayer, and quite unexpectedly, he was granted a sublime vision. A flood of divine light filled the room and he himself seemed to have turned into light. He did not know whether he was standing in heaven or on earth.

Another saint, Saint Elias the Presbyter in his *Gnomic Anthology* in the *Philokalia* writes that in concentrated prayer, the soul is inflamed with grace and glows like red-hot iron. In this radiant state the soul cannot be touched by the powers of the fallen world. It reaches virtual sinlessness, a state rarely achieved on earth. We must be careful in the use of these images. All these references counsel reserve in speaking too easily about *theosis* and making any claims about it for ourselves. The saints teach us that the Christian is better off practicing humble prayer and seeking God's guidance in daily life without yielding to thoughts of having achieved great spiritual heights, much less actual *theosis*.

When Jesus descended from the transfiguration mountain, He soon encountered the reality of human weakness, including that of His disciples who were unable to heal the epileptic boy. In exasperation Jesus cried out: "O faithless generation, how long am I to be with you? How long am I to bear with you?" (Mk 9:19). A sober lesson lies here. Prayer as communion may grant us life-changing moments of illumination and the desire to be always with the Lord. Nevertheless, we cannot live continuously on the mountain top. We must return to the plains of daily life engaging the obligations of family, work and community. Christ, who was transfigured, also had to bear the Cross from which he uttered the aching words: "My God, my God, why have you forsaken me" (Mk 15:34)? When great injustice, evil and pain come our way, it may seem that we have been abandoned by God and that despair may be engulfing our soul. It is in such moments that we must rely on our treasured experiences of true communion with God for strength and endurance. When we remain faithful no matter what happens, the darkness inevitably yields to light, because God is stronger than darkness.

CHAPTER SIX

SAINT SILOUAN: A MODEL OF SPIRITUAL LIFE

"O what a Lord is ours!... If the Lord is ours, then all things are ours. That is how rich we are."[1] Echoing the language of the Apostle Paul, Saint Silouan touches on the essence of Christian existence. For him Christian life is knowing Jesus Christ who became poor so that we might become rich (2 Cor. 8:9). Silouan lived in awe and wonder at the glory of the Lord and His love for all creation. The centrality of God's love for the world and Christ's glorious victory over sin and death mark Silouan's life with the special qualities observed in Orthodox saints: Easter joy, encompassing love and spiritual radiance. The opportunity to examine the life and thought of Silouan is an invitation to explore some of the rich dimensions of Orthodox spirituality.

Saint Silouan was a Russian "staretz" or spiritual elder who was proclaimed a saint some years ago. We are fortunate to know about the staretz through his disciple Archimandrite Sophrony. In 1948, ten years after Silouan's death, Sophrony wrote a volume in Russian about Silouan's life and writings which was subsequently published in Paris under the Saint's name (1952). An English translation of this volume was published in 1958 entitled *The Undistorted Image*.[2] Later a revised and expanded edition of this work came out in two volumes, one entitled *The Monk of Mount Athos* and the other *Wisdom from Mount Athos*[3] which are the main sources for the Saint's life and thought. The first is an interpretive account of the life and teaching of Silouan. It offers personal reflections of someone who intimately knew him and provides insights especially into the spiritual struggles of the Saint. The second book, edited also by Sophrony, contains the teachings of Silouan. These teachings were set down during the last years of the Saint's life in the form of inspired notations.

The title of the second book, *Wisdom from Mount Athos*, in one respect does not correctly reflect the spiritual message of Silouan.

The staretz's teachings are, to be sure, gems of spiritual wisdom but the Saint would not think of them in that way. What he has to communicate to his readers is a gospel, good news, a divine message: to know Jesus Christ through the power of the Holy Spirit. He writes with evangelical fervor and his words, even in translation, radiate apostolic power. Both of the above books are valuable contributions to the spiritual witness of Silouan whose life reaches down to modern times. The following appreciation of Saint Silouan and his teaching is based on these two books.

Born Simeon Ivanovich Antonov in the year 1866, Silouan lived the ordinary life of a Russian peasant. He was an honest, strong young man much impressed by the wisdom of his pious unlettered father. Simeon himself received little formal education. He went to school for only "two winters," as he said, probably just enough to learn how to read and write. However, his youth was marked by an inner yearning for God. This was highlighted by various incidents in his early life. At the age of nineteen he expressed the desire to enter the monastic life. Nevertheless, family considerations and sins of youth, by which the Saint was not untouched, diminished the divine calling in him.

A particular incident seems to have served as a turning point in his life. It was a jolting vision after a period of careless living. While Simeon on one occasion dozed off to sleep he dreamed that a snake crawled down his throat. He awakened full of horror and revulsion. He immediately heard a sweet voice saying: "Just as you found it loathsome to swallow a snake in your dream, so I find your ways ugly to look upon."[4] Simeon was convinced that the Virgin Mary had spoken to him and was trying to lift him up from a life of corruption and spiritual death. This experience generated in him a deep consciousness of sin and an equally profound need for repentance. These were the foundations for his later ascent to spiritual heights. At the age of twenty-six, as soon as he finished his military service, Simeon entered the Russian monastery of Saint Panteleimon on Mount Athos, the greatest monastic center of the Orthodox Church composed of more than twenty monastic communities and many hermitages.

The young novice set upon his monastic duties and the life of prayer with singular devotion. As in the case of each novice, Simeon was given a prayer rope (a "rosary") and was taught the Jesus Prayer – "Lord Jesus Christ, Son of God, have mercy on me, a sinner" –

which he practiced with great zeal. The first spiritual fruits soon appeared. He writes: "One day when I was a young novice I was praying before the icon of the Mother of God, and the Jesus Prayer entered into my heart."[5] This is a high state of spiritual prayer, known to Orthodox Saints and Church Fathers, in which the invocation of the Name of Jesus works spontaneously and uninterruptedly in the heart by the action of the Holy Spirit. Called the prayer of the heart, it is a high spiritual gift. Not long afterward Simeon was granted an even more sublime experience which he later intimated to his close disciple Sophrony. According to the latter,[6] Simeon, while at Vespers, near the icon of the Savior, beheld had a vision of the living Christ Himself. This was the decisive experience of his life. His whole being was filled with the grace of the Holy Spirit. He experienced a profound sense of forgiveness and reconciliation. Joy and peace flooded his soul. This was a new spiritual birth. Silouan himself is reticent about the actual vision. But he hints at this profound experience here and there as reflected in the following references:

> In the first year of my life in the monastery my soul apprehended God in the Holy Spirit . . . I turned to God for forgiveness, and He granted to me not forgiveness alone but the Holy Spirit, and I knew God in the Holy Spirit.[7]

And again: "It was given to me, a poor sinner, through the Holy Spirit to know that Jesus Christ is God."[8] Elsewhere he writes:

> I brought nothing but sins with me to the monastery, and I do not know why, when I was still a young novice, the Lord gave me the grace of the Holy Spirit. . . I did not ask the Lord for the Holy Spirit. I did not know about the Holy Spirit and how He enters the soul, nor what He does with the soul; but now it is a great joy for me to write of this. O Holy Spirit, how dear art Thou to the soul![9]

Three years later, at the age of thirty, Simeon was professed a monk, receiving the name of Silouan in accordance with the monastic tradition of changing name as a sign of a radical change in life. For most of his forty-six years as a monk, Silouan worked in the monastery flour mill and was also one of the monastery stewards serving in the kitchen and dining room. He never became outwardly significant. He quietly carried out his duties without attracting attention to himself. His disciple Sophrony cites several humorous incidents about important figures coming to seek the spiritual advice of the staretz to the surprise of some of his fellow monks who did not have eyes to see what treasure they had in Silouan.

In one such incident a learned monk, Father Stratonicos, came to visit Mount Athos from the Russian Caucasus. He was well-known for his spiritual wisdom. But he had come to the Holy Mountain to find someone with whom he could profitably discuss several matters of concern to him. After two months of visiting various monasteries he began to feel that his long and arduous journey had perhaps been in vain for he had not learned anything new. Then he incidentally discovered Silouan. They talked privately on several occasions. Afterwards Father Stratonicos became quiet and deeply thoughtful. Another monk engaged him in the following conversation:

> "What is wrong with you Father Stratonicos? I don't recognize you... You sit there mournfully, your inspired lips sealed. What is the matter?" "How should I answer your questions?" replied Stratonicos. "It is not good for me to speak. You have Silouan. Ask him." The monk who had asked the questions looked amazed. He had known Silouan for a long time and respected him. But he never thought of asking him for any advice.[10]

Silouan grew in the spiritual life but not without severe struggles. An initial period of spiritual exaltation followed his vision of Christ and his new birth by the Spirit. But this experience began to diminish in him. Severe struggles ensued. The questions that now emerged with great significance to him were: How can one remain alive to the gentle grace of the Holy Spirit? Once illumined, why does the mind become dark and dull again? How can one grow to spiritual stability? Silouan himself makes reference to his spiritual struggles. He is open about the cause of his soul's turmoil:

> Twice was I beguiled. The first time was at the beginning when I was a young novice, and came about because of my inexperience; and the Lord was swift to forgive me. But the second occasion was due to pride, and that time I suffered a long torment before the Lord healed me.[11]

It was through such struggles that Silouan learned more deeply about spiritual vigilance, the subtle warfare with pride, the cleansing of the heart, and complete reliance on God. In general Silouan's spiritual life was molded through the traditional Orthodox monastic disciplines such as worship, the life of prayer, reading of the Bible and hearing and reading works of the Church Fathers. Although the Saint had little formal education, he became well-schooled in the liturgical texts, Holy Scripture and the contemplative writings of Church Fathers. These were the sources, along with his devotion to private prayer, that provided the nourishment for Silouan's spiritual growth.

Silouan's most precious lesson was about humility. Humility seemed like a key which unlocked a deeper knowledge of the mysteries of God. Having discerned and renounced spiritual pride, Silouan was especially drawn to the humility of Christ. He received a richer illumination of grace which enabled him intuitively to understand the truths of Scripture and the spiritual teachings of the Church Fathers. Grace no longer seemed to leave him as before. Temptations diminished. Greater spiritual stability prevailed. His soul increased in joy and gratitude for all things. A deep love flowed from his heart for all people and for all creatures and wonders of creation.

One of the most distinctive aspects of Silouan's life was his personal witness or testimony, reminiscent of Saint Symeon the New Theologian (949-1022 AD). Silouan was a man of God. He had come to know God deeply and personally. The fire of divine love consumed him. Externally he was a quiet, simple, and gentle man who carried countless sacks of flour around the mill of Saint Panteleimon's monastery. Unlike Saint Symeon the New Theologian, he sought to instruct no one. He writes: "All my desire is to learn humility and the love of Christ that I may offend no man and pray for all as I pray for myself."[12] Inwardly his soul was a dwelling-place of the Holy Spirit. As in the case of the Prophet Jeremiah and of Saint Paul, the consuming fire that burned within his soul did not permit him to remain silent. Toward the end of his life he received a calling to write about God's love for the world. He exclaims:

> My soul loves the Lord, and how may I hide this fire which warms my soul? How shall I hide the Lord's mercies in which my soul delights? How can I hold my peace, with my soul captive to God? How shall I be silent when my spirit is consumed day and night with love for Him?[13]

Silouan did not stir up those immediately around him nor create any controversies. But his written word carries authority as a personal witness on behalf of God, such as in the case of the Prophets, Apostles and Evangelists. He states: "I write out of the grace of God. Yea, this is truth. The Lord Himself is my witness."[14]

Silouan did not write in order to write. Like many spiritual writers before him, he wrote because of the inner prompting of the Holy Spirit. He wrote at the end of his life, after his long spiritual struggles, when he had deeply matured in grace and was beyond the subtle influence of pride. He does not write about himself, although he seems to make the daring claim of having within him the same grace which empowered the Prophets and Apostles. He writes about the Lord. He thinks of himself as insignificant. His personal concerns completely recede behind the reality of the glory of God and the need to call all men to repentance. Can a single soul be saved? That was the crucial question. He says: "My soul knows His mercy towards me, and I write of it in hope that even one soul may come to love the Lord and be turned to Him by the fire of repentance."[15]

Silouan addressed himself not only to his contemporaries but to all. The love of God, the call to repentance, the need for forgiveness and the experience of reconciliation in the Holy Spirit are abiding issues for every generation. There is in the Saint a profound note of catholic truth and a genuine universal concern which flow from his soul. Silouan's heart burned with love not only for Orthodox Christians, not for Christians alone, but for all human beings. For him all persons on every corner of the earth were part of the people of God. Silouan's soul calls out to all. Here are some typical statements from his notations:

> I cannot remain silent concerning the people, whom I love so greatly that I must weep for them.[16]

> My heart aches for the whole world, and I pray and shed tears for the whole world, that all may repent and know God, and live in love, and delight in freedom in God.

> O all ye peoples of the earth, pray and weep for your sins, that the Lord may forgive them.[17]

> O ye peoples of the earth, fashioned by God, know your Creator and His love for us... Turn to Him, all ye peoples of the earth... Know all ye peoples that we are created for the glory of God... Cleave not to the earth, for God is our Father and He loves us like beloved children.[18]

Silouan was a man with a message. He was an evangelist. He wrote with a spiritual directness reminiscent of the proclamation of the Apostles. He is totally involved in a deeply personal way both with God and with man. Not infrequently, like Saint Paul, the ambassador of Christ who beseeched all to be reconciled to God (2 Cor. 5:20), Silouan pleads with people on behalf of God, as one pleads with dearly beloved brothers. His was an inner loving authority received directly from God. His notations have the character of a prophetic and evangelical witness. He does not write with intellectual arguments to convince the mind. He writes as a man of God to convert the heart. What follows are some major themes reflected in his writings such as knowledge of God, the Holy Spirit, prayer, the inner spiritual struggle, and the criteria of authentic spiritual life.

KNOWLEDGE OF GOD

Silouan's life was focused on seeking personal knowledge of God. Through his spiritual journey he had come to see with absolute clarity that what finally matters in life is just this: who comes to know God and who does not. He taught that the most precious thing in the world is to know God and to understand His will, even if only in part. Nothing is more precious than to know God; nothing is more disastrous than not to know Him. For Silouan, knowledge of God was direct and immediate, a personal communion with Him.

One may know *about* God and still not know Him personally. Many beheld Christ in human form, but not all knew Him as Lord. So it is now. Many may know about Christ but do not know Him by personal experience. Silouan distinguished between believing in Christ and knowing Christ. However, he did not criticize the implicit faith of Christians. To believe in Christ is also a blessed thing, he taught, according to the words of the Lord to Thomas: "Blessed are those who have not seen and yet believe" (Jn. 20:29). Yet there is another "seeing," not merely a "believing," open to every Christian. Such knowledge of Christ is a gift of the Holy Spirit, not a human achievement. When the soul which yearns for the Lord finds Him through the Holy Spirit, and knows Him, from that hour its love for the Lord is greater than any other love.

Silouan draws a similar distinction between learning about God through studies, books and research, and knowing Him through the Holy Spirit. Many philosophers and scholars may have arrived at a belief in God, but they have not come to know God. There is a great difference between affirming that God exists, or observing His works in nature, or even understanding His truths in Scripture, and, on the other hand, knowing God through personal communion with Him. No earthly science can adequately teach us about God.

Staretz Silouan knew educated men and respected them. He never talked against education. He was not an obscurantist. However, he was convinced that God is not made known through ordinary learning. There are those who spend their whole lives seeking knowledge of the world and the things in it; yet this is of no profit to the soul. A person can even earn a doctorate in theology and know what others have said and have thought about God, yet not know God personally. Sometimes knowledge through books can become an obstacle to knowing God, not because reason and human wisdom are negative in themselves, but because they can lead to pride and a false sense of self-sufficiency.

How is the Lord to be known? Silouan does not develop a theoretical answer to this question but simply points to daily Christian living, prayer and deep yearning for the Lord. He especially emphasizes that unless the Lord grants us knowledge of Himself, we cannot know Him as we should. Revelation is personal. Only God reveals God. We may study as much as we will and think as much as we will, but we cannot control or compel God through human skill, ingenuity or wisdom. The Lord makes Himself known to repentant hearts through the Holy Spirit. The Holy Spirit, sweet and gracious, draws the soul to love the Lord. Writes Silouan:

> If you would know of the Lord's love for us, hate sin and wrong thoughts, and day and night pray fervently. The Lord will then give you His grace and you will know Him through the Holy Spirit, and after death, when you enter into paradise, there too you will know the Lord through the Holy Spirit, as you knew Him on earth.[19]

According to Saint Silouan, knowledge of God is not a matter of speculation but of experience:

> We are able to truly speak of God only insofar as we have known the grace of the Holy Spirit. How can a man think on and consider a thing that he has not seen or heard tell of, and does not know? Now the saints declare that they have seen God…. The saints speak of that which they have actually seen, of that which they know.[20]

According to the Saint, each Christian should seek personal knowledge of God as his or her primary goal in life. A Christian does not need special learning nor special methods. He needs only to love his neighbor, be humble, obedient to God, and fervent in prayer. How personal knowledge of God occurs cannot be explained but that it does occur is an absolute certainty. The soul, graced by the Holy Spirit, suddenly sees the Lord and knows that it is He. Love and peace flood the soul. "Who shall describe this joy, this gladness?" asks Silouan. The soul experiences the Lord as a dear guest and seeks after Him with great yearning. Abiding in His presence and having daily fellowship with the divine Guest transform life into a spiritual feast in which the believer rejoices every day and every hour.

The Holy Spirit

According to the Saint, the Lord schools us through His Word and His Holy Spirit. He makes us kin with Him. The Holy Spirit dwells in us and transforms us into the likeness of Christ. By the Holy Spirit Christ unites us with God and makes us one family with the Father. Without the Holy Spirit the soul has no life. The person who has the Holy Spirit feels that he has paradise within himself.

The Holy Spirit is love and sweetness to the whole person. He pervades a person's entire soul, mind and body. A person who comes to know the Lord by the Holy Spirit stands in awe and wonder before the Lord. The Holy Spirit is like a dear mother. He lovingly cares for us, forgives and heals us, illumines and rejoices us. However, the staretz counsels, we must guard the grace of the Holy Spirit with prayerful vigilance. A single evil thought and He forsakes the soul. Unless we repent, the love of God remains no longer with us.

According to Silouan, the Holy Spirit is the power which unites the Church Triumphant and the Church Militant. The communion of glorified saints, the hosts of angels, and the faithful on earth are all bound together by the grace of the Holy Spirit. The same Holy Spirit is in heaven and on earth. He unites the whole wondrous assembly of God: the Virgin Mary, the angels, the saints, the patriarchs, the prophets, the apostles, the martyrs and all believers. We on earth are bound to the communion of saints through the Holy Spirit. Our spirits burn with love for them and their spirits burn with love for us. If love enables one not to forget a brother, how much more do the saints remember and pray for us.

It is by the power of the Holy Spirit that we can know and pray to the saints. When we pray to them, they hear our prayers in the Holy Spirit. Silouan exhorts Christians to pray to the Virgin Mary and to the saints. It was his conviction that they hear our prayers and even know our innermost thoughts. Intimates Silouan: "Marvel not at this. Heaven and all the saints live by the Holy Spirit, and in all the world there is nothing hidden from the Holy Spirit. . . they see us in the Holy Spirit and know our entire lives."[21]

Prayer

Prayer occupies a central position in the spirituality of the Orthodox Church. Progress in spiritual life is virtually identifiable with progress in prayer. By prayer is meant not only frequent private and corporate prayer, but a life of prayer, a spiritual condition of the heart by which the believer prayerfully lives, thinks and acts with spontaneous awareness of the presence of God. Because of the personal nature of prayer and the immediacy with which it brings the believer before the living God, prayer is the delicate instrument which, by its depth and warmth, measures a person's spiritual growth. Silouan's life was dominated by prayer. From the day he entered the monastery he practiced the Jesus Prayer and soon was granted true prayer of the heart through the grace of the Holy Spirit. It is no wonder that Silouan found prayer a mighty weapon in his struggles, a key to the spiritual life.

The staretz had some simple but profound thoughts to share with his readers on prayer. Prayer is equally for all. The best thing one can do is simply to pray with whatever strength and knowledge he may have. God will honor the longing and the efforts of one who struggles in prayer and will give him more strength and knowledge in prayer. A child cannot walk except by taking his first steps. Prayer comes with praying. But it must be contrite and sincere. Instructs Silouan:

> The Lord will give prayer to him who prays; and he of experience will know the assurance and love for God that comes to the mind. Although he be a sinful man, the Lord will grant him to taste the fruits of prayer.[22]

Silouan does not provide a formal definition of prayer. Yet it is clear from his notations that true spiritual prayer is to dwell with the mind and heart unceasingly with God. To think of God is already a prayer. The staretz counsels that he who makes it a habit to think of God always carries God in his soul, just as one who always thinks of worldly things is absorbed by them. The more a believer thinks of God, the more he is fired with love and fervor towards Him. He who loves the Lord is always mindful of Him. Remembrance of God begets prayer. But without prayer who can love God? If one is forgetful of God, he will not dwell in the love of God, for the grace of the Holy Spirit which inflames the soul with divine love comes through prayer.

Prayer is always and everywhere possible. The soul is the true temple of God. For the man who prays in his heart the whole universe is a church, says Silouan. Unceasing thanksgivings, spiritual songs and praises can go on in the believer's heart whose life is thus transformed into a living sacrifice to God. This is the true spiritual worship of which Christ spoke. No form of activity necessarily interferes with the person who yearns to abide in Christ and to practice daily inward prayer. The person who loves God can keep Him in mind day and night. But, warns Silouan, fault-finding, idle talk and self-indulgence are the death of prayer.

What is one to ask in prayer? The believer should pray for understanding in all things and about what to do in all situations. Genuine prayer is accompanied by peace of God in the soul and by a tender feeling towards every living thing. For the believer who prays in a humble manner, the Lord Himself is the teacher. The Lord, who mercifully watches over us, will not lead us astray. Silouan was aware of people's doubts about the efficacy of prayer and their fears about deception. For Silouan the fruits of prayer, such as divine love, humility, compassion, peace and joy, testify to the veracity of prayer:

> Some there are who say that prayer beguiles. This is not so. A man is beguiled by listening to his own self, and not by prayer. All the saints lived in prayer, and called others to prayer. Prayer is the path to God. By prayer we obtain humility, patience and every good gift. The man who speaks against prayer has manifestly never experienced the goodness of the Lord, and how greatly He loves us. No evil ever comes from God. All the saints prayed without ceasing: they filled every moment with prayer.[23]

What about the problem of unanswered prayer? According to Silouan, not one prayer nor a single good thought is lost with God. However, God sometimes seems remote to us. We pray but God seems not to hear us. There may be several reasons for this, says the Saint. First, what we ask may be improper. Secondly, it may not be to our spiritual benefit. Finally, pride may separate us from nearness to God and invalidate our prayers.

The highest form of prayer is the interior prayer of the heart, a spontaneous invocation of the Name of Jesus Christ This uninterrupted calling upon the Name of the Lord, which is a gift, must be sought with great care, love, and humility. God bestows His gifts on the humble. When a person is mindful of the Lord, obedient and humble in all things, he receives the gift of interior prayer from the Lord Himself, and such prayer continues without difficulty deep in the heart. When one attains to such perfect prayer and continually dwells in God, he acquires exceeding spiritual sensitivity. In all his conversations with others, and in all his dealings with things, he does not speak and act, as it were, from "his own mind" but he speaks and acts according to the promptings of the Holy Spirit. Such a person has become the dwelling place of the Holy Spirit and has acquired the mind of Christ This dynamic state of prayer is a sublime gift and, cautions Silouan, one should not be presumptuous to think for himself that he has attained it. It is best to keep one's mind on Christ and avoid self-conscious attention either to the fruits or heights of prayer.

THE SPIRITUAL STRUGGLE

In the tradition of Orthodox spirituality one meets recurrent themes about repentance, decision, firm resolve, vigilance, obedience, and inner spiritual warfare. These themes are not new but derive from the Bible. Jesus and John the Baptist radically called their hearers to repentance. Saint Paul frequently exhorted Christians to be sober, vigilant, and to put on the whole armor of God, always ready to wage spiritual battle. Jesus also said that it takes keen and daring persons to take hold of God's kingdom.

For all the apostles and saints grace is a gift; it is something to be received rather than to be earned. Salvation is primarily the work of God, not of human achievement. Nevertheless each Christian participates in the mystery of salvation through a personal response of his total being, beginning with a fundamental decision to turn from oneself and the world to God as the center and source of life. This is nothing less than a conversion to God and taking up battle against sin and evil. The Lord battled unceasingly with evil and lived in complete obedience to His Father. So also each Christian is called to wage ceaseless spiritual warfare against evil and sin in complete obedience to God. A human being cannot save himself. God alone saves. But to receive God's blessings and gifts, the Christian must respond to God with all of his inner and outer resources. God both demands and deserves a Christian's best in total surrender to Him.

Staretz Silouan was an accomplished warrior of Christ. He knew that spiritual warfare is at once simple and complex, easy and difficult. It is complex and difficult because of the cunning of the human heart. A human being does not easily abandon self-love nor quickly surrender the ego to God. The battle is simple and easy because of the grace of God. Writes Silouan:

> Fierce is the war we wage; yet it is a wise and simple one. If the soul grows to love humility, then all the snares of our enemies are overturned and his fortresses taken.... The war is a stubborn war, but only for the proud: the humble find it easy because they love the Lord and

He gives them the powerful armament of the grace of the Holy Spirit.[24]

The spiritual struggle begins with repentance, *metanoia*, a "change of mind." Repentance is a thorough conversion of the mind and heart to God. It is a profound yes to God which leads to the formation of new attitudes, new priorities and new values. A person cannot even begin spiritual warfare without this fundamental turning to God to receive His help. Without the Holy Spirit, declares Silouan, the soul is incapable even of starting out upon the race. The soul neither knows nor understands who and where her enemies are. Without God's unfailing guidance, the soul stumbles and falls at every turn.

Therefore, the whole basis of spiritual warfare is to place God at the center of life. Victory depends on complete reliance on God. But surrender and obedience to God do not at all imply passivity. What is surrendered is not action but self-will, not creative thought but selfish drives. The Christian can be highly active. In fact divine grace energizes and releases the believer's inner gifts in a most amazing manner. But a Christian's activity is always God-centered and love-centered. According to Orthodox saints, "passivity" is a state of being controlled by inner moods, drives and passions which the inner self obeys like a slave, whether or not a person is externally "active." True activity is prayer, a dynamic spiritual condition of being in conscious communion with God and freely choosing the good through cooperation with divine grace.

Because of pride which leads man to self-reliance, it is usually by affliction that a human being recognizes his insufficiency and turns to God. The Lord dearly loves man, teaches Silouan, but He allows affliction so that man may perceive his weakness, his need of God, and entrust himself to his Creator. When a Christian exalts himself or subtly lapses into self-reliance, God withdraws from him and delivers him to suffering.

Suffering is not only outward, such as some illness or physical hardship, which are unavoidable in life. But suffering is above all inward, the agonies and lacerations of the soul. Without God, the soul experiences distress, fear and conflict, or dejection, emptiness and unfulfillment. It often finds itself in darkness, tormented by fantasies, and beset by frustrations and evil thoughts. Silouan notes that the soul continues to suffer until it humbles itself and turns to the Lord in repentance. It is a short step to the light of God. After repentance, the simplest path to spiritual life is described as follows by the saint:

Be obedient and sober, do not find fault, and keep mind and heart from evil thoughts (through prayer). Remember that all men are good and beloved of the Lord. For such humility the grace of the Holy Spirit will dwell in you, and cause you to exclaim, "How merciful is the Lord!" But if you find fault and are rebellious, if you want your own way, your soul will fail and you will cry: "The Lord has forgotten me!" But it is not the Lord Who has forgotten you: it is you who have forgotten that you must humble yourself, and so the grace of God abides not in your soul.[25]

Spiritual warfare is primarily a matter of the mind and heart. Jesus said that all thoughts proceed from the heart, the inner world of the human being. The crucial battleground is mostly unseen. The Orthodox saints called the spiritual struggle "invisible warfare" (*aoratos polemos*). What is at stake is control of the inner thought world by grace or by other forces. Saint Paul spoke of having the mind of Christ. This exactly is the goal of spiritual life: to acquire the mind of Christ. The inner man can allow grace to control and transfigure all thinking, decisions and commitments. On the negative side, the inner person must alertly reject all evil thoughts and in no way obey sinful promptings. Silouan counsels his readers to cut off sin at the root by rejecting evil thoughts immediately through prayer. Should an evil thought arise in the mind, or an evil inclination disturb the heart, let the Christian quickly turn to Christ through inner prayer, such as the Jesus Prayer, which being brief and powerful, is most effective in invisible warfare.

If one becomes forgetful, fails to chase away evil thoughts, and assents to them, he must at once repent to God. Otherwise the force of evil will grow in him and soon will express itself through actions and then habits. It is easier to uproot a blade of grass than a tree, another Orthodox saint once remarked. Not only evil thoughts, but also day-dreaming, empty fantasies, and irrelevant thoughts often intrude, preoccupy the mind, confuse it, and subtly deceive it into evil. The outcome is the mind's separation from God which brings spiritual darkness. Another Orthodox saint called the mind "a wagon full of monkeys." There can be no inner relief from evil thoughts, no freedom from inner disturbance, without frequent prayer and vigilant resolve to follow the guidance of the Holy Spirit. According to Silouan, a Christian cannot fulfill the Lord's commandment to love God with all of his mind, heart and soul until useless thoughts are replaced by heavenly ones and the Christian is inwardly transformed through the renewal of his mind.

So the battle rages on and will not cease until death. Condemn your brother and you lose peace. Be boastful and grace leaves you. Tarry with evil thoughts and you lose confidence in prayer. Be fond of glory, power or material gains and you lose experience of God's love. Follow your own will and you are conquered by the enemy. Hate your brother, judge him, and you fall away from God into the control of an evil spirit.

Therefore, "be sober, be watchful. Your adversary the devil prowls around like a roaring lion, seeking someone to devour" (1 Pt. 5:8). Let not an hour pass without repentance, exhorts Saint Silouan. Do not lose the peace of the Holy Spirit over trifles. Surrender to the Lord so that He may guide you with His mighty hand. Guard the grace of God for without it, a human being is but sinful clay. As a person nourishes himself with food, so also he should sustain himself through the grace of the Holy Spirit. Without the Holy Spirit the soul is spiritually dead. Love your enemies, pray for those who insult or injure you, and offer thanks to God for all things. This is the narrow and hard way of the Christian struggle to spiritual victory by God's grace.

Two Criteria of Authentic Spirituality

"Test the spirits," admonishes Saint John (1 Jn. 4:1). What are the chief signs of genuine spiritual life? Staretz Silouan knew well the subtleties of the spiritual struggle and how easily we can fall prey to pride and vainglory. He especially emphasized two criteria of authentic Christian life: love and humility. In his own struggles Silouan was drawn more and more to Christ's humble, self-emptying love for all people and for all creation. Silouan lived the strict life of Athonite monasticism but his spirit was not rigid, doctrinaire, self-righteous or triumphalistic. He strove to understand and to serve every person. Those who differed with him, he treated with gentleness and respect. He was a man with a child-like, tender heart. Spontaneous love radiated from him and embraced all people and all things without differentiation.

Silouan held a remarkably enlightened view of people of other faiths. He would not pronounce judgment on any person, far or near. Sure of his own faith experience, he intuitively sensed that God has His ways with all of the world's people whom He loves dearly. Silouan constantly prayed that all people might turn to God and come to know His love. Once in a conversation with a certain hermit, the latter declared with evident satisfaction: "God will punish all atheists. They will burn in everlasting fire." Distressed with such an attitude, Saint Silouan replied: "Tell me, supposing you went to paradise and there looked down and saw somebody in hell-fire, would you feel happy?" The hermit responded: "it can't be helped. It would be their own fault." Silouan said: "Love could not bear that. We must pray for all."[26]

Silouan shed many tears especially for those who did not know God. He wrote: "Day and night I pray to the Lord for love, and the Lord gives me tears to weep for the whole world."[27] This is an image of how God loves us, gently and without reproach, just as the father of the Gospel story did not reproach his prodigal son. When a Christian experiences such love everything rejoices in him. When he loses awareness of it, he can not find peace, is troubled, blames others, and does not realize that he himself is at fault. Love of God and love of neighbor are the highest aspects of the Christian experience. Without them life becomes burdensome. Silouan is lyrical about God's love as reflected in the following references:

> O brethren, there is nothing better than the love of God when the Lord fires the soul with love for God and our fellow-man... The man who knows the delight of the love of God... loves both God and man (and) knows in part that the kingdom of God is within us. Blessed is the soul that loves her brother, for our brother is our life.[28]

Divine love, according to Silouan, reaches out to all things, including all creatures and plants. A story in the newspapers some time ago related how a dog jumped into a well after a three year old boy and held him up until the lad was rescued. Love is in all things and unites all things. A person must respond with love not only to people but also to nature and everything in it. Here are Silouan's words about a simple leaf:

> That green leaf on the tree which you needlessly plucked: it was not wrong, only rather a pity for the little leaf. The heart that has learned to love feels sorry for every created thing. But man is a supreme creation, and therefore if you see that he has gone astray and is bringing destruction upon himself pray for him... the soul that acts after this fashion is loved of the Lord, for she is like unto Him.[29]

The highest expression of love, and the surest criterion of Christian truth, is love of enemies, says the Saint. True love cannot suffer a single soul to perish. For Christ there are no "enemies," for the very word implies rejection. They are brothers and sisters who need our love and prayers. Christ prayed for those who crucified Him. Saint Stephen the First Martyr prayed for those who stoned him. So we must urge ourselves to love those who revile or injure us. If we cannot love, at least let us not revile. A person who reviles or despises those who are against him, brings spiritual injury to himself and shows that an evil spirit is working in him. But divine love cannot be attained by human beings without divine grace. We cannot love our enemies without having the Holy Spirit. When we humble ourselves and pray for those who affront us, God works impossible things in the heart. On one occasion Silouan states that the soul is so wounded by divine love that it "loses its wits." Even devils can rouse its pity because they were once God's creatures now fallen from the good.

The second criterion of authentic spiritual life is humility. "Were I to be asked," declares Staretz Silouan, "what would I have of God, what gifts, I should answer: 'The spirit of humility in which the Lord rejoices above all things.'"[30] Silouan learned true humility after years of intense struggles which seemed to cast him into the abyss of despair. According to the staretz, one night while yet in the midst of his struggles, his cell was filled with devils. A large devil stood in front of him so that Silouan could not pray before his icon without seemingly worshiping the foul creature. Silouan prayed fervently to God saying: "Tell me what I must do that they may leave me." The Lord's reply was: "The proud always suffer from many devils... Keep your mind in hell, and despair not."[31] According to Silouan's interpretation, this was not a counsel of despair but an admonition to check spiritual pride. Let the Christian keep his mind on his sinfulness and the judgment of hell, but let him despair not because of God's love which forgives, reconciles and saves.

True humility is the crucifixion of self-will and obedience to God's will under all circumstances and in all things. The whole spiritual warfare is waged around humility because the proud person does not want to obey God. He likes to be his own master. But where there is pride, there cannot be grace. Fight the evil one, exhorts Silouan, with the weapon of humility. Humility is the principal power. The soul of the humble person is like the sea: throw a stone into the water and for a moment it will disturb the surface. But then it sinks to the bottom. We are not humble and therefore we torment ourselves and others. We boast and compete over trifles, and so make ourselves and others unhappy. The humble soul enjoys great peace, while the proud soul is a torment to itself. The Christian can lapse into self-assurance and spiritual pride in subtle ways, as the Saint had learned from experience:

At first when a man begins to work for the Lord grace gives him the strength to be zealous after good, all is easy and effortless; and seeing this, in his inexperience he thinks to himself: "I shall continue thus zealously all my life long," and at the same time he exalts himself above those who live carelessly, and begins to pass judgment on them. And so he loses the grace that was helping him to keep God's commandments. And he does not understand what has happened – everything was going so well with him, but now it is all so difficult and he feels no desire to pray.[32]

If such a person who exalts himself over others does not humble himself and repent, a ravaging inner struggle begins. He becomes inwardly oppressed until he turns to the Lord. But suffering will profit him nothing if he does not humble himself. So long as the soul lacks humility, wrong thoughts and evil impulses will always torment it. But when the soul humbles itself, it will find forgiveness, serenity and holiness in God.

Silouan was greatly attracted to the humility of Christ who said: "Learn from me; for I am gentle and lowly in heart" (Mt. 11 :29). The staretz instructs Christians to take great pains to preserve the humble spirit of Christ, for without it the light of grace is extinguished and the soul dies. Some, says Silouan, after many years of struggle, do not understand why things are not well with them, why they do not feel peace and their souls are cast down. The reason is that they have not walked the humble way of the Lord but inwardly exalt themselves. But when the soul truly sees that the Lord is meek and lowly, it utterly humbles itself. Then the peace of Christ enters the soul and the soul, like the righteous Job of the Old Testament, is glad to sit among the ashes and behold others in glory. Out of love the soul wishes every human being more good than it wishes for itself. It delights when it sees others happier and grieves when it sees them suffering. This is the way of the Lord.

NOTES

[1] Archimandrite Sophrony, *Wisdom from Mount Athos*, translated by Rosemary Edmonds (New York, 1975), pp. 26-27.
[2] Translated by Rosemary Edmonds (London, 1958).
[3] Both were translated by Rosemary Edmonds but *The Monk of Mount Athos* was published in England (London & Oxford: Mowbrays, 1973), whereas *Wisdom from Mount Athos* was published in America (Crestwood: Saint Vladimir's Seminary Press, 1974).
[4] *Monk*, p. 11.

[5] *Wisdom*, p. 59.
[6] *Monk*, p. 19.
[7] *Wisdom*, p. 37.
[8] *Ibid.*, p. 19.
[9] *Ibid.*, p. 104.
[10] *Monk*, p. 41.
[11] *Wisdom*, p. 117.
[12] *Ibid.*, p. 86.
[13] Archimandrite Sophrony, *His Life Is Mine*, translated by Rosemary Edmonds (Oxford, 1977), p. 76.
[14] *Wisdom*, p.19.
[15] *Ibid.*, p. 42.
[16] *Ibid.*, p. 30.
[17] *Ibid.*, p. 76.
[18] *Ibid.*, p. 23.
[19] *Ibid.*, p. 21.
[20] *Ibid.*, p. 22.
[21] *Ibid.*, p. 59.
[22] *Ibid.*, pp. 102.
[23] *Ibid.*, p. 85.
[24] *Ibid.*, p. 111.
[25] *Ibid.*
[26] *Monk*, p. 32.
[27] *Wisdom*, p. 26.
[28] *Ibid.*, 30.
[29] *Ibid.*, p. 32.
[30] *Ibid.*, p. 120.
[31] *Ibid.*, pp. 118-119.
[32] *Ibid.*, pp. 91-92.

CHAPTER SEVEN

DISCERNMENT AND DIAGNOSIS IN HUMAN DEVELOPMENT

The Gospel account of the woman caught in adultery who was brought to Christ for judgment (Jn 8:2-11) is a dramatic example of discernment and diagnosis in religious life. "Teacher," Jesus was challenged by some religious leaders of his time, "the law of Moses commanded that such should be stoned – what do you say about her?" Put on the spot in the presence of a crowd, Jesus remained silent, scribbling on the ground. When the question persisted, He stood up and said to the accusers: "Let him who is sinless among you be the first to cast a stone." And again He bent down to scribble. Hearing His words, the accusers, one by one, beginning with the oldest, went away. Jesus then said to the woman: "No one has condemned you? Neither do I condemn you. Go, and do not sin again."

Although scant in historical detail, this dramatic account leads us to perceive divergent kinds of religious discernment and diagnostic action. On the one hand, the religious leaders discerned that a serious breach of God's law had occurred and apparently arrived at the decision that the law's provision had to be applied lest God's will be subverted and the authority of the tradition be compromised. On the other hand, Christ's teaching about God's love and mercy toward sinners dictated a chance at a new start for the woman, that is, both forgiveness and a call to responsible future behavior. The religious leaders were concerned about upholding the authority of the law and tradition. Jesus was concerned about God's ultimate purpose behind the law and God's will for this woman – to be saved and not to be condemned.

Moreover, there was a trap in the question. Christ's adversaries intended to expose Him before the crowd either as advocating subversion of God's law or contradicting His own principle of mercy toward sinners. Religious values and warrants were being used in an attempt to destroy the woman as well as Jesus who undoubtedly appeared the greater threat to the religious tradition. In a masterful way Jesus not only escaped the trap but also succeeded in His salutary purposes. He granted a new start to the woman. He also provided a way of escape for his adversaries who, hopefully, withdrew with much food for thought about religious values. And the crowd witnessed a concrete, dramatic expression of God's love and forgiveness toward a sinner through Christ.

SOME DEFINITIONS

What is discernment and what is diagnosis in the religious realm? More importantly, what is true discernment and how is correct diagnosis spiritually and theologically grounded? And how can such discernment and diagnosis, in consultation with other fields of knowledge, such as education, psychology and medicine, be applied to human development? These questions involve complex issues. Formally speaking discernment and diagnosis are parallel terms having to do with knowing and knowledge. Both derive from verbs meaning to recognize, distinguish, and come to know something in a penetrating way. Discernment is the power and skill to see, analyze, and arrive at a deep insight about any given matter. Diagnosis is the ability to compare, assess, and come to a conclusion as a result of the exercise of discernment. Often inseparable and indistinguishable from one another, discernment and diagnosis may well be at times largely intuitive and inspirational. Yet they are also part of a process of observation, thought, and aptitudes developed through accumulated wisdom and trained skill.

At the heart of the issue is the question of truth both theoretically and functionally; truth as the basis of fulness of life. But truth is as comprehensive as it is complex, an all-embracing reality. There are consequently different kinds and various levels of discernment and diagnosis pertaining to the diverse yet related dimensions of human existence and fields of knowledge including religion, philosophy, politics, sociology, economics, and physics, as well as medicine and psychology. An engineer who discerns cracks in the structure of a bridge will make the necessary diagnosis for repairs lest it collapse and cause harm. A marriage counselor who discerns cracks in a marriage will provide the diagnosis for healing lest the marriage break apart. A pastor who discerns cracks in a Christian's life of prayer will provide the diagnosis for spiritual growth lest the Christian lose all sense of relatedness to God. The obvious challenge is how the tasks of discernment and diagnosis in various fields can become cooperative and mutually supportive in the pursuit of truth and the enhancement of all life in its ecological totality.

Two Presuppositions

From the perspective of classic Christian tradition which Eastern Orthodoxy represents, an assessment of the nature of theological discernment and diagnosis must take into account at least two fundamental presuppositions. The first is the ecclesial character of theology and theological truth as sources of discernment and diagnosis. By ecclesial is meant not something abstract but the Church in all its concreteness – its experience of God, worship, core teachings and values, disciplines of piety, and spiritual ethos. Of course all fields of knowledge are in various degrees sociologically conditioned because the very language and symbols used for communication are part of the given cultural heritage. Yet such culturally conditioned elements can in most fields of human affairs be modified, corrected, and even rejected or replaced by new elements in the course of the interaction of cultures and the progressive accumulation of human knowledge. In the case of classical theology, however, there are a number of deep and abiding truths and values which are not open to revision because they are grounded in revelation, that is, the self-disclosure of God Himself as a gift to be received by the community of faith but not be controlled by human will, reason or skill. Although such truths must also be received, understood, and interpreted by human beings, nevertheless they pertain to core experiences, principles and values constitutive of the deep nature and self-understanding of the religious community born in integral connection with great moments of revelation such as the incarnation of Christ, His death and resurrection, and the gift of the Spirit on Pentecost as events of the new covenant enjoyed by Christians.

In addition, the ecclesial experience of God is not a reality located only in the past but also in the present, namely, in the worship, prayer, study, work, recreation, and Christian living of believers. In other words, the Church as a community is a concentrated locus of God's gracious action and the healing context within which Christian discernment and diagnosis, as well as their application, occur. Unless engagement of the divine presence is taken with utter seriousness, talk about spiritual or theological discernment and diagnosis remains hollow and easily coopted by psychological models and considerations. The religious context then becomes a sociological frame, a pretext, for the application of psychological methods and principles.

The integrity, power and efficacy of Christian discernment and diagnosis derive not simply from theoretical considerations, as accurate as they may be, but from the actual cooperative dynamics between God's saving presence and the grateful response of human beings who pray, worship, and live together in spirit and truth. The prayers and supportive love of a simple Christian may be far more healing for a hurting soul than the counsel of a professionally trained pastor filled with psychological knowledge but empty of the divine presence. The integrity of the pastor himself *qua* pastor is always rooted in one's God-given call to and empowerment in that ministry.

The second fundamental presupposition which determines the nature of theological discernment and diagnosis is the universal vision of Christian theology. Classical theology stands on the truth claim that it seeks to understand and interpret all of reality from the standpoint of God. The adjective theological and the noun theology do not signify the knowledge of God as metaphysical speculation but the revealed knowledge of God, as we know it especially from Scripture, appropriately applied to all spheres of life. Therefore, theological discernment and diagnosis do not pertain only to specifically religious behavior or to a narrowly defined religious realm, but rather to all human endeavors valued and interpreted from the standpoint of the revealed Creator, His truths, His purposes, and his will for humanity and creation.

Thus a Christian going out to the world – whether a doctor, psychologist, engineer, economist, lawyer, politician, businessman, or even a consumer in a shopping mall – cannot leave his or her Christian convictions at home. The dynamic process of discernment and diagnosis, just as the struggle for truth and life, is always at hand. If this reality of revealed truth in its universal scope is not taken seriously, any theological judgment is rendered impotent. Theology itself becomes either sectarian or a coopted vehicle of a culture's latest wisdom and favored values. However, when theology holds to its true position and function as reflection on and interpretation of God's self-disclosure for the whole world, it retains its authenticity and power, and remains the queen of the sciences, a service it should perform in humility.

I have emphasized the ecclesial or communal character of theological truth grounded in the experience of God in the life of the Church. I have also insisted on both the personal and universal scope of theological truth applicable to all walks and areas of life. I have also suggested what now may be stated directly, namely, that theological discernment and diagnosis constitute responsibilities not only of the Christian pastor, teacher, counselor or other professional, but also of every Christian. Each Christian is a free and synergistic agent in the process of one's spiritual growth and ultimate salvation. Each Christian, with the help of others, especially pastors, must always seek to discern deeper and wider aspects of God's presence and God's truth, make the appropriate diagnosis regarding personal and social considerations, and live by this truth with faith and integrity. Even in a close pastor-parishioner relationship, the Christian's personal responsibility of discernment is never eclipsed by obedience to a spiritual father, as for example in the case of temptation to violate a clear spiritual principle or biblical commandment. The same goal is set before all Christians, lay and clergy, that is, in the words of the Epistle to the Ephesians, to grow "to mature personhood, to the measure of the stature of the fulness of Christ" (Eph. 4:13). As Saint John of the Ladder much later put it, the essence of true Christian life is "to imitate Christ in thought, word, and deed as far as this is humanly possible."

Stages of Spiritual Growth

In Orthodox theology and spirituality masters and students of the subject have proposed several patterns or stages, variously named, for measuring spiritual growth. A basic one consists of a paradigm of three stages: (a) purification (*katharsis*), (b) illumination (*photisis*), and (c) perfection (*teleiosis*). One might use this three-stage pattern as a heuristic model to discuss three levels of theological discernment and diagnosis in Christian life. We should not think that these levels or stages are sharply separated. On the contrary, they are dynamically connected, interpenetrating each other especially at the points of their boundaries, and each level includes gradations of considerable range. To give them titles for discussion, these three levels of discernment may be called: (a) practical, (b) spiritual, and (c) mystical. Some remarks on each may be in order.

The practical level of discernment pertains to the entire range of Christian practices such as worship, study, ethical obedience, fasting, service to others, and unceasing struggle against evil. Practical discernment has to do with such matters as learning to pray, finding time to pray, perceiving and cultivating patterns of Christian behavior at home and work, distinguishing and choosing priorities according to Christian teaching, finding ways of seeking forgiveness and reconciling with others, anticipating and avoiding occasions of sin, and many other similar nuts and bolts of Christian life. Such insights deserve to be called theological because they involve elementary knowledge of God's truths and God's will about what is good and evil, right and wrong, appropriate and inappropriate, pursuable and avoidable, based on received tradition. This practical theological discernment is strongly guided by the community of faith and its leaders. To be sure, the personal faith, innate moral sense, and individual reason of the Christian are intimately and intricately involved as well, and not without profound and complex struggles beginning with true repentance, a deep conversion of the mind and heart to Christ. Yet one's own discernment is elementary, based on the teaching, guidance, and way of life of the Christian community.

The goal of this first stage is purity of heart from evil passions, that is, the liberation of personhood from the bonds of fallen humanity – the whole corporate and personal pattern of selfishness, manipulation, greed, exploitation, corruption, anger, hatred, cynicism, and despair. The saints teach that sin and evil are foreign to human nature, a distortion of the image and likeness of God, a beclouding of reason and moral sense, a sickness of the soul, a corruption of humanity and creation. By sin is not meant some moralistic transgression, as sin is often trivialized by some, but the power of sin expressed in human life through wrong choices, wrong goals, wrong relationships, wrong attitudes, wrong values, wrong acts, wrong use of things – all those things which define the forces of alienation and disintegration in humanity, community, as well as the environment. The way to health and wholeness is through the grace of God and the stable practice of the evangelical virtues such as faithfulness, humility, self-control, service, holiness, and love, as well renouncement of self-will, egomania, and indulgence to evil passions.

Because unruly human nature easily follows its own ways and falls prey to many temptations, the ascetic disciplines of regular prayer, fasting, and meditative reading help in centering the mind on the living God, freeing persons from ingrained habits of sin, purifying the heart, restoring human rationality and moral capacity, and opening the way to ongoing inner transformation. Among the fruits and criteria of progress in this way of life are growing stability of Christian behavior, an inner sense of purpose and well-being, moments of true peace and joy in the Lord, and desire to learn more about and to grow closer to the mystery of the living Christ.

The grace of the Holy Spirit is active in all the stages of Christian growth but its gracious action in the Christian becomes more conscious in the second stage of illumination. Spiritual discernment, a critical mark of illumination, already begins in the higher levels of the previous stage, that of purification, and is signified by the occasional warm and joyful stirrings of the Holy Spirit in the depths of one's being. As these stirrings become more frequent, the Christian experiences illumination at the same time. At this second stage the Spirit becomes a more abiding presence, a growing flame, a lantern of the soul, and a source of living waters as Christ said (Jn 4:14). At this level discernment may be called truly spiritual primarily because it is a gift of the Holy Spirit and secondarily because the Christian through illumination acquires a deeper understanding of the meaning of what he practices as a Christian.

We need not quibble about terminology. In the patristic tradition this second stage is called *theoria*, often translated "contemplation." However, it is not contemplation in the sense of meditative cogitation on a verse of Scripture, a Christian truth, or an aspect of creation, things which in themselves are of course commendable. Rather *theoria* is a dynamic state of being in which the Christian can testify to an inner conscious awareness of grace working in the heart, a profound sense of being surrounded and penetrated by the divine presence, and a radiant sense of awe, wonder, and gratitude about everything. *Theoria* may be translated consciousness of grace, awareness of God's presence, spiritual vision, that is, vision of God, as the etymology of the term *theoria* (*theoro*="see God") indicates. However, it is not yet an actual mystical vision of the uncreated glory of God in its greater reality, nor certainly a psychological vision in terms of created images, but an abiding lively awareness of God's presence – precisely a spiritual vision of all things in the light of the divine presence.

At this level of illumination, spiritual discernment is neither directly connected, nor necessarily dependent on acquired theological knowledge. One may possess a theological doctorate and be known as a famous scholar in theology, but be entirely devoid of spiritual discernment (and, alas, sometimes even practical discernment). However, this level coherently builds on and also transcends practical discernment just as *theoria* builds on and transcends the first stage of *praxis* ("practice") without ever leaving behind the *praxis*. To give some examples, practical discernment perceives the Christian obligation to speak the truth, spiritual discernment perceives the freedom that truth works. Practical discernment distinguishes the importance of love, spiritual discernment is guided by the power of love. Practical discernment knows that prayer brings one before God's presence, spiritual discernment delights in prayerful communion with God. In the former case discernment is based on theological knowledge, whether elementary or expert, acquired from the ongoing tradition of the community and also based on God-given abilities of reason and moral sense. In the latter case discernment is a gift of the Holy Spirit which has cleansed the powers of the soul and crowned the received knowledge with a spiritual light. In the full stage of *theoria*, knowledge of God is no longer simply pedagogical or abstract, it is personal communion with God. Theology becomes spirituality and spirituality is true theology. The Orthodox definition of theologian is not merely a person who is professionally trained and holds a theological degree but a person who knows God through faith, goodness, purity, and a life of deep prayer.

Many examples of spiritual discernment can be given from the saints. There is a story in the Desert Fathers similar to the account of the adulterous woman brought before Christ. A certain brother in a monastery fell into disgrace. He came before the Elder Anthony and together with him came many brothers who, wishful to restore him to proper monastic discipline, overwhelmed him with reproaches. Now the Elder Paphnoutios was also present and told the brothers a parable they had never heard before. "I saw," said Abba Paphnoutios, "on the bank of the river a man sunk to his knees in the mud; and some came up with outstretched arms to pull him out, and they sunk him to the neck." Then Abba Anthony said: "Behold a man who can truly heal the soul." Hearing these words the brothers were cut to the heart, repented of their overzealous tactics, and restored the erring brother to the community. In a similar spirit Abba Makarios used to say: "A proud and ill word would turn good men to evil, but a good and humble word would turn evil men to better." And another Father, echoing the words of Jesus, said: "The devil cannot cast out devils."

One has of course much to learn from such stories and all the treasures of the wisdom of the saints. One should also seek, with humility and prudence, to practices such teachings and principles even while striving at the first stage of purification. However, at the stage of *theoria*, which is the level of illumination, spiritual discernment is *ad hoc*, that is, spontaneous, intuitive, truly inspired by the Holy Spirit. Spiritual discernment perceives not only spiritual insights but expresses and applies them with spiritual power and freedom appropriate to the needs and circumstances of the moment, often transcending and even seemingly going against Christian convention. The Jewish religious leaders who came before Jesus, just as the accusing brothers who came before Anthony and Paphnoutios, had a legitimate claim to uphold their respective traditions. Yet Jesus and the two elders of the desert perceived a far greater truth, a truth of love, which did not necessarily reject the demand of the law but affirmed the more profound purpose of the law, that is, to give life.

The third stage of Christian growth, the stage of perfection, cannot occupy our attention long because only the perfect can speak about perfection. The lives and writings of Saint Isaac the Syrian, Saint Symeon the New Theologian, and others, give evidence of a truly mystical level of union with God in His uncreated light and glory. These saints speak of actual visions of the risen Christ as uncreated light which penetrates the beholder and transforms him into light as fire radiates through glowing iron. Such saints, including Moses, the great prophets, the apostles, Saint Paul converted on the Damascus road by a vision of divine light, and many others, known and unknown in the Christian tradition, are primary witnesses of revelation and pillars of the life of the Church. At this level one might speak of a truly mystical cognition, mystical discernment, grounded in the actual experience of *theosis* ("divinization"), and often prophetic, radical, and disturbing in its bold call for repentance and a life worthy of God. "It is not [your] theological knowledge which is the light," cried out Saint Symeon to Byzantine theologians of his time, "but the [uncreated] light which is the knowledge." He called emperors, patriarchs, bishops, priests, monastics and lay people to deep repentance and to apostolic life through an adult baptism of the Holy Spirit. He was cast out of Constantinople and died in exile. Within one or two generations the Church proclaimed him a saint and gave him the distinct title New Theologian.

COOPERATION AMONG PROFESSIONALS

Now a few words pertaining to Christian professionals, especially those who occupy leadership positions in the Church such as priests, teachers, administrators, missionaries – all those who share in the guidance ministry of the Church – and others who work outside the Church but who take the adjective Christian seriously. What benefits can we derive from the above paradigm of Christian life and growth so integrally representative of the essence of the Orthodox way of life? First, we must be vitally concerned with our own continued spiritual growth to the attainment of spiritual discernment. We may remember the exhortations of Saint Gregory the Theologian and of Saint John Chrysostom that those who seek to guide others to purification must themselves be first purified. The chief qualification of Church leadership is spiritual life. From this viewpoint, for example, it is a question whether or not one should in the first place be ordained unless one has reached at least the beginnings of the stage of illumination or *theoria*. How can God's people be guided with spiritual discernment otherwise? The spiritual vigor of the Church and the efficacy of its witness as Church to society is directly related to the depth of spiritual life of its leaders.

Secondly, Christian professionals can work together to develop patterns of diagnosis based on Orthodox spirituality to be used in teaching, counseling, and pastoral care. Such work would not guarantee higher degrees of spiritual discernment to anyone on the basis of professional credentials alone, but would surely support the process of spiritual growth. The Church Fathers have already conducted extensive analysis of personhood and life, and have written detailed instructions on basic virtues and vices, making various diagnoses, and offering diverse therapies for healing and growth. Saint Nikodemos of the Holy Mountain composed a handbook on confession discussing the person of the confessor, the nature and dynamics of various sins, and the application of spiritual therapy. A number of handbooks on confession have been written in our own century. All of these resources need to be studied, compared, interpreted, and presented in a form useful to the ministry of the Church today. If the professionals in the fields of psychiatry and psychology have devoted such ongoing, systematic attention to the dynamics of the human personality, should not theologians do the same on the basis of the riches of the Christian tradition? One of our great sins of omission as Orthodox leaders and theologians in modern times is our virtual surrender and abandonment of the Church's ministry of counseling to secular psychiatry and psychology which have eagerly filled the vacuum.

Various models or patterns of discernment and diagnosis could be proposed. One is the above paradigm of the three stages. Another might be a paradigm constructed on the basis of fundamental relationships which define the meaning and quality of human life. There are four such fundamental relationships, namely, to God, to self, to others (including the Church), and to things. These can serve as structural categories for the development of flexible and dynamic diagnoses and application of therapies toward spiritual growth. For example, under the category of the relationship to God the pastor could appropriately assess a Christian's or even a congregation's depth of relationship with God in terms of specific criteria such as formal or living faith, personal trust or doubt, love or fear, and sense of distance from or communion with God. He then could apply therapy with genuine openness to the Holy Spirit through renewed emphasis on worship, prayer, and relevant topics in preaching and teaching.

Under the category of relationship to self, the pastor could explore with a Christian the degree of honesty, self-acceptance, willingness to take responsibility, self-critique, participation in the sacraments, and evidence of the fruit of the Spirit in a Christian's life. Under the category of relationship to others the defining criteria of diagnosis might be openness or capacity to enter into relationship with others, respect for the personhood of others, service to others, responsibility for and enjoyment of community, and the like. Under the category of relationship to things the critical referentials might be the following: degree of attachment or detachment, use or abuse, whether self-worth is derived from things, whether things have become more important than people, and degree of appreciation of things as God's gifts to be enjoyed, shared, and protected. All of these elements could be flexibly organized and prayerfully offered to Christian professionals as they seek to fulfil their ministries with constant openness to the Holy Spirit.

In this essay we have not touched on issues pertaining to psychopathology, demonology, or addiction to substances such as alcohol. To lift an example, there is a strange case reported by Dorotheos of Gaza in his *Discourses*. A brother came to him and confessed that he constantly stole food to eat. Dorotheos asked the steward to give the man all the food he wanted so as not to steal. But the brother kept stealing and hiding scraps of bread, dates, figs, and onions under his bed and in other places, or just giving the food to the monastery's donkey. "My dear brother," Dorotheos asked, "did I not give you everything you wanted? Why do you steal?" The brother replied, "Forgive me, I don't know why. I simply feel the urge to steal." Dorotheos lifted up this case as an example of the plight to which indulgence to passions can lead but provides no detailed diagnosis or specific therapy. The poor man who was stealing obviously suffered from kleptomania. In such areas it may well be that the modern sciences provide specific discernment and diagnosis, as well as therapies, which go further than the wisdom of the ancient Christian tradition. Such cases deserve special attention and close cooperation between pastors and professionals in the medical and psychological fields. Since all truth in life is God's truth, theologians, pastors, doctors, therapists and others, all can cooperatively and fruitfully engage in the enormous, ongoing process of understanding and healing in human development.

PART THREE

FAITH, TRADITION
AND RENEWAL

CHAPTER EIGHT

FAITH AND CULTURE IN SAINT PAUL

The issue of renewal in Christian perspective cannot properly be treated only in the context and challenges of modern times. A holistic perspective must take into consideration all of the Church's historical life, particularly its earliest period marked by the most dramatic changes when the Christian faith was seen as a new, subversive force threatening both Jewish and Gentile traditions. Indeed, Christianity emerged as a powerful renewal movement from the matrix of Judaism and rapidly spread among Gentiles in the Graeco-Roman world already during the first generation of its adherents. By the middle 50's it had made what perhaps can be seen as the greatest cultural leap of its entire history, a remarkable transition from the Aramaic-speaking Jewish culture of Palestinian towns and villages to the cosmopolitan culture of the major Hellenistic cities of the East, such as Antioch, Ephesus, and Corinth, as well as of the center of the Empire, Rome itself. The amazing success of Christianity is eloquent testimony to its own internal vitality, its distinctive developing character over against both Judaism and Hellenism, as well as its capacity to adapt to new circumstances and to use both Jewish and hellenistic elements to its own advantage.

In the eye of this dynamic and complex religious and cultural interaction stands the great figure of Saint Paul, Roman citizen (Acts 22:27-28), zealous Pharisee (Phil. 3:5-6), cultural Hellene (1 Cor. 9:21; Rom. 9:14), and most successful Christian missionary (Rom. 15:16-29). Far from being an individualist working in splendid isolation, as some have portrayed him in the past, Saint Paul consciously lived, thought and worked with the strongest, albeit paradoxical, sense of solidarity with Jews, Gentiles, as well as Christians. He is after all the one who said, "I have become all things to all that I might by all means save some" (1 Cor. 9:22). But he also said, "Neither circumcision counts for anything, nor uncircumcision, but a new creation" (Gal. 6:15), signaling his conviction about the new faith in Christ for which he fought both to disseminate and define with all his apos-

141

tolic zeal, theological skill and pastoral capacity. The great Apostle epitomizes the dramatic interaction of faith and culture in early Christianity. In him we find evidence of powerful continuities and discontinuities between Christianity, Judaism and Hellenism. Furthermore, insofar as Saint Paul helped shape basic Christian perspectives during this most creative and canonical epoch of Christianity, we may also gain from him some challenging insights into the tumultuous interaction of faiths and cultures in our own times as we stand at the beginning of the twenty-first century.

A MODERN PARABLE

A modern parable will bring home to us the revolutionary nature of Saint Paul's witness. Think of a strongly traditional Greek Orthodox family in cosmopolitan New York, or Boston, the Athens of America. Imagine them to be American citizens having established roots in American business and society, yet powerfully attached to their own religious and ethnic heritage which for them is a single, undifferentiated unity. Their ties with Greece are such that they send off the son to study in Greece and be thoroughly infused with the Greek Orthodox mindset and way of life. While in Greece the young man visits the Holy Mountain of Athos and has a profound religious experience. Suddenly the young man has a changed heart and a new set of priorities. What really matter to him now are Christ, the Church as His mystical Body, the Liturgy, and the theology and spirituality of the Church Fathers, all of which, according to his awareness, are only dimly perceived by his fellow Greek Orthodox living in an immensely rich culture of religious and ethnic traditions.

The young man then returns to America with a new vision and with glowing convictions about the opportunity of Orthodox mission in this free and open society. He tries to arouse local Greek Orthodox congregations to the same grand vision. He tells them that in order to have a true and vigorous Orthodox mission, they must have a renewal of identity centered on Christ and the fundamental Orthodox truths, which defines in any case their true baptismal identity, and not an ambiguous kind of sociological identity based on their sense of peoplehood and on their humanly justifiable pride in their ethno-religious culture and language. To be sure, he is not at all opposed to the rich ethnic heritage for the Greek Orthodox; only the mission of Christ and His Church have for him an incomparably higher priority. He welcomes converts into the Greek Orthodox

Church and points to them as being the first fruits of a renewed identity, a renewed humanity in Christ, just as in the case of the Book of Acts when the flow of Gentiles into Christianity transformed the identity of the nascent Jewish Christian Church.

For him, all this would be consistent with Orthodox theology and history, since Orthodoxy itself has made several great moves into new nations and cultures over the ages. Indeed, such renewal of baptismal identity centered on Christ and His Church, even at the risk of losing some precious cultural traditions and gaining new ones, is exactly the essence of the matter and the pledge of the future destiny of the Orthodox Church in America for the glory of Christ. Such a zealous man, you can imagine, would create quite a stir preaching his message to Greek-Americans and all at once trying to relate to family, friends, converts, and the general public.

While the parable is not analogical in every detail, it gives us an illuminating perspective in which to understand Saint Paul and his personal and theological struggle with faith and culture. Born in Tarsus, arguably the Athens of the Eastern Mediterranean, he was of a family of "Hebrew of Hebrews" (Phil. 3:5), apparently well-established, and possessing Roman citizenship (Acts 22:27-28). He learned Greek there but went off to Jerusalem for high Jewish studies, where he joined the strict party of the Pharisees, if he were not already a member of it (Phil. 3:5). But while heavily involved in the persecution against Christian Jews who were "Hellenists," that is, spoke Greek and were raising issues about the Temple and other Jewish customs (Acts 6:1,8-14; 9:1-18) he was granted a Christophany, a vision of the risen Christ, which transformed his whole life and simultaneously called him to a new mission in the Gentile world (Rom. 11:13). The person of the risen Lord was such a powerful reality for him that he could say, "For me to live is Christ" (Phil. 1:23) and "It is no longer I who live but Christ who lives in me" (Gal. 2:20). From Law-centered he became Christ-centered. The Christ-focus was so immense that the Apostle came to view all other values, whether Jewish or Hellenic, as relative, including the Mosaic Law, and he was willing to live out the consequences. Some twenty years after his call and conversion he could still write that he counted all things, including his attainments in Judaism, a "loss" and "refuse," in order "to gain" Christ and to continue to pursue the "surpassing worth" of Jesus his Lord (Phil. 3:8-9).

SAINT PAUL AND JUDAISM

From this perspective we can appreciate the dramatic struggle of faith and culture reflected in Saint Paul's Epistles. In his *magnum opus*, the Epistle to the Romans, he takes up the theme of continuity and discontinuity between Jews, Gentiles, as well as Christians in a rather conscious way. Of course he is not concerned with this theme in the abstract but in terms of the direction of salvation history in his times. His concern was about what God was doing in Christ among Jews and Gentiles which the Apostle understands as the revelation of God's righteousness – the demonstration of God's saving action in fulfillment of His promises in the Old Testament. It is in Romans (chaps 1-3) that the Apostle presents a christocentric survey of universal history which finds that ultimately neither Jews nor Gentiles have much to boast about morally or spiritually. All have gone astray and all need Christ through whom God offers universal salvation by means of faith in Christ and apart from the Law of Moses. In what follows, our first focus will be on aspects of Saint Paul's life and thought in continuity and discontinuity with his own tradition of Judaism of which he was a zealous and strict adherent.

Chapters 9-11 of Romans are of special relevance to our discussion. The chief issue here is the fact of the corporate unbelief of the Jewish people. To the Apostle, this fact presents a painful personal and theological problem of the greatest magnitude, wrapped in the mystery of God's inscrutable ways. How can his fellow Jews not believe in their own Messiah? What is one to think about God's faithfulness to His promises? What is God's plan about Jews and Gentiles now that messianic times have arrived? Saint Paul's complex and laborious argumentation in part reaches a high point with his illustration of the good olive tree in Rom. 11:17-14. The illustration is not accurate horticulture – a wild shoot is not grafted on a good tree but the reverse – and Saint Paul is aware of it (Rom. 11:24). However, his extended use of this forced image indicates that Saint Paul is grappling in an agonizing way with the problem of the relations between Jews, Gentiles and Christians, and can thus serve as a key by which to outline some main aspects our topic.

First, we note that the illustration unequivocally assumes the essential continuity between the Jewish tradition and all Christian believers. The good olive tree (*kallielaios*) with its richness (or "fatness," *piotes*) is the whole Jewish heritage glowing with divine revelation. Saint Paul earlier sums up this heritage when enumerating

God's many gifts to the Jews: "the sonship, the glory, the covenants, the giving of the Law, the worship,... the promises,... the patriarchs, and... the Christ" (Rom. 9:4-5). Elsewhere in Romans he mentions the privilege of "the oracles of God" (*ta logia Theou*), the Scriptures, with which the Jews have been entrusted by God. According to Saint Paul's train of thought in Romans 9-11, there are two kinds of branches on the good olive tree, natural and honorary. The honorary branches are the Gentile Christians, formerly shoots of a wild olive (*agrielaios*), but now organically "grafted" to the good olive tree of whose richness they partake. The natural branches are the minority of Jewish Christians, mentioned not in the illustration itself but earlier in Romans 9-11, who constitute "the faithful remnant" of the Old Testament prophecies and who have attained to God's righteousness in Christ (Rom. 9:24; 11:5-7). These two kinds of branches representing the Jewish and Gentile Christians are united by their common call in Christ (Rom. 9:24) and their mutual participation in the blessings of the Jewish heritage. They are the ones who "confess with [their] lips that Jesus is Lord and believe in [their] hearts that God raised Him from the dead," and who consequently make up the saved community in which "there is no distinction between Jew and Greek [because] the same Lord is the Lord of all" (Rom. 10:9-13).

For Saint Paul, therefore, salvation history marks an essential and intrinsic continuity between Christianity and Judaism. Unlike Marcion of old and some theologians in modern times, Saint Paul has a completely positive view of the revelatory value of the Old Testament and the Jewish heritage. In agreement with the overall witness of the New Testament, the Apostle holds to the fundamental view that the Christian faith and life are to be interpreted in the category of renewal and fulfillment, rather than negation or abolition of the Jewish heritage. This line of theological thinking continues in the classic patristic tradition which affirms not only the workings of grace but also the sainthood of numerous figures in the Jewish tradition down to the Maccabean martyrs.

Secondly, however, the illustration of the olive tree also emphasizes a sharp discontinuity between Judaism and Christianity centering on Christ. Here the qualification must be made that Saint Paul, in his own view, has a lover's quarrel not with the Jewish heritage as such but with contemporary unbelieving Jews. Without mincing his words, the Apostle holds that in the new stage of salvation history marked by the lordship of Christ, some natural branches were indeed "broken off" the good olive tree by reason of unbelief (*apistia*), just as "in their place" previously wild branches have been organically "grafted" by reason of faith (*pistis*, Rom. 11:17-20). In vain modern thinkers involved in the Jewish-Christian dialogue have tried to find support in Romans 11 for a theology of two equally valid covenants by God, one for Jews and the other for (Gentile) Christians. According to Saint Paul's illustration, the unbelieving Jews in messianic times are clearly cut off from the good olive tree. Earlier in Romans 9 the Apostle states that they are not the spiritual but the physical Israel (Rom. 9:6-8). He considers that they are "vessels of wrath," who stand over against the "vessels of mercy," the Christian Jews and Gentiles with whom the Apostle himself identifies using the plural "we" (Rom. 9:22-24). Thus a double discontinuity exists, not only between Christians and unbelieving Jews, but also between unbelieving Jews and their own heritage!

This precisely is the agonizing problem of Romans 9-11 over which Saint Paul struggles to provide various answers. The two important qualifications he makes are (1) that the unbelief of the Jewish people serves the positive cause of a large-scale conversion of Gentiles and (2) that it is provisional rather than final (Rom. 11:11,25-26). The Jews have indeed stumbled but they have not ultimately been rejected by God as His people – "by no means!" (*me genoito!*), says the Apostle, for otherwise the faithfulness of God to His own promises would be in question (Rom.11:1,11,29). They may now be "enemies of God" pertaining to the Gospel and for the sake of Gentiles, but they are the irrevocably beloved and elect people of God, although now paradoxically in a state of disobedience, just like Gentiles Christians were previously in a state of disobedience (Rom. 11:28-32). God's plan is to consign all to disobedience that He may show mercy upon all (Rom. 9:32). Saint Paul's profound conviction, which he reveals as a divine mystery, is that by God's power all Israel will finally believe and be saved (Rom. 11:23,25-26). He concludes with a doxological affirmation of God's inscrutable wisdom (Rom. 11:33).

It is of great importance to note that Saint Paul, despite his harsh language – there was no ecumenical politeness in antiquity – refrains from pronouncing judgment on the Jews as being accursed by God. Rather, he expresses astonishing solidarity with them, solemnly stating that he would be willing "to be cut off from Christ for the sake of my brethren and kinsmen by race" (Rom. 9:3). These words of the Apostle, as well as similar words by Moses in Ex. 32:32, have been lifted up by various Church Fathers as the highest examples of selfless love. In the illustration of the olive tree Saint Paul on the contrary warns Gentile Christians three times not to be haughty or conceited toward unbelieving Jews but to stand in awe before the mystery of God (Rom. 11:18,20,25). However, later Christian generations were often to forget the Apostle's admonitions. Without any sense of solidarity with the Jewish people, they turned the lover's quarrel and the "in-house" biblical critique of Jews into a hateful source of prejudice, polemics, and persecution, despising and mistreating the Jewish people. It is one of the darkest ironies of history that the "honorary Israelites," the Gentile Christians engrafted on the good olive tree, chose many times to stomp on the broken branches rather than to long and pray with Saint Paul for their salvation.

The final major discontinuity between Judaism and Christianity pertains to Saint Paul's hermeneutical perspectives. Saint Paul's quarrel of love with contemporary Jews was not only over Christ but also over the interpretation of the Jewish tradition. The experience of Christ gave the Apostle and the early Church a new hermeneutical key by which to appropriate the Jewish heritage. It is a fact that the developing Christian tradition consciously or unconsciously embraced numerous individual elements as well as patterns of Jewish thought, worship and practice from a new theological perspective, yet with a great deal of variety and diversity. At certain points, however, the christological criterion yielded interpretive results quite conflicting with those of the Jewish scribal tradition. Of course Saint Paul would claim that the coming of Christ and the gift of the Spirit led quite naturally to the Christian interpretation of the Jewish heritage as the fulfillment of prophecies. But the scribal teachers would vehemently disagree, viewing the christological interpretations as radical departures, even an apostasy, from Judaism. What we observe in history is two communities of faith with differing hermeneutical perspectives.

The most crucial discontinuity in interpretation, and one which hastened the historical separation between Judaism and Christianity, centered on the role of the Mosaic Law. Already the Hellenists of Acts, that is to say, the Greek-speaking Jews who had become Christians, seemed to have questioned the authority of the Temple, the Law and Jewish customs in messianic times, which generated a fierce persecution against them (Acts 6:13-14; 8:1). The Apostle Paul, erstwhile zealous persecutor of these same kind of Christians, took up their cause and was himself, after Damascus, persecuted not only by unbelieving Jews but also by right-wing Jewish Christians, those whom he names "false brethren" (Gal. 1:4) and "the circumcision party" (*hoi ek peritomes*, Gal. 1:12) who wanted, along with Christ, to maintain Jewish customs in strictness. When Saint Paul speaks about "his Gospel," he surely means not a different Gospel from that preached by all (1 Cor. 15:11), but rather preaching Christ to the Gentiles apart from the requirements of the Mosaic Law, a Gospel with which "the pillars" of the Jerusalem Church agreed (Gal. 2:1-9).

The essence of the complex problem of the Law in Saint Paul and early Christianity, as more and more scholars have come to perceive in recent years, has nothing to do with the alleged Jewish attitude of meritorious "work righteousness," but with the concrete question of how Gentile converts were to be received into the Church. Some of the Jewish Christians insisted that Gentiles Christians had to be circumcised to be saved (Acts 15:1). Gentile Christians in the Galatian churches actually began to practice circumcision, eat kosher foods and celebrate Jewish festivals (Gal. 4:10; 5:2), which the Apostle describes as "Judaizing" or living like Jews (Gal. 2:14). His uncompromising answer is well known: justification is by faith in Christ not by works of the Law (Gal. 2:16).

The Pauline phrase "works of the Law," contrasted to faith, points essentially to the Jewish religious customs and not to ethical works which Saint Paul everywhere requires (Rom. 2:6-10; 1 Cor. 7:19; 2 Cor. 5:10; 5:20-21), especially in his frequent pastoral exhortations. Although the Apostle does not explicitly make a distinction between moral and ceremonial parts of the Law, he does implicitly draw such a differentiation (Rom. 2:21-29; 1 Cor. 7:19). The focus of his objections to the Law, after all, centers on circumcision and other religious signs which visibly identified Jews as Jews (Gal. 2:3; 4:10; 5:2,11; Rom. 2:25-29; Phil. 3:2-3,19), and not on moral elements assumed to be valid for all. His sharp critique of the Galatians is that they were "Judaizing" by observing circumcision and the like, not that they were either wrongly or excessively given to moral works!

Where Saint Paul theologizes about the Law, the Apostle conceives of it in its totality as a God-given, holy, but temporary dispensation which Christ has ended and from which Christians are now free (Gal. 3:15:4:7; Rom. 7; 10:4). That the term *telos* (Rom. 10:4) should not be understood as "goal" or "fulfillment," as many exegetes would have it, but rather as "termination" or "end" is indicated by the contrasts which follow as explanation of the point (Rom. 10:5-9). Obviously a dispensation that is temporary according to God's plan has a beginning (Moses) and an end (Christ). In Saint Paul's theological thought what is really fulfilled in Christ is God's promise to Abraham, not God's gift to Moses (Gal. 3).

The Apostolic Council (Acts 15; Gal. 2) by supporting Saint Paul's position on the Mosaic Law regarding Christian Gentiles, succeeded in securing the unity of the Church but sealed Christianity's accelerated separation from Judaism. Saint Paul was not against observance of the Law by Jews, although the Law for him had become in the final analysis a matter of indifference as a saving criterion. But the Jewish people as a whole could not accept the new faith if it involved such a substantive revision of a core part of the tradition which defined their identity. In Romans 9-11 Saint Paul expressly links the corporate unbelief of the Jews to their zealous attachment to the Law (Rom. 9:30-32). At a time in history, from the Maccabean Revolt to the Jewish Rebellion against the Romans (*ca.* 165 BC-73 AD), when the Jews were struggling to preserve their identity over against Gentile cultural, political and military onslaughts, they probably sensed only too well that the Christian relativization of the Law of Moses was life-threatening to the Jewish community. No wonder that they were aroused to persecution of Jewish Christians and their expulsion from the synagogues.

However, the Apostle Paul and others like him were willing to risk that sacrifice toward a new universal identity in Christ. The Apostle was not of course opposed to a Jewish identity on a sociological level any more than he was opposed to a Roman, Greek or Scythian identity. Nor does he suggest anywhere that Hellenic culture was "higher" or "nobler" than the Jewish. He does not appeal to any humanistic reasons in moving beyond what, from the Christian point of view, came to be regarded as sacred Jewish religious culture. Rather, for him as well as for the developing Church, the very nature of faith in a universal Lord and the very nature of the Church as a universal community, required this historically fateful passage toward the universalization of the essence of the Jewish faith discovered in Christ and the new humanity, the Church, which is His Body.

Here we may note that Saint Paul's bold move for the cause of Christ and the Church in the Graeco-Roman world has much to say to us Orthodox Christians with the blessings and burdens of our own rich ethno-religious heritage today as we face the interaction of faiths and cultures in a global context. Our challenge is to consider how far our own Christian identity is shaped by the experience and convictions of Saint Paul regarding Christ as the universal Savior, the Gospel as the universal message, and the Church as the universal new humanity; and how far it is variously shaped by the immense and rich ethno-religious heritages of the various Orthodox Churches developed over many centuries. To be sure, as peoples with concrete histories we can rejoice in our particular ethnic cultures and share in the variegated culture of today's global village. But what of our universal identity in Christ which transcends all cultures and adapts to new ones? What are the measures of appropriate unity and diversity? To what extent can we move beyond the sense of necessary uniformity and see that new cultural forms can express the essential experience and truth of the Orthodox faith? These and such questions will become more and more burning concerns in the future and tremendously important for our mission on a global scale. To understand more deeply our true identity as Christ's Church is also to grasp more clearly the great mission to which He calls us today.

PAUL AND HELLENISM

As part of his self-introduction to the Christians in Rome, the Apostle Paul writes that, "I am under obligation both to Greeks and barbarians, both to the wise and to the foolish: so I am eager to preach the Gospel to you also who are in Rome" (Rom. 1:15). With these words, the great Apostle seems at first blush to commit a social blunder by referring to his future hosts, the Romans, as barbarians and fools. But, of course, this is not the case. Rather he simply assumes that the Romans are cultural Greeks, because they are versed in the Greek language and share in the Hellenic culture pervasive in Rome itself. His words indicate how far the meaning of the word "Hellene" has widened by the first century. There is little doubt that, as far as the social distinction between Greek and barbarian is concerned, the Apostle would classify himself not as a barbarian but as a cultural Greek, too.

We have mentioned that he was born in Tarsus, a thriving Greek city. He received the name *Pavlos* which, although originally Roman, was quite likely given to him in its Greek version and most always was used as such. He was well versed in the Greek language as his letters show. By the time he had written any letters at all, his Christian evangelizing and tent-making involved him for at least fifteen years (35-50 AD) in the hustle and bustle of all the major centers of Hellenistic culture except Alexandria. It is no surprise at all that Saint Paul's letters reflect numerous Hellenistic elements, including language, epistolary form, dialogic manner of exposition and, on occasion, key terms. Once he anonymously quotes a proverbial statement of a Greek poet (Menander) with approval, "bad company ruins good morals" (1 Cor. 15:33). In Phil. 4:8, his eloquent exhortation about whatever is true, honorable, just, pure, lovely, gracious, and so on, could have been said by any Greek philosopher or moralist. He even uses a Stoic term such as *syneidesis* (Rom. 12:15; 1 Cor. 8:7; 2 Cor. 4:2) from the popular terminology of his time.

Saint Paul's affinities with Hellenistic culture already had deep roots in Judaism which had had direct and welcome contacts with Hellenism since the days of Alexander the Great (356-323 BC). The Jews in Alexandria, where they strived for citizenship, translated the Hebrew Scriptures into Greek primarily for their own use. Jewish cemetery inscriptions found throughout the empire are mostly in Greek. The later Hasmonean Kings in Palestine issued coins with Greek inscriptions. A gymnasium had been built in Jerusalem one hundred and fifty years before Christ. When Jesus and His disciples "reclined" to eat the Last Supper, they were in fact following a Greek custom long in use. By the era of Saint Paul Hellenic culture had penetrated Palestine to such an extent that scholars no longer consider the distinction between Palestinian and Hellenistic Judaism useful. Although there was a variety of reactions to Hellenism, including fierce opposition by some, the ideal among most Jews was to create a synthesis between Judaism and Hellenism as expressed by a rabbinic saying: "May the beauty of the Greeks dwell in the tents of the Jews." Again, it is not surprising that Jews would embrace many aspects of the prevailing culture. Earlier the prophet Daniel and the three youths had adopted Babylonian names and used Babylonian wisdom (Daniel 1-6)! Today both Jews and Greeks in the United States not only have eagerly absorbed American patterns of life and thought, but also have in part contributed to the shaping of American culture itself.

For a minority group living in a dominant culture the question is not whether or not to acculturate but how much. The remarkable feature about the Jewish people in Graeco-Roman times, given the historical upheavals of that period, is that they vigorously maintained a distinctive identity. Although Judaism exhibited great diversity both in the Diaspora as well as in Palestine – recall the variety of religious groups such as the Sadducees, Pharisees, Scribes, and Essenes – virtually all Jews shared a common identity centered on faith in the one God, the Law and a profound sense of peoplehood. Philo of Alexandria was deeply hellenized in thought, but nevertheless was a sincerely observant Jew who chided other hellenizing Jews for not keeping the Jewish customs. The Apostle Paul who calls himself "a Hebrew of Hebrews [and] as to the law a Pharisee" (Phil. 3:5) was much less hellenized than his contemporary Philo. Saint Paul's Greek is distinctly less literary than Philo's and his cast of thought basically Hebraic. It is true that several generations ago scholars were fond of interpreting every major aspect of Saint Paul's thought, such as the christological titles Son of God and Lord, the contrast between flesh and spirit, and the sacred rites of Baptism and the Lord's Supper, in terms of hellenistic syncretism. But in the last two generations a great reversal has taken place in biblical scholarship. A consensus of scholars now views these important aspects of the life and thought of Saint Paul and the early Church as intrinsic developments of the new Christian movement which are entirely understandable within the context of its Jewish background.

Saint Paul's openness to the Graeco-Roman world and its culture, an amazing phenomenon for a former zealous Pharisee, was theologically grounded and derived from his understanding of his vision of the risen Christ. In Gal. 1:11-17, where he appeals to this momentous event as his frontline defense of the divine origin and authority of the Gospel, he describes his conversion as a "call" from God using the language of Jeremiah and Isaiah. God had set him apart "from his mother's womb" and "called" him to evangelize His Son among the Gentiles (Gal. 1:15-16). The Apostle contends for "the Gospel which [he] preach[es] among the Gentiles," the Gospel to the uncircumcised "entrusted" to him by God (Gal. 2:1,7). In this special "commission" from God lies his "necessity" to evangelize and his "obligation" to "Greeks and barbarians" (1 Cor. 9:16-17; Rom. 1:14). Elsewhere he names himself "the Apostle to the Gentiles" (Rom. 11:13). Saint Paul thus understood himself as fulfilling a special role in God's design pertaining to the Gentiles entirely consistent with the Old Testament.

In a book entitled *The Early Christians: Their World Mission and Self-Discovery* (1986), Ben Meyer convincingly develops the thesis that, of all the religious groups in first-century Judaism, including the Jewish Christians, only the Christian Hellenists and Saint Paul were able to conceive of and carry out a seemingly impossible world mission against all odds, and that for theological reasons. The Christian Hebraists understood themselves as the vanguard of a restored Israel and resisted the outreach to Gentiles. But the Christian Hellenists and Saint Paul understood themselves as the first fruits of a new humanity in Christ in which "there is neither Jew nor Greek... neither slave nor free... neither male nor female; for... all are one in Christ" (Gal. 3:28). The key difference was that the Hellenists and Saint Paul interpreted the death and resurrection of Christ as His enthronement as universal Lord (*Kyrios*). The experience and theology of the universal lordship of Christ, and the resulting universal soteriology, were thus the driving force behind the world mission. As the Epistle to the Ephesians puts it: Christ "has broken down the dividing wall of hostility, by abolishing in his flesh the law of commandments and ordinances, that He might create in Himself one new man in place of the two, so making peace, and might reconcile us both to God in one body" (Eph. 2:14-16).

But what was the content of Saint Paul's openness to the world? Surely he did not come to Hellenistic society with empty hands. Yet by what insights and criteria did he strive to give shape to the life of the congregations he founded? Christ did not give him a blueprint but the grace of the Holy Spirit. It was by his daily union with Christ, and the power of the Spirit, that Saint Paul preached, taught, ministered, organized, and theologized. The Church Fathers correctly say that it was Christ who acted in Saint Paul for the Apostle himself had said that he possessed the mind of Christ (1 Cor. 2:16). Nor was he unaware that certain boundaries were not to be crossed. A former Pharisee inclined to see even eating with Gentiles as defiling, the Apostle would indeed be highly conscious of the road he traveled in pagan society. He nowhere reflects on the matter of continuity and discontinuity between faith and culture in a systematic way. He deals with *ad hoc* issues and develops distinctive positions, using all appropriate elements, whether Jewish or Greek, according to his new discernment in Christ. Examples abound. The Roman Christians must shun drunkenness and debauchery (Rom. 13:13), but they may eat of whatever food according to their own judgment in good faith (Rom. 14). The Corinthian widows would do better to stay unmarried but if they cannot exercise self-control, they should marry (1 Cor. 7:9). The slave Onesimus is returned to his master, but Philemon must now treat him no longer simply as a slave but as beloved brother in Christ (Philemon 12 and 16).

An extended example of the dynamic interplay between Saint Paul's theological discernment, spiritual sensitivity and pastoral flexibility is the Apostle's long discussion on idol meats in 1 Corinthians, chapters 8-10. Are Christians allowed to eat the meat of animals previously offered to pagan deities? The Apostle answers yes, agreeing with the "strong" or theologically knowledgeable of Corinth because, although there are many mythical gods and lords, yet for Christians there is one God, the Father, and one Lord, Jesus Christ. Idol gods are nothing, he says. Nevertheless, the Apostle pastorally sides with the "weak" Corinthians whose conscience is offended by such practice (1 Cor. 8). Saint Paul's spiritual insight is that "knowledge puffs up, but love builds up" (8:1). His pastoral principle is that a Christian should sacrifice her or his rights if the upbuilding of another is at stake. He presents himself as an example by sacrificing his apostolic rights to material support and also by becoming all things to all for their salvation (1 Cor. 9).

However, eating idol meats is one thing (1 Cor. 10:23) which is permissible. Participating in ceremonies and banquets at pagan temples is quite another which is not. The Jews have their sacrifices and the pagans have theirs as well. But the Christians have their own distinctive identity in the Lord's Supper, participating in the one bread and becoming the one body of Christ (10:14-22). While the Christians are permitted table fellowship with pagan friends in pagan homes, they are not to eat meat about which a scandalous question is raised (10:27-29). The Apostle's last words on the subject eloquently indicate both an open-ended discernment and a clear awareness of the Church as a distinctive community. "Whether you eat or drink, or whatever you do, do all to the glory of God. Give no offense to Jews or to Greeks or to the Church of God" (10:31-32).

How could the early Church spread in the Graeco-Roman world with such openness and flexibility, and yet develop its own distinctive identity? For a long time many New Testament scholars, especially on the Protestant side, have reveled in the great variety of patterns of life and thought in the New Testament. They have gleaned "many gospels." They have talked about the utter disunity of early Christianity. One cannot help but sense a hidden agenda somewhere. In more recent times, however, a corrective to this tendency is taking hold especially in the area of the study of early Christianity and its social environment. For example, the comprehensive study by Wayne Meeks, *The First Urban Christians* (1983), builds up a detailed case for the powerful unitive forces in the Pauline congregations both on a local and universal level. Meeks shows that, along with the undeniable diversity, Pauline Christianity is marked by a broad but distinct convergence through developing patterns of language of belonging and separation, a sense of spiritual and moral purity, the rituals of Baptism and the Lord's Supper, and patterns of belief, practice and governance. When the Epistle to the Ephesians states that there is "one Lord, one faith, one baptism, one God and Father of us all" (Eph. 4:56), it is not speaking idly but expressing a powerful drive of the early Church to develop and maintain its unique character and witness in the Graeco-Roman world, just as Judaism had done long before. It is this same drive that eventually led to the clear consciousness among Christians that they constituted, along with Jews and Gentiles, *to triton genos*, the third race.

Ben Meyer in his book, *The Early Christians* (1986), takes to task a number of scholars such as Walter Bauer, Hermann Gunkel, Walter Bauer, Rudolf Bultmann, and others, who have treated ancient Christianity of the first and second century as an excessively variegated and syncretistic phenomenon. Meyer cautions that the diversity should not conceal the drive toward identity and unity. Nor should "orthodoxy" be defined as something static and fixed in order then to be superficially dismissed, for "orthodoxy" itself is dynamic and developing. Meyer finds that behind all the talk about conflicting diversity and syncretism by modern scholars lies "a massive cultural phenomenon: the recoil of the West from its religious heritage, or at least from the classical form of its religious heritage" or, to put it more simply, a hidden resistance to truth-claims and dogmatic teaching (Meyer, p. 196).

As for myself, whenever I have encountered the writings of "thorough-going diversity scholars" over the years, I have genuinely wondered whether or not we were reading the same Apostle Paul, the same Clement of Rome, the same Ignatios of Antioch, the same Polycarp, the same Justin Martyr and the same Eirenaios – the leaders of the ancient Church who express the Church's deep integrative movement toward doctrinal, sacramental and administrative unity. To my understanding, one of the most astonishing aspects of the interaction of faith and culture in Saint Paul and the early Church is that, as the young Christian movement was leaving behind the distinctive signs of Jewish identity mentioned above, it did not move into the Hellenistic world in a syncretistic manner borrowing and mixing elements indiscriminately. On the contrary, it had a powerful sense of its own uniqueness, an invincible conviction of possessing the truth, a dynamic ability to develop its own patterns of faith, worship, teaching, and organization – the building blocks of what in time emerged as the institutional signs of a highly visible apostolic and catholic Church putting its own seal on culture! To be sure, there was great diversity and even divisions and heresies in ancient Christianity as a historical phenomenon. Some groups seeking to preserve forms of Jewish Christianity, and other groups, the wild variety of Gnostic sects hopelessly syncretistic, are evident until the mid-second century and beyond. But the primitive Church of Jerusalem, the Gentile Church of Saint Paul (who did his utmost to maintain the unity of the whole Church), the Church of Clement of Rome, and later the Churches of other leading Christian figures such as Saints Ignatios, Polycarp, Justin Martyr and Eirenaios, form a golden cord of amazing historical continuity, catholic identity and theological coherence which shines all the more against the background of Graeco-Roman unbridled religious syncretism.

The dynamic interplay of faith and culture in Saint Paul and the early Church carries significant and challenging insights for Orthodox Christians today as we face the dramatic interaction of diverse faiths and secular pluralistic cultures on a global scale. Perhaps the greatest challenge for us is Saint Paul's conviction about world mission grounded in the universal lordship of Christ. Dare we, like Saint Paul, claim the modern world in Christ's name, rather than maintain a basically defensive and protective posture over against contemporary society? What kind of discernment and what measures of flexibility are truly appropriate to the catholicity of the Orthodox faith so that it may be lived and expressed incarnationally through new cultural forms? The Church of Saint Paul was like a vehicle with four-wheel drive, efficient and able to travel the cultural topography of the time with power and amazing success. The Orthodox Church today presents more the image of a stretch limousine, self-conscious about its image and using a lot of energy to maintain itself rather than carry out its mission. The future holds opportunities and risks. The closer we are to Christ, the more clearly we can discern our way under the law of Christ (*ennomoi Christou*, 1 Cor. 9:21). The deeper our union with Him, the stronger our conscious identity as His Body, the more securely we can be "all things to all... for the sake of the Gospel" (1 Cor. 9:19, 22-23).

CHAPTER NINE

CHRIST: THE JEWEL OF ORTHODOXY

In the previous chapter we examined the life and thought of Saint Paul in relationship to Judaism and Hellenism. We reflected on the dynamics of early Christianity as a renewal movement emerging from Judaism and adapting to the new cultural milieu of the Graeco-Roman world. In this process of development the early Church struggled to define and express its own identity, distinct from both Judaism and Hellenism, by foundational beliefs and ritual acts, for example, the proclamation of the Gospel, the initiation act of Baptism, the sacred meal of the Eucharist, and new perceptions of moral conduct. The powerful impetus driving forward the new Christian movement was the experience of the risen Christ and the gift of the Holy Spirit, events by which the entire ministry of Jesus was interpreted and proclaimed as the decisive arrival of the new age in fulfillment of the Old Testament promises. The central focus was the person of Christ Himself, not simply as a great figure of the past but as living Lord present and active through His Spirit. Saint Paul counted all things as a "loss" and "rubbish" for the "sake of Christ" and "the surpassing worth of the knowledge of Christ" (Phil. 3:7-8). The Apostle applied these words not only to his personal religious achievements but also to his rich Jewish traditions. Centered on Christ and inspired by the Holy Spirit, he "pressed forward to what lies ahead" as he carried himself and the early Church to new horizons of faith and life. He did so in vigorous conversation with both Judaism and Hellenism, yet always in uncompromising faithfulness to the truth of the Gospel of Christ.

Twenty centuries later the Orthodox Church, now spread throughout the globe, finds itself in a situation both similar to and different from that of Saint Paul and the early Church. Now the Church is no longer a nascent community seeking to define its developing identity through distinct beliefs and forms of expression. Its theology is highly defined. Its worship is greatly elaborated. Its religious life, for example fasting, is specified down to minutiae. Its

157

canonical order, although not without disputes, is established by a host of laws. Nevertheless, the Church still struggles with its sense of self-understanding, unity, identity and mission. Theology as concepts and definitions cannot reach ordinary people unless theological principles and themes are simplified and applied to daily life through inspirational preaching and teaching. Worship in its traditional forms and language is enjoyed as sacred ceremonies but without sufficient impact on the actual life of worshipers. The religious life of the faithful in terms of customs and morals is in a dire state because the majority of the baptized are influenced more by the world than by the Church's traditions. Canonical harmony itself seems always debatable in view of rival claims regarding jurisdictional authority and the long-standing divisions over the ecclesiastical calendar. Historically, these are facts, and facts must been seen with realism.

The radical cultural changes of the last century, as well as the internal developments within Orthodoxy itself, make the Church's need for self-assessment more urgent. The task belongs not only to Church leaders and theologians, but also the entire body of the faithful as a whole. And the challenge is not to achieve a revision of the abiding essentials in terms of dogma, worship, canonical order, ethical values and the spirituality of Orthodoxy. Rather the challenge is to achieve a sense of renewal of hearts and minds, resembling that of Saint Paul and the early Christians, in order to see the treasures of the tradition in their appropriate light and function. The challenge is to attain to a level of trust and unity among all Orthodox leaders and theologians, clergy and laity alike, to the extent that the Church can present a clear and powerful message to its own people and the world. Such a task cannot be accomplished apart from our personal conversion to Christ and our existential appreciation of the centrality of Christ in the Orthodox tradition. In what follows, we present reflections for further meditation on the subject of renewal based on the Sunday of Orthodoxy, the great liturgical celebration of Christ and the Orthodox Faith.

CHRIST AS REVEALER OF THE FATHER AND THE HOLY SPIRIT

We begin with a story about the jewel and the jewel box. Many ages ago, so the story goes, a family clan acquired a jewel of priceless value. Its beauty and power were of unsurpassed quality. In order to safeguard it, the family placed this jewel in a jewel box crafted with exquisite care. The next generation marveled not only at the jewel but also at the beautiful jewel box. For safekeeping, it made a larger jewel box in which it put both the jewel and the first jewel box. As ages passed, generation after generation saw the making of more and ever larger jewel boxes until at last a great and magnificent treasure chest had been built – itself adorned with intricate carvings, precious stones, artful symbols, and mystical paintings. The family clan, now grown quite large, was very proud of its noble inheritance. Outsiders, too, would come and admire the antique beauty of the enormous treasure chest. "How fortunate you are," they would often say, "to possess such a truly rich tradition." Then one day someone asked: "By the way, what is *in* the treasure chest?" No one could offer a clear answer. Few seemed to know for sure.

As we celebrate the Sunday of Orthodoxy each year, we rejoice in the treasures of the Orthodox Faith. We delight in the veneration of icons, our symbolic windows to heaven that unite us with the communion of saints. We proclaim the truth and glory of Orthodoxy. We triumphantly declare: "This is the faith of the Apostles! This is the faith of the Fathers! This is the faith of the Orthodox! This is the faith that upholds the universe!"

But what is the content of this Faith? What is the essence of our celebration? What is the center of our joy? What is the priceless jewel? Let us recall the words of the Gospel lesson recited on the Sunday of Orthodoxy (Jn 1:43-51). The Gospel lesson recounts the conversion of the first disciples of Christ. Philip proclaimed: "We have found Him of whom Moses and also the Prophets wrote!" And Nathaniel cried out: "Teacher, You are the Son of God! You are the King of Israel!" Commenting on this passage, Saint John Chrysostom writes: "See how Nathaniel's soul is filled with joy? See how he embraces Christ with his words of faith? See how he leaps and dances with delight? So should we all also rejoice, who have been made worthy to know the Son of God."

And, surely, the Sunday of Orthodoxy invites us to do just that: to embrace Christ with fervent faith; to delight in Him with true joy; to glorify Him as our Lord and Savior; and to see that, above all, He Himself is the good news, the beauty and truth, the grace and glory, behind all the treasures of our Orthodox Faith. He, and He alone, is the priceless jewel of Orthodoxy. Let me be clear: Orthodoxy is Christ and Christ is Orthodoxy. Without Christ, (that is, without His living presence among us), Orthodoxy is but a historical ornament fit for a museum. But with Christ, (that is, with His empowering grace and love in our hearts and lives), Orthodoxy is a living and vibrant witness to God, a burning bush glowing with the fire of the Holy Spirit, a bright beacon shining on the path to a lost but ever seeking world.

What would you reply if someone asked you: "What's in the treasure chest"? Would you say, "Christ our Lord, the Leader of our Church, the One who said, 'I am the light of the world' (Jn 8:12) and who taught us, 'Love one another as I have loved you' (Jn 13:34). But what more could you say about the importance of Christ for Orthodoxy? What else could you say to answer more clearly and convincingly? And what if you were asked, "What does Christ really mean to you? What difference does Christ really make in your life?" What would you say then to a potential convert to Orthodoxy?

Let us draw three lessons from the New Testament and see what we can learn about Christ, the eternal Word and Wisdom of God, "who became flesh and dwelt among us, full of grace and truth" (Jn 1:12). His first disciples testify: "We have beheld His glory, glory as of the only Son of the Father" (Jn 1:12). And again: "That which we have seen with our eyes, and touched with our hands – the eternal life which was with the Father and was made manifest to us – we proclaim to you, so that you may have communion with us. And our communion is with the Father and with His Son, Jesus Christ. And we are writing this that your joy may be complete" (1 Jn 1:1-4).

Here we have the first great lesson of what the mystery of Christ means to Orthodoxy: Christ reveals to us the life of God, indeed, the fullness of God, the very character of God as light and life. The most magnificent words ever written are the opening words of the Gospel of John: "In the beginning was the Word…. He was in the beginning with God and all things were made through Him, and without Him was not anything made that was made. In Him was life, and the life was the light of humanity. The light shines in the darkness, and the darkness has not overcome it" (Jn 1:1-5).

The marvelous good news of the Gospel is that the eternal Son who, united with the Father and dwelling in the bosom of the Father, "has made Him known" (Jn 1:18). The Greek verb behind the expression "has made Him known" is *exegesato*. From this verb also comes the word *exegesis* which scholars use for the interpretation of the Bible. *Exegesato* means that Christ has shown to us the full meaning of God. As no one else before Him or after Him, Christ has clearly explained or interpreted for us the mystery of the true and living

God. Why? In order that we may have communion with God, that we may share God's personal life, that we may live in the same spiritual realm of the Father – the Kingdom of light, life, truth, love, grace and glory.

Let me be specific. Recall the Parable of the Prodigal Son, particularly the image of God as a loving Father. What an unusual Father Jesus presents to us: a Father who utterly respects the freedom and dignity of each human person; a Father who shared with his young rebel son His own property and let him go to squander it without questions! I can well imagine if one of my two sons came to ask me for his share of the family property. I would say: "Wait a minute, I am still living and want to manage my household. Besides, what are the reasons for your considerable request? Is it for college or a graduate program? Is it to get married, or buy a house, or start a business?" Anything else would hardly count. But not for God who freely gives of His attributes and possessions to His sons and daughters. And it is of course God who is pictured as the Father in that parable. God gave His property, freely and generously, even though He knew it would be squandered. What an unusual Father, a Father of generous freedom, impressive dignity, and incomparable love.

We may ask: What "property" does God give to each one of us? For He truly does give and has given to us of His "property" – that is His very life and likeness. God has given us the capacity to be free, the capacity to know what is true and good, the capacity to think and decide, the capacity to create and build things, the capacity to love and show compassion toward others, the capacity to forgive and begin anew, the capacity to bond and create friendships, the capacity to enjoy family relationships and to live in loving and supportive communities. All these are His enormously generous gifts to us – all packaged in what we call the gift of the image and likeness of God in which we have been created. In other words, we too have the inner capacities, just as Christ did, to show who God is, to explain and interpret God the Father by how we live and use His gifts. One of the Church Fathers has said that of all things in creation it is a human being herself or himself who can provide by word and action the most glorious testimony to the goodness, greatness and wisdom of God.

Yet we often squander God's property by in fact abusing His gifts. Freedom becomes arbitrariness. Knowledge becomes cunning to gain advantage over others. Creativity becomes the tool of pride, or greed, or other wicked passions and evil imaginations. Love is shortchanged by selfishness. Compassion is hamstrung by short-lived emotions. Forgiveness seems impossible. Friendships, family relationships, and social ties are scarred by petty human weaknesses and unrepented sins. What is sin but the abuse of gifts, the abuse of people, the abuse of things, the abuse of relationships. Sin is the corruption of what is good; and we know that everything that God has created is good.

What is the result? We often live in resentment and anger. We find ourselves in conflict and alienation from God, ourselves, and others. We cannot make peace even with the natural environment in which we live. Not infrequently we abuse our very bodies which are the temple of the Holy Spirit. Thus, in various ways, we share the misfortune of the Prodigal Son – being away from home, experiencing exile in a foreign land, and living like slaves to the evil passions and the wrong choices which lead us to abuse God's gifts.

But the loving Father is waiting as He waited for the Prodigal Son. When the young son utterly crashed and hit bottom, he remembered home, the plentitude of home. Surely, he also remembered the goodness and the love of the Father on which he counted to be accepted at least as a servant, if not a son again. He had prepared a speech of repentance, but his very decision to return for a new start was sufficient. The waiting Father ran out to him, embraced him, and welcomed him as a son. He would not hear of any words of lament or long explanation. Rather, he commanded: Bring a new robe, bring new shoes, bring a ring as a sign of restored sonship, prepare a banquet and let's have music and dancing. "For this my son was dead, and is alive again; he was lost, and is found" (Lk. 15:24).

See what a glorious image of God our Lord Jesus has shown to us? See what hope the loving Father who is revealed to us through the Son inspires in us? See what good news the gospel announces to us? No matter how far we have departed from the Father, no matter how deeply we have fallen, no matter how much we have abused His gifts and have been enslaved by the wretchedness of evil – there is the path of return and recovery, there is the path of going home, there is the path of true renewal and joy! And what is this path, or better, *who* is this path, but Christ Himself, who said: "I am the way and the truth and the life" (Jn 14:6). The way to what? The way to the Father, the way to communion with Him, the way to share again the Father's fullness of property – life, light, love, grace and glory.

We have come to the second lesson from the New Testament about why Christ is the jewel of Orthodoxy. Christ leads us to the Father not only by His teaching such as in the Parable of the Prodigal Son, but also through His example of humility and sacrifice, particularly His sacrifice on the Cross. Our hymns and prayers often mention the death of Christ as a sacrifice for forgiveness and redemption. The main hymn of the Sunday of Orthodoxy does the same: "We venerate Your pure icon, O Good One, asking for forgiveness of our sins, Christ our God. For by Your own free will you deigned in the flesh to ascend on the Cross to save Your creation from the bondage of the enemy. Therefore, we cry out to You in thanksgiving: You have filled all things with joy, O Savior, having come to save the world."

Christ came not only to teach but to save the world. Christ is not only the supreme example of love and goodness, He is also the only Savior and Redeemer. He is "the Lamb of God who takes away the sin of the world" (Jn 1:29). Recall the night before His death when He ate the Last Supper with His disciples. With certain solemn words and actions, Christ signified the meaning of His death. He broke the bread and said: "Take eat; this is my body." Then He took the cup and said: "Drink of it, all of you; for this is my blood of the new covenant, which is poured out for many for the forgiveness of sins" (Mt. 26:26-28).

In modern times we can hardly fathom the profound meaning of ritual sacrifice in the religion in which Jesus grew up. By way of analogy, we might catch a glimpse of its significance when we hear or read in the newspapers that someone gives a kidney that someone else might live; or that someone jumps into a burning house to rescue another, and then himself perishes. Christ died on our behalf. Although sinless, He became a curse, a sin, that is, a sacrificial sin offering according to the Jewish tradition. He died that we might be cleansed, sanctified, and have full access to the mercy and forgiveness of God.

Do not ask now for an exegesis of the paradox of how our loving Father in heaven both offered and accepted as sacrifice His beloved Son on the Cross. Rather, receive the mystery in faith and rejoice in the blessings which flow from it. In the Old Testament, God stopped Abraham from offering his son Isaac as a sacrifice. However, out of his boundless love for the world, God did not spare His own Son to establish the New Covenant and reconcile a sinful world to Himself. In the words of St. Paul: "God shows His love for us in that while we were yet sinners Christ died for us.... We rejoice in God through our Lord Jesus Christ, through whom we have now received our reconciliation" (Rom. 5:8,11). And again: "If God is for us, who is against us? If God did not spare His own Son but gave Him up for us all, will He not also give us all things with Him" (Rom. 8: 31-32)? Saint Paul goes on triumphantly to proclaim that no one and nothing can separate from the love of God in Jesus Christ – neither tribulation, or distress, or persecution, or famine, or nakedness, or anything else saint or sinner, prodigal or righteous can suffer. Why? Because Christ died and rose again for our salvation. Through His Cross and Resurrection, Christ the Victor, defeated the powers of evil, sin, corruption, death and the Devil. He liberated humanity from these evil forces and ushered in the new age of grace – a new time in which we can return home and share the life of our Father in heaven.

The third lesson from the New Testament about why Christ is so decisively important and absolutely central to our Orthodox life and tradition is that Christ is the Giver of the Holy Spirit. Christ promised His disciples: "I shall send to you from the Father, even the Spirit of truth, who proceeds from the Father, [and] He will bear witness to me" (Jn 15:26). In Christ we come to know not only the Father but also the gift of the Spirit through whom all of God's gifts and mercies are energized and become effective in the Church, as well as our personal lives. In other words, Christ has shown to us the fullness of the mystery of God, the eternal three-foldness of the one, true and living God, namely, the great mystery of the Holy Trinity which is the alpha and the omega of all things.

Recall how during His earthly ministry, Jesus spoke of the Holy Spirit as God's finger or power by which Christ taught, healed, and cast out demons. On one occasion Jesus said: "I came to cast fire on the earth; and how I wish it were already kindled" (Lk. 12:49)! He was speaking of the fire of the Holy Spirit that the flock of His faithful followers were to receive on Pentecost. They were about 120 of them, including Jesus' mother, the other women followers, and the brothers of Jesus, according to the Book of Acts (1:12-15). On that awesome day, as the little Church had gathered for prayer, the Holy Spirit was poured out upon them from heaven "like the rush of a mighty wind ...and there appeared to them tongues as of fire, distributed and resting on each one of them" (Acts 2:1). On that day the risen Christ became a fire starter and His Church became a burning bush ablaze with the grace of the Spirit.

What does all that mean for us today? The gift of the Spirit on Pentecost means that we, the body of believers who are the Church, are not so much an institution defined by so many forms and regulations. Rather we are a spiritual movement alive with the presence and power of Christ. We are the body of Christ. We are God's holy people. We are the community of the Holy Spirit. We are the keepers of holy fire. And our vocation is to be united together and to form a mighty torch of fire witnessing to the world the light and the glory of God.

Why is Christ the precious jewel of Orthodoxy? He is the eternal Word of God who reveals to us the loving Father. He is the Son who offered His life on the Cross for our redemption. He is the Lord who gives the Spirit to empower us in the life of new creation. In Christ we know and worship the Holy Trinity. In Christ we transcend human boundaries and conventions to witness to the One, Holy, Catholic and Apostolic Church, "the Church of the living God, the pillar and bulwark of the truth" (1 Tim. 3:15).

ORTHODOXY: TRIUMPH OF TRIUMPHALISM?

The Sunday of Orthodoxy is called the Triumph of Orthodoxy. This title is connected to the historical origins, as well as the theological meaning of the Feast. The Sunday of Orthodoxy began more than eleven hundred years ago in 878. It was established as a celebration of the restoration of the holy icons, an event that occurred in 843. After nearly two centuries of bitter controversy, the heresy of iconoclasm (or "icon-smashing") was defeated. The holy icons were returned to the churches and the homes of the faithful. Orthodox Christians were again permitted to venerate icons in remembrance and honor of Christ and the saints. Thus the restoration of icons signaled a historical triumph in the life and piety of the Church.

The Feast of Orthodoxy celebrates a theological triumph as well. Icons reflect the mystery of our salvation and define our destiny as children of God. The most important icon, and that featured on the Sunday of Orthodoxy, is the icon of Christ. The icon of Christ symbolizes His incarnation by which He embraced our humanity and called us brothers and sisters. Created in His image and likeness, we strive to be living icons of Christ and sharers in the new creation, the mystery of the transfigured cosmos. We kiss and reverence icons as sacred symbols, not idols. The honor passes on to the Lord and his saints. Icons are "windows to heaven." They remind us of the Church triumphant, the communion of Saints, the victory of righteous men and women in Scripture and tradition. In the words of Saint John of Damascus: "The icon is a song of triumph, and revelation, and an enduring monument to the victory of the saints."

Yet we must ask about our understanding and application of this triumph of the Orthodox Faith today. What is our part and claim, indeed our duty and mission, in the light of this triumph? Do we present ourselves in the manner of Christ's love and service to others or in terms of exalted traditions and privileged status over against other people? What is the difference between a true triumph and false triumphalism in Christ's terms? I invite you to reflect with me on these questions as we bring to mind the past and present of Orthodoxy, the unity and mission of the Church, the true faith and life in Christ.

The triumph of Christ is His coming to Jerusalem for his holy Passion and glorious Resurrection. He came with a group of fishermen and others whose dialect betrayed them as village Galileans. He entered Jerusalem riding on a donkey, fulfilling Zechariah's prophecy that He was coming as the Prince of Peace. A spontaneous crowd of ordinary people waved palms and welcomed him with the words: "Blessed is He who comes in the name of the Lord!" He went on to cleanse the Temple to make it a house of prayer, not trade. He faced arrest, beatings, mockings, and finally shameful death on the Cross in obedience to God's will. And God raised Him from the dead, smashing the gates of hell, shattering the power of death, and, in the words of the Epistle to the Colossians, stripping "the principalities and powers [of evil], triumphing (*thriambeusas*) over them in Christ" (Col. 2:15). The triumph was God's, a true triumph accomplished by Christ, who came not to be served but to serve, and to give His life for many, as He said. The triumph was life and resurrection for all humanity, a splendid victory over the powers of sin and death through sacrifice, a source of abundant grace poured out by the Holy Spirit on the day of Pentecost.

About thirty years after our Lord's resurrection, there was another triumph, the triumph of Titus, the Roman general and son of Vespasian Caesar. He had returned to Rome from a great war with the Jews during which he had destroyed Jerusalem and burned the Temple. A magnificent parade, which the ancients called triumph (*thriambos*), was prepared in his honor. Titus entered Rome riding on a shining chariot with all the trimmings of worldly pomp and military power. Soldiers and officers in full uniform marched ahead of him. Behind him came captured slaves and behind them wagon after wagon of booty. Excited on his arrival, all Rome shouted with one voice as to a god: "Hail, Caesar's son! Hail, Caesar!" His was an awesome procession memorialized to this day by the colossal arch in Rome bearing his name – the Arch of Titus – and depicting carved scenes of his victory. His triumph was an exaltation of the power of man, the might of Rome, symbolized in the Book of Revelation as a harlot riding on the beast and drunken with the blood of Christian martyrs. But in God's eyes this was not a triumph at all – it was an expression of self-glorification, *hubris*, human pride. It was empty, false triumphalism.

Today Orthodoxy is resplendent with majestic worship, sublime doctrines and impressive offices. Orthodoxy claims a rich legacy of hymnology, spirituality and canon law. Orthodoxy exhibits the universal Faith of the One, Holy, Catholic and Apostolic Church to the whole world – Protestants, Catholics, Jews, Muslims, Hindus, Buddhists and so many others. But what does Orthodoxy have to celebrate at the beginning of the third millennium as we consider its day-to-day life and witness in actual practice?

A generation ago Father Alexander Schmemann wrote three classic articles on the "Problems of Orthodoxy" – the canonical problem, the liturgical problem and the spiritual problem.[1] The same problems burden Orthodoxy today, much as they did thirty-five years ago when Father Schmemann wrote. About ten years ago, His Eminence Chrysostomos Konstantinides of the Ecumenical Patriarchate, wrote an article with the title *"Ekklesia gerasmene?"* (*"A Church Grown Old?"*), in which he touched on the ordination of women deacons, changes in the canons about fasting, and the activation of the laity in the Church.[2] We are still talking about these subjects but are in fact reluctant to deal with them in substance. More recently, Father Thomas Hopko, of Saint Vladimir's Theological Seminary, used the following words to describe the position of Orthodoxy in the post-modern world: "Orthodoxy [is] still a minority Church riddled with massive inner confusions, fears, pretensions and divisions from its 2000 year odyssey through history [and] now finds itself in a 'global village'… moving toward a [secular, post-modern] way of life which has already begun to dominate the planet."[3]

As Orthodoxy celebrates the Sunday of Orthodoxy around the globe each year, it is therefore both pertinent and justifiable to ask whether Orthodoxy is celebrating a triumph or triumphalism. Are we following the way of Christ's triumph through His example of humility, service and sacrifice for the life and resurrection of the world? Or are we following the way of another kind of triumph based on external splendor, institutional weight, and self-glorification which in God's eyes is not a triumph at all, but hollow triumphalism? Given its treasures and triumphs, does Orthodoxy truly ascribe the credit and the glory to God, being grateful for His gifts and repentant for failing to use them adequately? Or is Orthodoxy self-absorbed with its identity problems, looking backwards to past glories, and drawing up the bridges because it neither understands nor is able to help a spiritually starving world?

In his article on Orthodoxy in the post-modern world, which is one of the most prophetic statements I have ever read by an Orthodox theologian, Father Hopko shows the true way for Orthodoxy. It is a way which Jesus called narrow and hard, but the only way that leads to life. I focus on this article in part because it is a rare example of how theology applies to life. It is not often that we theologians descend from our ivory towers to look at the actual life of the Church and speaks prophetically within it. Yet theology is not merely a repetitive but also a critical and guiding discipline. Theologians are obliged not only to expound the truths in the abstract, or to recite the triumphs of the past, but also to apply them concretely. A fully adequate theology includes a prophetic, cleansing, even cauterizing function. The ancient prophets loved God and loved God's people, and because of this burning love, they spoke boldly God's word in order to bring about repentance and correction of life. To be prophetic in the classic sense means to speak on behalf of God – to be inspired, forthright, stirring, exposing institutional pretensions, denouncing hypocrisies on high, and calling all faithful to accountability before God. The aim of Father Hopko as a prophetic theologian is positive: to awaken the community to its actual conditions, abandon its illusions, and return to the path of God. For those who long to celebrate a true, sobering triumph on behalf of Orthodoxy, here are his insightful and weighty directives:

1) We must compel ourselves to put Christ, and only Christ and His Gospel, at the center of our concerns, and do only that which is pleasing to the Holy Spirit and according to the mind of Christ (Acts 15:28; 1 Cor. 2:16).

2) We must practice conciliarity, the principle of working together, which is one of the defining truths of authentic Orthodoxy, applicable as much to parishes, dioceses, local Churches and patriarchates as to individual persons – working together and dying to our own narrow, selfish interests for the sake of Christ and the Gospel.

3) We must abandon the lie that we can live by Christ's Gospel and still retain all the riches and glories of our respective ethnic cultures and identities in America. This is not a denial of our ethnic heritages but a true appreciation of them in the light of Christ who affirms and blesses all that is good and beautiful in every culture and every ethnic heritage. Our Orthodox Faith and our ethnic heritages are by no means contrary treasures, but keeping the priorities straight is of immense importance for the universal mission of Orthodoxy in America and elsewhere.

4) We must die – as the seed dies in the ground to bring new life – to aspects of ecclesiastical institutionalism and notions of Orthodoxy as sectarian ideology. We must live Orthodoxy and present it to the world as the way of universal truth and life; and in doing so we must be ready to talk and discuss, to question and be questioned, to dialog and persuade on the basis of all the challenges of modern life and without recourse to special pleading.

5) We must reject all forms of coercion, control or dominance, and be prepared to put up with error and evil, while unmasking its falsehood and rebuking sin. On the one hand we must follow the way of love and affirm whatever in the world is true, honorable, just, and lovely (Phil. 4:8), doing so with joy, not reluctance. On the other hand we must intercede before God on behalf of all, witnessing to and serving all people, without dreams of conquest and domination, indeed, without even the desire to convert others which is God's job, not ours. Thus, being free ourselves, we can bring God's gift of freedom to others by the only way possible – proclaiming, learning, embracing, loving and doing the truth.

6) Finally we must recognize that we live in what Pope John Paul II has called a "culture of death." We live in a society that is morally decomposing and bears the stench of death exuding from its very soul. And yet we must love this dying world and offer to it the message of life. As intercessors and advocates before God, we must, just as Christ did, love evil-doers with an unconditional love which alone can redeem sinners and draw them to the Kingdom of love. Orthodoxy is nothing if not this inexhaustible divine love and invincible

paschal proclamation of Christ's victory over death bringing new life to creation.

These are six golden points, six principles of prophetic vision, six ways by which to celebrate the triumph of Orthodoxy in integrity and authenticity. It is not enough for us to glory in that a crowd has gathered to witness the grandeur of Orthodox worship. It is not enough for us to leave the liturgical gathering self-satisfied that we have done our part in observing the great festival of the Sunday of Orthodoxy. It is not enough for us to go home reassured that we possess the superior Faith. Such sentiments smack of triumphalism. The true triumph of Orthodoxy is God's triumph, not ours. The victory of the true Faith is God's victory, not ours. The mission to which we are called to rededicate ourselves today is God's mission, not ours. We cannot claim the praise and the glory because they belong to God alone. We are but participants in God's triumph, sharers of His victory, co-workers in His mission. We are God's servants, His hands and feet, His voice and instruments, to bring Orthodoxy's universal light and truth to all peoples.

Christ exposes false triumphalism, the pride and boasting of empty religiosity, through the Parable of the Publican and the Pharisee. Certainly not all Pharisees were hypocrites. It was because most were respected teachers of wisdom and sincere practitioners of their religion, that Jesus chose precisely a Pharisee to expose the dangers of religious triumphalism. The Gospel text notes that Christ said the parable for those who trusted in themselves that they were righteous, and despised others (Lk. 18:9). It is astonishing that Jesus does not deny the Pharisee's righteousness according to the Law. The Pharisee was not an adulterer, nor an extortioner, nor unjust like the tax collector. He fasted according to the sacred tradition and gave 10% of his income to the Temple. And yet it was this righteous man that lost all standing before God because of his boastful pride and contempt for others. Do we, especially the most zealous of us, not often exhibit prideful self-righteousness and unconcealed disdain for sinners and peoples of other faiths? Saint John the Baptist uttered a powerful prophetic word to triumphalists in all ages: "Do not presume to say to yourselves, 'We have Abraham as our father'; for I tell you, God is able from these stones to raise up children of Abraham" (Mt. 3:9).

However, let us follow the way of another Pharisee who became an exemplary servant of Christ. The Apostle Paul was a Pharisee, and a "Hebrew of Hebrews," who viewed himself as blameless according to the Law (Phil. 3:5-6)? He was so zealous for ancestral Jewish traditions that he persecuted the early Church to destroy it. But when he met Christ and converted to the mind of Christ everything changed! It is amazing that Saint Paul put aside essential aspects of the Jewish tradition, what Jews considered as integral to the Jewish ethno-religious identity, in order to preach and promote the universal Gospel and the one Church of Christ which is His Body. In many ways he died to what he was before in order to live his new Christian identity and to serve Christ as fully as possible. Are there not some lessons here about ourselves as Orthodox Christians in America seeking to affirm our common identity in Christ even at the risk of perhaps losing some of our cherished ethnic traditions? I leave that to your prayerful reflection.

Saint Paul's life and work teach us what true triumph is. On account of his courageous stance, the Apostle was himself persecuted by Jews, Jewish Christians, Gentiles and sometimes even members of his own congregations. Once he was compelled to write a letter of anguish and tears to the Christians in Corinth (2 Cor. 2:4). Strangely, those who are closest to us sometimes cause us the greatest pain. The Apostle's great sufferings brought him closer to the sufferings of Christ and taught him to rely not on himself but on God whom he calls the God of all comfort who raises the dead (2 Cor. 1:3-10). In the early chapters of 2 Corinthians Saint Paul describes how, amidst pain and sorrows unto death, he nevertheless proclaimed the Gospel and carried the aroma of the new life in Christ to all who were being saved. Not that he, of his own power or talents, was sufficient for Christian ministry. He writes: "But thanks be to God, who in Christ always leads us in triumph (*thriambeuonti hymas*) and through us spreads the fragrance of the knowledge of Christ everywhere" (2 Cor. 2:14).

For Saint Paul, just as in the case of Christ, true triumph is achieved by way of humble service and sacrifice, the way of the Cross. There is, certainly, not only the Cross, but also the Resurrection. Yet, no one can have a share in the Resurrection apart from the Cross. Saint Paul well knew of the treasure of the soul inwardly beholding the glory of the Lord and being changed "from glory to glory" (2 Cor. 3:18). But he also knew that "we have this treasure in earthen vessels, to show that the transcendent power belongs to God and not to us. We are afflicted in every way, but not crushed; perplexed, but not driven to despair; persecuted, but not forsaken; struck down, but not destroyed" (2 Cor. 4:7-9). Later on in the same epistle, the great Apostle tells us that Christ had spoken to him saying: "My grace is sufficient for you, for my power is made perfect in weakness." Saint Paul concludes: "For the sake of Christ, then, I am content with weaknesses, insults, hardships, persecutions, and calamities; for when I am weak, then I am strong" (2 Cor. 12:9-10).

The triumph of Orthodoxy is the way of Christ. Behind the symbols, the icons, the hymns and prayers, the worship and theology, is the crucified and risen Christ, the heart of Orthodoxy, the inner mystery of its radiant beauty, the source of invincible life against which the gates of hell cannot prevail. On this day in particular, the Sunday of Orthodoxy, Christ through His icon looks upon us with eyes of love and tells us: "Take up your cross and follow me. If you truly wish to honor me, believe in me and commit yourselves to the great triumph of God in the world. Delight in me and love one another as I have loved you, so that others will know that you are my disciple and want to join you. Do not keep the treasure locked in colorful boxes while being boastful of your spiritual heritage as if it were your family inheritance. Follow the example of my servant Paul who renounced all to gain all, who became all things to all people for my sake and the Gospel's. And, behold, I am with you to the end of ages." To Christ, together with the Father and the Spirit, be all the glory, honor and worship now and forever.

NOTES

¹ Fr. Alexander Schmemann's articles were published in *St. Vladimir's Seminary Quarterly*, Vol. 8, Numbers 2 and 4, and Vol. 9, Number 4 (1964-65).,
² Metropolitan Chrysostomos' article was published in *Episkepsis*, February 1, 1991, a bulletin of the Orthodox Center of the Ecumenical Patriarchate in Geneva, Switzerland.
³ Fr. Thomas Hopko, "Orthodoxy in Post-Modern Pluralistic Societies," *Orthodoxy and Cultures* (Geneva: World Council of Churches, 1996), pp. 137-150.

CHAPTER TEN

HOLY FIRE: THE INNER TRADITION

THE TREASURE OF HOLY FIRE

Life is a journey with many stages from birth to death. As the journey progresses new challenges arise. Significant decisions must be made. When we are young, we usually ask: What kind of friends do I really want to have? What goals should I pursue? Later, other questions come up. What kind of job or profession should I seek? Whom will I marry? By what principles and values shall I live? Finally, the deeper issues confront us. Who am I? What is life all about? Am I living or merely existing?

For Orthodox Christians the highest goal of human existence is life with God. Jesus said: "What does it profit a person to gain the whole world and to lose one's soul? What can a person give in exchange of one's soul" (Mk 8:36-37)? The word "soul" (*psyche*) in Jesus' statement is often translated as "life" following the Jewish word behind it (*nephesh*) which means the living principle or life. Essentially the two words are co-equal because each person's unique gift of life is his or her soul – one's personal being and existence. Nothing is more precious than a person's soul. No goal, no pursuit, no value, no achievement is higher than the fulfillment of one's life in Christ and the attainment of one's eternal salvation.

Among the Desert Fathers, the ancient monastics in the Egyptian wilderness who led a life of prayer, a story is told about an elder giving instruction on the spiritual life. Enthused by the talk, one of his disciples asked a question: "Abba, how far can one grow in the life with God?" The elder raised his hand toward heaven and suddenly his whole arm became like a flaming torch. He turned to his disciple and said: "If you want, if you truly desire it, you can become all fire!"

Christ has been called a "fire-starter." He came "to baptize with the Holy Spirit and with fire" (Mt. 3:11; Lk 3:16). He once said: "I came to cast fire upon the earth; and how I wish it were already kindled" (Lk. 12:29). On the day of Pentecost, the fullest moment of divine revelation, the Holy Spirit was poured out on Jesus' followers. Divine grace came to rest on them like "tongues of fire" (Acts 2:3). Christianity began as a spiritual movement through baptism by divine fire.

What is the Orthodox way of life? How can we live it with full awareness? Preeminent theologians of the past, such as Vladimir Lossky, have taught us that the essence of the Orthodox Tradition is the life of the Holy Spirit in the Church. Authentic Orthodoxy, not as an abstraction but as reality, is not merely a religion of rituals, rules and regulations, but the personal self-disclosure of the living God, His self-giving to us in love. Orthodoxy is the treasure of the holy presence and transforming power of the Holy Trinity dwelling among God's people who are His holy temple. As God has promised, "I will live in them and move among them, and I will be their God and they shall be my people" (2 Cor. 6:16; cf. Lev. 26:11-12). To live an Orthodox way of life is to be part of a burning bush glowing with all the blessings that flow from God: His love, mercy, truth, righteousness, freedom, light, life and joy. Orthodoxy in its essence is the gift of "holy fire," the inner, dynamic and transforming Tradition.

Do you want to be an Orthodox Christian with full awareness? When your parents, the priest and many friends and parishioners baptized you, they chanted the baptismal hymn, "As many of you as have been baptized in Christ, you have put on Christ" (cf. Gal. 3:29). At each Liturgy, you hear and receive the priest's blessing, "May the grace of our Lord Jesus Christ and the love of God the Father and the communion of the Holy Spirit be with all of you" (cf. 2 Cor. 13:13). In the Communion Prayers you recite, you pray, "It is good for me to cling to my God and to place in Him the hope of my salvation." If you want to be an Orthodox Christian with full awareness, be what you are! If you truly desire the gift and seek it earnestly, as the ancient elder said, you can become all fire by the grace of the Spirit.

Of course the task is difficult and the way is narrow because we must wage war against our unredeemed self, the power of sin, and the idols of the world. We also have to face obligations, trials, sickness, and other hardships. Saint Paul himself well knew of the way of the cross when he wrote: "We are afflicted in every way, but not crushed; perplexed, but not driven to despair; persecuted, but not forsaken; struck down but not destroyed" (2 Cor. 4:8). We struggle with the forces of life and death. In Saint Paul's words we carry the treasure of holy fire in "earthen vessels," our fragile human nature, showing that the sustaining power comes not from us but from God. God is the One who shines within our hearts the light of the glory of Christ. "Therefore we do not lose heart: although our outer nature is wasting away, our inner nature is being renewed every day" (2 Cor. 4:16). When we speak of renewal in the Church, this is the primary renewal we have in view: the renewal of our minds and hearts in Christ, the full recovery of holy fire in our daily lives, the spiritual renewal of the community shining with the radiance of God.

Recognizing Our Situation

We need humbly to acknowledge that the highest claims of Orthodoxy are often subverted by lack of tangible evidence and actualization, by our own lack of sufficient self-awareness, by our failure as Orthodox Christians to nurture the holy fire of the presence and power of the Spirit. Look around you and ask yourself: How many of the faithful go to Church with a sense of eagerness and joy? How many of us are present and ready at the beginning of the Divine Liturgy to sing the Doxology and to confirm with a resounding "Amen" the priest's invocation, "Blessed is the Kingdom of the Father and of the Son and of the Holy Spirit?" How many of us come out of the Liturgy spiritually renewed and strengthened, in the words of St. John Chrysostom, "like lions breathing fire?" How many of us have placed the love of Christ and the cause of His kingdom as the primary priorities in life?

Certainly, not all Orthodoxy, nor all Orthodox Christians, make up a burning bush glowing with the holiness and transforming presence of God. If it were so – and how we wish that it were so! – the world would surely notice and soon be converted. Orthodoxy has developed an enormously rich tradition – elaborate worship, high doctrines, impressive offices, appealing customs and innumerable canons. Orthodoxy is often viewed like a beautiful antique, or a grand fireplace in which the fire, however, is not burning with intensity in all places and at all times. Not that the fire of the Holy Spirit has ever diminished in power or availability – far from it. Rather, it is that the firewood needs stoking. In some instances, the fire seems virtually extinguished, perhaps only smoking, or the ashes need to be poked to find some hot coals below in order to rejuvenate the fire. This situation may be true of our own personal fireplace, or the fireplace of a local parish, or even the fireplace of an entire regional Church.

What to do? We must imitate the example of the Prodigal Son who "came to himself" and returned to his father's home. If we wish to attain to the high calling of holy fire, an Orthodoxy in full awareness, we must heighten our sensitivities at several levels. The first level is honest and courageous appraisal of our actual situation. We need diagnosis in order to apply measures of therapy. The problems are not new. They have been called by various names ending in "ism" – institutionalism, factionalism, minimalism, nominalism and so on. Nominalism is being a Christian in name only and having little or no significant interest in God, the Church, or Christianity. The Bible calls this condition spiritual deadness. Minimalism is picking and choosing from the Church's table whatever suits our interests and convenience, without strong commitment and enduring motivation to learn more about and to grow in the Faith. The Bible calls this condition lukewarmness. Factionalism is a divisive spirit based on ego and arbitrary choice. The Bible calls this heresy, whether theological or ethical. Institutionalism is a way of thought and practice that relies strictly on, or is satisfied with, merely outward forms, while neglecting or even denying the inner spirit of the Tradition. This the Bible calls hypocrisy and self-righteousness. In modern times, add to all of these "isms" secularism, a total indifference to and even hostility toward God, while worshiping other gods of the present age. This the Bible calls idolatry, the worship of false gods.

But let us not despair. The above phenomena in various mixtures have existed in every era. The fourth century, the golden age of the Church Fathers – Saint Athanasios, Saint Basil, Saint Gregory the Theologian, Saint Gregory of Nyssa, and Saint John Chrysostom – was engulfed by as much evil, sin, callousness, pretension, injustice, conflict, and division as our own times. Facing widespread conflict and schism in the Church, Saint Basil devoted his theological and pastoral talents to the task of unity according to the ideal of the early Church in the Book of Acts. Saint Gregory the Theologian, who presided for a time at the Second Ecumenical Council (381) was exceedingly distressed by the chatter and manipulations of ecclesiastical authorities. Saint John Chrysostom did not hesitate to critique the Church of his day. For example, in an astonishing homily on 1 Corinthians, chapter 14, Saint John exalts the spiritual gifts of the early Church and laments the situation of the contemporary Church. He portrays the Church of his day as an aged woman who had lost her inspired leaders, as well as her spiritual jewels, and is satisfied merely by exhibiting her empty jewelry boxes to the world. Here is what he says:

> In truth the Church was a heaven [back] then, the Spirit governing all things and moving each one of the leaders and making him inspired. But now we retain only the symbols of those gifts... The present Church is like a woman who has fallen from her former prosperous days... displaying indeed the repositories and caskets of her golden ornaments, but bereft of her wealth (1 Corinthians, *Homily* 34.7).

Saint John Chrysostom, whose prophetic voice thunders across the centuries to reach our own ears, fought like a lion of God against unacceptable ecclesiastical conditions. As a result, he was persecuted by emperors, bishops, priests, as well as monastics in name only – but not by the people themselves who loved him and loved to hear him, although they did not necessarily practice all that he preached and taught. Saint John was exiled and died in great suffering. However, he lost hope neither in the power of the Gospel of Christ, nor in the mission of the Church. He had the spiritual maturity to go to his Lord in peace, his last words being: "Glory be to God for all things!"

RENEWING OUR MINDS

Next to recognizing our true situation realistically, a second and even more important level of Orthodox awakening is learning, knowing, and applying our own essential Orthodox principles and values as a faith community. Of course we do not presume to become Chrysostoms, or Basils, or Athanasioses. However, we can contribute our part, small or large, and above all ourselves, to the ongoing task of the spiritual revitalization of the Church. For example, one of the distinctive marks of Orthodoxy is what theologians call "conciliarity" – the principle of working together by consensus as bishops, priests and lay people, granted the hierarchy of authority in the Church. This is not the political principle of democracy, nor is it against democracy, but something higher and better than democracy. It is the affirmation of Christ and the Holy Spirit in each baptized Orthodox Christian which makes each believer a profound agent and witness of the life and truth of God. Orthodoxy knows hierarchy and ordained leadership based on love and service according to the model of Christ. Orthodoxy also knows conciliarity (*sobornost*) – praying, thinking, and working together on the basis of the authentic tradition which rejects erroneous notions of clericalism, that is, the dominance of clergy as if God's presence and truth is manifested primarily through clergy. True Christian leadership is listening to the voice of God's people, being responsive to their needs, discerning their hopes and ideals, drawing out and actualizing their noble insights and talents. The principle of conciliarity is of such depth and significance in Orthodoxy that a number of Orthodox theologians have connected it with the life of God as Holy Trinity. Just as in the life of God, Father, Son and Holy Spirit, there is mutual indwelling, shared communion, and plentitude of love, so also in the life of the Church there should be free self-giving, full sharing and mutual service reflecting the presence and light of the Holy Trinity.

The Church is our spiritual home, our spiritual family, and we are all members of it – members of the Body of Christ. In the words of Saint Paul, "the eye cannot say to the hand, 'I have no need of you,' nor again the head to the feet, 'I have no need of you'" (1 Cor. 12:21). Just as in a family, we in the Church are all both responsible for and accountable to each other. Just as in a family, so also in the Church, when persistent problems cause dysfunction, all family members must recognize the issues and work together toward their solution for the entire family's well-being. We cannot say that we are part of the Body, nor that we love our brother and sister, and then stand apart in indifference and cynicism, or complain and merely wring our hands while doing nothing positive. And the Church, your spiritual home and spiritual family, indeed your spiritual mother, needs you, your energy, your creativity, your idealism, your commitment, your talents. She needs you to put new logs in the fireplace. She needs you to stoke the fireplace, to furnish a new supply of wood. And know this: the fire of the Spirit is always eager to kindle the wood and let the fireplace burn brilliantly with holy fire.

About ten years ago a theological commission of the Greek Orthodox Archdiocese published a wide-ranging report, a kind of theological agenda for the twenty-first century,[1] in which a number of relevant issues were taken up concerning the future of Greek Orthodoxy in America. One of the key problems was what the report defined as a "cultural crisis of faith," a general drifting away from traditional religious and moral values in a secular society marked by selfish individualism, family instability, substance abuse of all kinds, consumerism, pornography and other dehumanizing aspects of modern life. These phenomena were seen as amounting not only to the breakdown of community in our nation but also the breakdown of personal integrity among its citizens as well as leaders across the board.

The report's suggestion for a solution to this problem is still on target and applies to all Orthodox jurisdictions. The report is instructive as follows:

> The contemporary crisis of faith can be countered at its roots by raising the consciousness of the whole Church to the abiding goals of the Church and by placing these goals at the center of our thinking, deciding, and planning for the future. A new spiritual vision must be set to work among clergy and laity alike, not by means of high-sounding promotional statements or radical institutional changes, but by means of a conscious, deliberate, and consistent focus on the true goals and priorities of the Church.

According to the report, the Orthodox Church existing in a free, pluralistic society must assume for itself the responsibility to recover and strengthen Orthodox identity both as an intrinsic goal and as empowerment for the fulfillment of its mission in the world. In a society where ethnicity is inevitably fading and interfaith marriages have exponentially increased, drifting away from the Faith will continue unless common ecclesial and spiritual bonds are built. Formal adherence to tradition without insightful knowledge will not win the day in a world where novelty and excitement are at premium. All Orthodox together must look to the essence of their common spiritual heritage and lift up those treasures which unite us and can serve as guiding lights in the present and future. These shared treasures, in the words of the report, "must become the conscious focus of preaching, teaching, meetings, conferences, clergy-laity assemblies, administrative polity, church departments, and parish life."

Let me repeat for clarity: I am not advocating substantive renewal in the magnificent forms and objective content of Orthodoxy. Of course, some practical matters and certain other more difficult issues need attention. We can use better and standard translations of our liturgical texts. We need to encourage congregational singing and perhaps some modifications in liturgical services to make worship a truly meaningful and participatory experience for all the faithful. We certainly need to update the canons or at least to develop clear criteria for their interpretation and use in the spirit of Christ. Also, no theological impediments exist to the recovery of the ordination of women deacons nor even to the ordination of married clergy to the episcopate, both of which were honored traditions in the early centuries of the Church. And we have only begun to activate the talents of the laity, both men and women, that massive reservoir of spiritual power which was decisive in the growth and expansion of early Christianity. And all these difficult issues can be faced most effectively precisely on the basis of the renewal of our minds and hearts.

The gifts are in front of our eyes. Beautiful forms of worship, the message of the Gospel enriched by unsurpassed hymnology, a theology which rings true to anyone who delves into it. In a word, the Orthodox tradition embodies an exquisite balance between such things as Scripture and Tradition, worship and teaching, faith and works, prayer and action, freedom and responsibility, clergy and laity. The urgency lies in the study, understanding, and appropriation of the inner Tradition. We are advocating that Orthodox Christians, as they grow to adulthood, ought to be moving beyond a childish understanding of Orthodoxy to a renewal of minds, a renewal of vision, a renewal of confidence on the basis of the fullness of truth about God, life, creation, heaven and hell. Orthodoxy is concerned with truth about all things and invites intellectual comprehension of the truth through the use of our reason, which according to the Church Fathers is the noblest element of the image of God in human beings. Christ came, as has been said, to take away our sins, not our minds. In an age when education is absolutely crucial for life, we must be well informed about our Faith and apply the insights of the Orthodox legacy about the meaning of personhood, freedom, moral responsibility, the goodness of humanity, human rights, civic duty, the gift of creation, and the like, to contemporary life and society.

When it is true to itself, Orthodoxy has explosive potential. Twenty years ago, Jaroslav Pelikan, a preeminent Lutheran theologian and Church historian, gave a keynote address at a large gathering at the University of Chicago on a festive occasion celebrating the 450th anniversary of the Augsburg Confession, a milestone in the Protestant Reformation. Along with his usual insightful gems and personal charm, Pelikan startled the audience with the remark that the Eastern Orthodox tradition may well be the most authentic guardian of the classic, universal Christian faith.[2] We rejoice that a few years ago, Jaroslav Pelikan joined the Orthodox Church, as many others have done as well in our generation. We welcome all into the Orthodox Faith, and our welcome is not an expression of narrow, selfish satisfaction, nor a triumphalistic celebration of victory over others, but rather a joyous sharing of the gifts we ourselves have received from Christ, the Apostles and the Church Fathers. Because Orthodoxy is indeed the universal expression of Christianity for all peoples and cultures, Orthodoxy in essence and at its best is not a diminishment or negation of other faiths but an affirmation and ful-fillment of them.

RENEWING OUR HEARTS

The third and deepest level of Orthodox awareness is the renewal of our hearts. The "heart" in Holy Scripture and the Orthodox Tra-dition is the deep self, the center of consciousness, the deep mystery of the inner person, which qualifies everything that we are, feel, think, do, see and appear to others. Saint Paul spoke of the new creation in Christ in terms of "God's love poured into our hearts through the Holy Spirit" (Rom. 5:5). In a stirring passage, he exhorts Christian believers "by the mercies of God, to present your bodies as a living sacrifice, holy and acceptable to God, which is your spiritual wor-ship. Do not be conformed to this world but be transformed by the renewal of your mind that you may know what is the will of God" (Rom. 12:1-2). "The renewal of mind" here means something more than intellectual comprehension which, as noted above, is praise-worthy in itself. In Saint Paul "renewal of mind" is equivalent to "renewal of heart" – the deep conversion of the inner self to Christ. It happens when, by the grace of the Spirit, the veil of spiritual in-sensitivity is removed from the heart and the believer inwardly be-gins to perceive her or his Lord, "beholding the glory of the Lord [and] being changed from glory to glory" (2 Cor. 4:14-18).

We have now come to the most crucial issue. The greatest prob-lem of Orthodoxy today is a spiritual problem, as Alexander Schmemann said years ago.[3] More accurately, it is not the problem of Orthodoxy but the problem of Orthodox Christians. It is the former because it is the latter. It involves all Orthodox Christians, lay people, priests and bishops who, by God's grace, are called to be energizing bearers of the fire of Orthodoxy. We mouth love and forgiveness, but really do neither very deeply. We glory in the icons and legacy of the saints, but do not fully imitate their example. We point to the magnificent Pantocrator, the All-ruling Christ, in the domes of our Churches, but we are reluctant to place ourselves fully under His rule. We extol our spirituality and parade the teaching about *theosis* (union with God, divinization), but we have not yet properly re-pented and many are afraid of the words "spiritual renewal." We point to the grand fireplace, but where is the fire?

The question is once again about authenticity, genuineness, in-tegrity, connecting ideals and life, letting heaven touch the earth, bridging the yawning gap between what we preach and what we do, a gap which sometimes appears as wide as the Grand Canyon. The tragedy is that, not only we do not rise to a modest level of lived spirituality, but we may instead be filled with sinful passions, cor-ruption, immorality, hypocrisy, and the odor of spiritual death – all the while, as Saint Chrysostom put it, exhibiting the Church's empty jewel boxes!

But again, let us not despair. In the New Testament itself we read about "times of stress" when some false Christians and false Chris-tian leaders were people of "corrupt mind and counterfeit faith," showing themselves to be "lovers of self, lovers of money, proud, arrogant, abusive ...holding the form of religion but denying the power of it" (see 2 Tim. 3:1-9). Let us recall once again the example of the Prodigal Son and let us pray with the words of the Lenten hymn: "I am captive, O Savior, in the depths of sin and I am drown-ing in the sea of life. But as You brought Jonah out of the belly of the whale, bring me also out of the evil passions and save me."[4] Yes, deliverance from the depths of darkness, escape from the belly of the beast, that is what we need. "For we are not contending against flesh and blood, but against the principalities, against the powers, against the world rulers of this present darkness, against the spiri-tual hosts of wickedness in high places" (Eph. 6:12).

Let Saint Symeon the New Theologian give us an illustration of Orthodox life and renewal. An Orthodox Christian, he says, is like an oil lamp (*kandili*) which consists of the oil, the wick, and the flame. The oil is the whole life of the Christian, one's prayers, fasting, sac-ramental participation, and all other good works of piety. The wick is the soul, trimmed, straight and reaching upward to receive the light. The flame is the gift of grace which God alone kindles. All three elements are integral to and work together in the oil lamp. Without the oil of a righteous life, the wick would soon smoulder and die out. Without the wick of the soul yearning for Christ, no amount of good works could receive and sustain the holy flame. The flame of the Holy Spirit, which God alone can give, burns brightly only when the wick is trimmed and soaked with oil. Where the Spirit finds eagerness of soul and abundance of goodness, according to Saint Symeon, the whole lamp of the Christian becomes full of light burning with holy fire.

FAITH, REPENTANCE AND OBEDIENCE

Saint Symeon and other saints provide practical instruction on renewal. They tell us that growth in spiritual life is not a hit or miss proposition involving unclear or unknown factors. Rather it is an assured promise and gift of God which entails specific knowledge and clear spiritual principles. God is always the source of life and salvation, the One who says: "Behold, I make all things new" (Rev. 21:5). We are the joyful respondents to God's renewing grace, the active recipients of His gracious gifts. God, like the golden sun, always shines His light upon all. He shines even when clouds and storms appear. It is up to us to open our inner world to God's sunshine, to allow His sunbeams to burn away the dark clouds of sin surrounding the soul, and thus let the inner cosmos of the heart radiate with the brightness of God's grace.

The abiding center and focus of renewal is Christ Himself in Whom we know the Father and through Whom we receive the Spirit. Christ said: "I am the way, and the truth, and the life" (Jn 14:6). And again: "I am the first and the last, and the One living; I died, and behold I am alive forever, and I have the keys of Death and Hades" (Rev. 1:17). Christ and His Gospel is the foundation of the Church, the sacraments, our personal and family lives, all our Christian striving, and our hope of glory. Spiritual life and renewal result from the active response to Christ and the Gospel: that Christ died for our sins and that He rose from the dead granting new life to all. We call this active response faith, followed closely by repentance and obedience. What are faith, repentance and obedience? When we reflect on these words, we begin to see how this integrated trilogy of responses to Christ and the good news constitutes the nuts and bolts of Christian spirituality.

Faith (*pistis*) can be defined according to objective content as well as personal disposition. Faith as content indicates the objective teachings of the Bible and the Church, as I have spoken above, which serve as basis for the renewal our minds. Faith as personal disposition, which is our concern in the present context, is defined by the personal act of trust not in something but in someone. Christian faith as personal disposition is intimate trust, existential commitment, unwavering reliance, abiding dependence on Christ as risen Lord, present and active in the Church and the world. Christian faith is not faith in faith as a subjective sentiment, a kind of admirable but shallow optimism, nor is it a leap into the unknown, because it involves the historical witness of Christ and a clear way of life. Christian faith is free trust and commitment to Christ, the supreme revelation of God, as well as to His presence and power, His truth and righteousness, His love and goodness, His mercy and compassion, His demands and promise of eternal life. This kind of faith as a way of life is the indispensable spiritual principle which, when activated, transforms us into Christ-centered believers and into a Christ-centered Church.

According to the teaching of the Church Fathers, there is a formal faith we inherit from our parents called "thin" or "formal faith" (*psile pistis*) and there is a "living faith" (*zosa pistis*) which is an energizing divine force. Formal faith is an implicit faith which can range from a vague sense of belief in the existence of God to a deep but unexamined commitment to our ethno-religious group and all its traditions. We do not denigrate formal faith but welcome it and seek to build on it. Living faith is an active gift of God, the working of holy fire in our lives, a spiritual force which transforms human existence according to the beauty and goodness of Christ. Everyone has the capacity to move from formal faith to living faith by turning to God with one's whole heart. "God is love" (1 Jn 4:8). The essence of our faith response to God is but "to love the Lord your God with all your heart, and with all your soul, and with all your mind, and with all your strength ...and your neighbor as yourself," Christ said (Mk 12:30-31). As soon as we begin to act on our faith, feeble as it may be, God's grace lifts it up, cleanses and empowers it, transforming it into living faith. By putting our faith to action, always by the grace of God, we ourselves become love and the Church becomes a community of love, overflowing with concern and love for a lost and suffering world. Living faith is the driving force of spiritual renewal.

However, living faith is not activated without its close counter-part, repentance, the second indispensable principle of Orthodox spirituality. It is futile to speak of living faith without genuine repentance. Repentance is *metanoia* (literally, "change of mind"), a spiritual about face, a thorough conversion of the heart, which testifies to the stirrings of living faith. Repentance is not mere regret and tears over past sins, although these are salutary as well, but above all a new way of life according to Christ. The Church Fathers have called repentance "the mother of life," "new birth," "second baptism," "renewal of the soul," and "gateway to heaven." The spiritual principle of repentance in its essence involves the conversion of the soul, an unceasing receptivity to the mystery of God, a forward movement of spiritual progress in the image and likeness of Christ, a decisive and abiding turning to God evidenced by a way of life pleasing to Him. The proof of true repentance is a changed way of life in Christ – and nothing else. God's word through the Prophet Ezekiel is this: "Repent and turn from all your transgressions… and get yourselves a new heart and a new spirit" (Ez. 18:30-31). Again through the Prophet Isaiah: "Wash yourselves: make yourselves clean; remove the evil of your doings from before my eyes; cease to do evil, learn to do good" (Is. 1:16-17). Christianity as a spiritual movement has its inception in the words of Jesus: "The time is fulfilled, and the kingdom of God is at hand; repent, and believe in the Gospel" (Mk 1:15). Repentance as unceasing receptivity of God and essential orientation to His kingdom serves as the context of spiritual renewal.

Because repentance involves free decision, a deliberate and conscious act of the will, which is to be affirmed again and again, it also amounts to a personal crisis, a coming to a crossroad where one must choose one way or the other. It is in this way that repentance energizes faith and, by God's grace, transforms formal faith into living faith, as I said. In the setting of modern life, unless we wish to be enfeebled Christians burdened with an inferiority complex, we need to know and internalize the treasures of our faith, and more, to make our faith a personal matter, a personal decision, actualizing the gift of faith through repentance. Repentance is the answer to the problem of many Orthodox Christians being born and baptized in the Church but not truly converted to the life of the Holy Spirit. Repentance makes our knowledge of Christ existential. It gives us not merely intellectual, but experiential knowledge of God's love. It brings us closer to the mystery of the living Christ. It stokes the fire of holy love. It brings us to the banquet of God's kingdom where our loving Father, as in the case of the Prodigal Son, waits to welcome our homecoming with music and dancing in heaven.

Finally, from the human side of things, there is the ground of renewal which is obedience (*hypakoe*), a word which in Greek literally means to listen well and to come under what is heard. This third spiritual principle is loving obedience and service to the Lord and His people. The essence of the principle of obedience is found in Christ's words: "If one loves me, he will keep my word, and my Father and I will love him, and we will come to him and make our home with him" (Jn 14:23). Obedience is above all loving obedience to Christ and His truth, an obedience that unites us with Christ and grants the celebration of a perpetual Pascha in communion with Christ. Whoever asks for obedience, priest or parent, must oneself first be obedient to Christ and be ready to serve Him and others, being motivated by the example of Christ's love and service. Otherwise, obedience is license for wrongdoing and abuse. Moreover, obedience to wrongdoers who violate the spirit and the truth of Christ, who in a word violate divine love, is to enable them in their wrongdoing, and thus to aid in the corruption of the larger fabric of the community.

The Orthodox tradition in its many forms knows of active obedience and service, just as it knows of faith and repentance. Jesus challenged His hearers to be bold and take the kingdom by storm. Saint Paul compared himself to a runner and a boxer in training. The ancient ascetics, literally the "athletes" of Christian spirituality, invoked the axiom, "Give blood to get spirit." This rule, correctly interpreted, is not a slogan for extreme asceticism as another "-ism" – that is, strict observance of extreme rigors which harm the body and deny the goodness of creation – but a challenging call to take up the inner warfare of the heart, the deepest seat of good and evil. Christ said: "For out of the heart come evil thoughts, murder, adultery, fornication, theft, false witness, slander [which] defile a person" (Mt. 15:19-20).

Orthodoxy breathes a heroic spirit over against our fallen nature and against the Devil and his works. Careful attention to the inner disciplines of the soul, such as inward vigilance and prayer, as well as to the outer disciplines of the body, such as fasting and good works, establish the firm ground for authentic obedience and renewal in Christ. Obedience is meant as a way not of control but of freedom for service, not of stifling self-righteousness but of wise and joyful use of God's gifts, not of demeaning personal dignity but of presenting the soul as a pure virgin to Christ. True obedience taps the well of the heart and, by God's grace, releases the energies and treasures of the inner person created in the image and likeness of God. The more perfect our obedience, the deeper our experience of Christ, and the more effective our service and witness for His glory.

To conclude, the Church Fathers and saints teach no other way to the new life in Christ than centering on Christ and practicing the trilogy of faith, repentance and obedience, all working together as permanent dispositions of Christian life. Although the gate is narrow and the path difficult, so the Lord has said, the burden is also light and the yoke is easy (Mt. 7:13-14; 11:30). Do you recall the icon of the Ladder of Divine Ascent? Climb the ladder one step at a time. Christ looks down from heaven encouraging you and waiting to welcome you. The safe way is by way of deeds, not mere words, for words without deeds, as a spiritual elder has said, is like an unrepentant sinner expounding on virtue.

Yes, life is a journey, a pilgrimage toward God. It has many difficulties, many burdens. But let us focus on Christ. All of us possess the holy flame of God's grace through baptism. Every person, clergy or laity, and every parish or regional Church can reach as high as inner yearning gives them motivation and strength. You are like a powerful light on a dimmer switch. The dimmer switch can be on, but so low that no light shines. Your task, as well as the task of all, is to turn on that switch to high in order that the grace of Christ may glow to its full power. If you desire it and seek it diligently, you can become all light and fire!

NOTES

[1] Published in *The Greek Orthodox Theological Review*, Vol. 34 (3, 1989), pp. 283-306, and also separately under the title *Report to His Eminence Archbishop Iakovos Concerning the Future Theological Agenda of the Greek Orthodox Archdiocese* by Holy Cross Orthodox Press (1990).

[2] See the news report "Celebrating a Confession," in the *Christian Century*, November 12, 1980, p. 1085.

[3] Alexander Schmemann, "Problems of Orthodoxy in America: III. The Spiritual Problem," *St. Vladimir's Seminary Quarterly*, Vol. 9 (4, 1965), pp. 171-193.

[4] A hymn taken from the sixth canticle of Matins of the Sunday of the Prodigal Son.

CHAPTER ELEVEN

FAITHFULNESS TO THE PAST
AND COMMITMENT TO THE FUTURE

Human history is replete with conflicts between races, nations, and social groups, as well as religious traditions. A sad aspect of this tragic story is that religion, presumably a liberating force meant to improve the lot of humanity, has often been a significant contributor to human strife causing great loss of life and acute suffering in the human family. With rare exceptions, it is only in modern times that many religious leaders of major faiths have called for the renouncement of polemics, prejudice, proselytism, discrimination, misrepresentation, persecution, or denigration of others. Instead of the path of polemics they have sought to lead people on the way of mutual understanding through respectful dialogue. The primary aim of religious dialogue is neither intellectual contests over beliefs, nor agreement in constitutive values, but rather the clarification of positions, mutual respect, and the encouragement of human cooperation in such matters as justice, freedom, peace, employment, health, and the environment.

In a shrinking and pluralistic world, the ultimate challenge of religious people is how to maintain the integrity of their particular communities, how to enjoy the freedom of fostering their own cherished beliefs and values, while developing a positive acceptance of the right of others to exist and to do the same. A creative approach, away from negativism and bias, is that of respectful mutual acceptance and peaceful cooperation on the level of basic human relationships. This challenge confronts not only religions on a world scale but also their specific adherents in their personal relationships as they meet in the neighborhood, the school, the place of work, recreation, and even the family through marriage, especially in America.

Orthodox leaders and theologians have conducted numerous dialogues in the twentieth century, notably in the context of the World

189

Council of Churches, for the purpose of both greater understanding, as well as an opportunity for irenic witness to their faith. In addition several bilateral dialogues have continued with representatives of the Roman Catholic Church and of Protestant denominations including Lutherans, Anglicans, Methodists, and Presbyterians. A few instances have seen separate official contacts with Jews[1] and Muslims,[2] with whose religions Orthodox history has been variously entwined for centuries. In 1993, a large conference of Orthodox and Jewish scholars took place in Athens, Greece, in which I participated.[3] The theme of the conference was "Continuity and Renewal." What follows is essentially the my contribution to the conference on the topic "Faithfulness to Roots and Commitment Toward the Future." This essay has been incorporated in the present book as part of the theme of renewal pertaining to positive relationships with people of other faiths. Aspects of how Orthodox Christians can relate to the Jewish community are of course applicable to relationships with other religious people, Christian, Jewish, or not. At the Athens Conference, I prefaced the delivery of my paper with the following oral remarks now lightly edited.

PERSONAL REMARKS

Let me begin with some personal statements about the presuppositions of my presentation. I am not here to debate or negotiate issues of ultimate value related to transcendent claims of my faith. I am here to seek clarification and understanding; to let the light of truth build trust in such a way that freedom and mutual respect will develop between Christian and Jew. My Jewish colleague and I, dealing with our specific topic, walk down a beautiful seashore, as it were, witnessing to the treasures of each other's faith without the slightest desire to manipulate the other to one's own position. That is what I call good faith. In Romans 14:23, Saint Paul writes, "for whatever does not proceed from faith (or faithfulness) is sin" before God and before humanity.

What is the thesis of my paper? That it is possible for two peoples such as Jews and Orthodox Christians to hold on with faithfulness to their convictions, their ultimate beliefs, their transcendent values, and still foster mutual respect and friendship. I do not say merely tolerance, but positive tolerance and friendship. I seek not only to state the thesis but to provide as well a theological construction for its actualization. Yet, I have another purpose in mind, and that is to expose as clearly as I can the diabolical abuse of religion, if not directly, then indirectly through culture. The abuse of religion is to marginalize, oppress, hurt, and even to destroy others in the name of religion. In this connection, I have several stories to tell, some which have long defined my thinking, and some which have moved me deeply as recently as last night visiting the Jewish museum in Athens.

When I was a child living in the town of Gargalianoi in the southwestern Peloponnese, we used to have an annual celebration in honor of an ethnic martyr who had died battling the Bulgarians in the early twentieth century. As the Ottoman Empire was weakening and losing its grip on its Balkan holdings, Greeks and Bulgarians themselves, although partners against the Turks, conflicted over boundary claims. History lessons in school had taught us to hate not only the Turks but the Bulgarians as well. My personal animosity toward the latter, without ever having seen a single Bulgarian, intensified one day when I saw in our history book a picture of Bulgarians literally holding decapitated Greek heads. Our local hero had died in such confrontations. We had a statue of him in our town and celebrated his memory with religious ceremonies each year.

Then suddenly one day I discovered, to my great shock, that Bulgarians were Orthodox Christians! Another picture in the same book featured Bulgarian Orthodox priests together with Bulgarian soldiers in full weaponry! "Are the Bulgarians Orthodox?" I asked my father. "Yes! Don't you know?" he replied somewhat impatiently. I did not say anything more, not even to my father whom I deeply respected, but that occasion was my first religious scandal and revelation showing how skin deep Orthodox Christianity was for Orthodox Christians themselves. If our Orthodox faith is so embracing and precious, I said to my self, why is it that Greeks and Bulgarians could not settle their affairs peacefully instead of killing each other? From then on I decided to do my own thinking about what is true and right rather than absorb what everybody else was telling me.

The second story comes from a friend who lived out the events of the Asia Minor "catastrophe" in the early 1920s. After an unwise and futile attempt by the mainland Greek army to reconquer Byzantine territory in Turkey following World War I, two million Greeks native to Asia Minor were driven from their ancestral homes by the Turks in horrific ways. My friend, only ten years of age at that time, lingered behind as Smyrna was being emptied by fleeing Greeks.

He and a friend went into a house to find something of value to take with them, when suddenly two Turkish soldiers burst into the house. The boys froze in their tracks. One soldier said: "Let's kill them!" The other replied, "No, they are only children." The lives of the two Christian boys were spared on that day because one of the Turkish soldiers, like the biblical Good Samaritan, was of a noble character.

The last story is of a Jewish widow in Greece during the German occupation. It comes from a pamphlet, published by the museum we visited yesterday, which I read last night virtually in tears. The woman lived in Thessalonike and, sensing the danger of the Germans, moved her family to Athens, but then returned home alone to fetch her belongings. There she was captured and imprisoned, her only crime being that she was a Jew. From prison she wrote the following words in part to her children:

Dear Children,

In spite of my trying not to upset you, I see that the last hour is near. I do not find comfort being separated from dear children that I wish with all my heart to see, and in these last days to have the unique joy of my life.

For two nights we sat on the bed dressed, waiting for the knock at the door to wake us and to take us away. Everyone is selling their things in the street. The cries, the moans, the tragedy cannot be described... We are living a bad dream, day and night in indescribable anguish. God, who sees my tears, should pity you and keep you alive.

Live happily if you can. May God preserve you from evil. This is my prayer every night.

The children survived but the woman was taken away and eventually killed. Is it possible to read to read this poignant story of this widow and not be moved with deep compassion? What is it about religious misconceptions and prejudice, as well as the mixture of religion and culture, that has led people to commit acts of unspeakable injustice and cruelty against those of different faiths? What is our responsibility as religious leaders and theologians in this matter as we look into the past and face the future? At the first international meeting in Lucerne (1977) Shemaryahu Talmon had already proposed that even academic discussions are inevitably concerned with the life of individuals and of society and that they should aim at clarifying principles, rules, and attitudes which help regulate everyday life. To quote him: "Every debate among sages… must have as its end not the mere elucidation of theories in the form of a scholastic exercise, but should – at any rate ideally – lead to practical conclusions."[4] Let us hope and pray that continued dialogue, on the one hand, will expose the pernicious use of religion as what it actually is, a denial of both religion and our common humanity, and, on the other hand, will encourage a renewed sense of positive and respectful relations between all religious communities.

FAITHFULNESS TO ROOTS

The biblical concept of "faithfulness" is based on the word "faith," one of the richest words in the biblical vocabulary. Faithfulness literally means a state of fullness of faith, a spiritual quality anchored on the faithfulness of God in His covenants and promises, a theme deeply ingrained in the consciousness of Jews and Christians. Alternate terms are fidelity, steadfastness, loyalty, reliance, unwavering commitment, and the like. All of these words and expressions resound with powerful echoes in the self-understanding and history of both the Jewish and Christian Orthodox peoples for whom tradition has been the force of survival over the millennia. Faith and faithfulness constitute the very ground of Jewish and Christian life from the human as well as the divine sides. For those who believe in the God of Abraham, Isaac and Jacob, and for those who believe in God as the Father of Jesus Christ, faith and life are co-equal realities.

The more problematic concept is that of "roots." This word is not particularly biblical and has a sociological rather than theological ring to it. Why not formulate the topic as follows: "Faithfulness to the *Past* and Commitment to the *Future*" in order to achieve a smoother historical and linguistic parallel? I assume that the reason has to do with the vagueness of the term "past" and the intent of this academic meeting to guide the discussion in part to "the roots," that is, to the concrete and fundamental areas of faithfulness. Moreover, the term "roots" can also possess theological significance precisely because the faith and the concrete expressions of faithfulness of our respective religious communities are closely woven theologically and sociologically. By "sociologically" I mean the whole complex of the institutions, religious rites, customs, educational traditions, system of values, operative attitudes, and patterns of behavior which mark the multi-dimensional identity and consciousness of the Greek and Jewish people.

We may ask, then, faithfulness to *what* roots? Here, although I would not presume to speak for the Jewish side, I would neverthe-less suggest a basic outline of "roots" which may have relevance for both religious communities. The first and great subject and goal of faithfulness is the living God, the One who was, who is, and who comes (Ex. 3:14; Rev. 1:8). Despite the decisive difference of the Chris-tian trinitarian understanding of God, both Jews and Christians are bound together by their faith in the one God, historically revealed according to the Scriptures as Creator, Lord, and Father, a God of glory and majesty, love and mercy, justice and peace, righteousness and judgment. His true servants, whether Jews or Christians, are called to walk humbly before Him and to live as thankful witnesses to His goodness and mercy before all peoples.

The second subject and goal of faithfulness is the religious com-munity called into existence by God's self-disclosure, now painfully divided into variegated Jewish communities[5] and a multitude of Christian traditions. The Scriptures teach us that the living God re-vealed Himself in order to establish His people as a light to the na-tions. God and people, Messiah and people, go together. Knowl-edge of God and of Christ are integrally connected with the life of the respective communities as the concrete contexts of worship, life, service and witness. One of the ten commandments is to honor our fathers and mothers who have struggled to preserve and communi-cate to us God and His ways. Whatever the historical vicissitudes, doctrinal differences, divergent concepts, and shortcomings of each community of faith, we must be faithful to our respective religious communities. Genuine dialogue at any level cannot occur without genuine faithfulness to the communities that have nourished us in the experience and knowledge of God.

The third goal or area of faithfulness is comprised of God's gifts, covenants, great acts of deliverance, laws, faithful agents in salva-tion history, as well as promises. These constitute the heart of the self-understanding of our faith communities. Although we differ in the interpretation of the meaning, duration, and present validity of these gifts, nevertheless we are bound, for faithfulness' sake, to rec-ognize them precisely as God's gifts and to regard them with requi-site awe and thankfulness. Should we fail to honor God's gifts by viewing them superficially or even negatively in polemical critique of one another, we dishonor God Himself and diminish the dignity of our faith communities.

The fourth and final major area of faithfulness is the whole integrated complex of institutions, practices, teachings, values, customs, offices, structures, and ways of conduct which seek to manifest the good order and spiritual vision of our communities in ongoing history. It would indeed be both arrogant and foolish to regard lightly, from an allegedly superior modernistic critical viewpoint, time-honored expressions of faith, however culture-bound they may seem, which in their totality enshrine not only the deep experiences, constitutive truths, and ultimate values, but also the very cohesiveness, strength, and vital spirit of our communities.

You may by now object that I have placed all things under blessed faithfulness and you would be right. But if so, one would ask, how is it possible to conduct any meaningful dialogue at any level between sharply different traditional communities such as ours, though they may manifest a number of formal parallels? That is the crux of the problem in the Christian Orthodox-Jewish dialogue. We both possess, if I may use the key terminology of our consultation, deep faithfulness, canonical Scriptures, rich traditions, and long memories, all invested with an embracing sanctity that seems as inviolate as the principle of faithfulness itself. And yet, according to the fourth sub-theme of the consultation, we all live "in the contemporary world." It is this element of our experience of the modern world and of multi-faceted modernity that inevitably thrusts us toward dialogue, as in the case of all religions. Significant reasons validate the dialogue. Above all, a violent, unjust, exploitative, and perhaps dying world, both spiritually and ecologically, urgently needs the sacred treasures of our living traditions.

Dialogue, as is well known, is a fairly recent and distinctively modern phenomenon. The histories of our religious communities, with rare exceptions (for example, Justin's *Dialogue With Trypho* in which the Christian and the Jew disagree but part as friends), have been marked since New Testament times by conflicts, polemics, disdain, persecution, and even killings, although there have also been periods of tolerated co-existence.[6] The reality is that our religious communities, although sharing common spiritual roots, also have clashing beliefs and conflicting interests which readily impinge on daily life up to and including the present, for example most notably in the Holy Land.[7] Past conflicts, suspicions, enmity, and recriminations have had plenty of theoretical and practical ground from which to rise. The crucial question now is whether or not our communities have sufficiently discerning and courageous leadership, as well as the necessary moral and spiritual strength, to seek and to find both in their common roots as well as in their own respective traditions, principles and values upon which to build bases for a gradual great reversal. That reversal can only be positive, respectful, just, and co-operative relationships worthy of the God of mercy and justice whom they claim to worship. In so doing, they would also serve as faithful and luminous witnesses to other conflicting religious communities.

We must be realistic and admit our human limitations, as much as we may be inspired by the divine possibilities, because of an additional strong reason. On both sides we have many co-religionists for whom dialogue, as modernity itself, is contrary to faithfulness. For them dialogue, especially between Jews and Christians, is not only too late in history but also a betrayal of our particular histories. For such faithful people, and admittedly claimants of a longer historical polemical tradition than the dialogical one, "Commitment to the Future" is exactly the same as "Faithfulness to Roots."[8] The two parts of the present topic would be tautological! These are brothers and sisters whom we must constantly seek to include both in our field of vision as well as, wherever and whenever possible, in the dialogical process itself. This call does not signify merely strategic interests to win them over to the principle of dialogue but also, and more so, to consider respectfully their witness and learn from it in order that the dialogical process itself may be authenticated and enriched to the maximum degree of faithfulness and truth.

As for me, I should lay my cards on the table and say that, after much prayer and long thinking, I have long been committed to the principle of dialogue on intrinsic theological and spiritual grounds. I firmly believe that my personal faith in Christ and my commitment to the Orthodox Church do not merely permit but actually propel me toward dialogue which, without compromise to the transcendent claims of the Christian Orthodox faith, seeks God's love, truth, justice, and peace among all peoples. The perspective of this personal testimony, I should openly admit, certainly informs the treatment of my whole topic but especially what I am about to say concerning "Commitment to the Future."

COMMITMENT TO THE FUTURE

One of the primary nuances of the verb "to commit," should one consult an English dictionary, is to put someone into charge of something or, even more appropriately for our topic, to entrust or consign something of value for future preservation. Indeed, faithfulness to the roots necessarily implies commitment to the preservation of the gifts and treasures of those roots. It was wise of the organizers of the conference not to use the superficial expression "openness to the future" because commitment, as well as faithfulness, imply an obligation, indeed a binding pledge, to matters of the highest importance for our respective communities. Both as Jews and Orthodox Christians we do not come to the contemporary world and face the future with empty hands. On the contrary we carry on our backs rich heritages and immeasurable treasures, even if our hands sometimes seem shamefully empty to us and to others.

But another significant nuance of the verb "to commit" is to make available or to put something at someone's disposal. Commitment implies not only preservation but also responsible use and effective availability of the treasures of our roots for the present and future generations. I submit that faithfulness, too, carries a similar equivalent force of meaning. True faithfulness bears within itself the responsibility of the discerning and effective use and application of God's gifts in the present and the future for the benefit of humanity and for the glory of God. In the ongoing process of change and adaptation in changing historical circumstances, a blind faithfulness to roots may well turn out to be unfaithfulness! No one, but a stubborn and blind person, can possibly deny change and growth in the traditions of our religious communities. The critical question is how to guide the continuity of tradition in such an authentically faithful way that its gifts and treasures may shine brightly and usefully for the urgent issues of our times as well as the practical needs of daily life. From this perspective, continuity and renewal, involving both spiritual and practical aspects, go together and make available the treasures of our roots as living realities. Thus the religious community, and each member thereof, ought to be faithful to a living tradition, always penetrated by the spirit of renewal, and not merely be enslaved to the forms of a dead past.

I must now try to exemplify the above concepts on the basis of the outline of "the roots" given earlier in the paper. This indeed is a very delicate and most difficult task. Permit me the caveat that what follows are suggestive lines of thought rather than well-defined principles. In view of the subjects and questions raised, I would be utterly presumptuous to offer anything but expressions of my own lifelong struggles with continuity and renewal within my own religious community. I do so in good faith, trusting in the loving correction of my Orthodox colleagues to whom I mainly speak, as well as counting on the principle of consensus so highly valued in the Christian Orthodox community. If my words have some meaning and relevance for the Jewish participants as well, I would be delighted and thankful to the One whom we address as Father in heaven.

The earlier outline of "the roots" or fundamental areas of faithfulness is intentionally hierarchical. Our primary faithfulness is to the living God, the sovereign Lord Himself, who stands within but also over the community of faith and all its innumerable institutions, teachings, and practices which constitute the ongoing life of His people. The first and greatest commandment is: "The Lord is our God, the Lord alone, and you shall love the Lord your God with all your heart, and with all your soul, and with all your might" (Deut. 6:4-5). And the second great commandment is: "You shall love your neighbor as yourself" (Lev. 19:18). Jesus and another Jewish sage agreed that these two commandments are "much more than all whole burnt offerings and sacrifices" (Mk 12:29-34) and sum up the entire biblical heritage of "the law and the prophets" (Mt. 22:30). Here is the essence of our shared spirituality as Jews and Christians in obedience to the living God.

Continuity and renewal meet and interact most essentially at the point in which we worship, pray, and live in such faithfulness to and intimacy with the Holy One that we put nothing in His place or even above Him, not even His precious gifts to us, which would constitute a kind of idolatry. All conflicts between Jews and Christians have ultimately derived from either unwitting or willful forgetfulness of our common rootedness in and disobedience of the two greatest commandments. We have tended too easily to put "our religion" in the place of the transcendent God, and in the place of the dignity of our neighbor, and thus made our religion God instead of God our religion. If I walk humbly before the Lord my God, and truly love Him as the One who commands love and mercy, justice and peace towards all, how could I long entertain evil thoughts of prejudice and enmity – much less raise up audaciously a hand of violence, injustice, or exploitation – against any people, even those with whom I may strongly disagree? Christ has taught His followers to love even their enemies and to pray for those who persecute them, yet not necessarily to agree with their principles and values.

Deep renewal in inter-religious relations cannot occur without such a humble and fervent faith in God, and without discerning the great difference between godly respect for others and disagreement with them over transcendent values.

The sharpest difference between Christian and Jews is Christ who paradoxically both binds and separates us. It is said by scholars that Christ and Christianity do not constitute a theological problem for Judaism but rather that Judaism constitutes such a problem for Christianity.[9] But Rabbi Jacob B. Agus has wisely observed: "If our self-awareness as Jews is determined by our overview of Jewish history, we cannot but regard the emergence of the Christian branch out of the Jewish stem as the most momentous event in our millennial experience."[10]

Along with the historical results, Rabbi Agus goes on to point out that, through Christianity, "the God of Israel triumphed over the pagan deities and all of their works… a magnificent triumph," which paradoxically "was associated with a systematic denigration, even the demonization of, the Jew." I tend to agree with this view but abhor the pernicious Christian backwash for Jews. Yet I do not see how history and theology can be separated pertaining to these painful issues. We are, as Jews and Christians, both historically and theologically, not only problems but also gifts, one might dare say, to one another, and should be, precisely because of our common spiritual roots and mutual experiences in history. Apart from the sufferings inflicted upon Jews, and sometimes upon Christians, perhaps God would not have it any other way! Certainly the Apostle Paul, a Hebrew of Hebrews (Phil. 3:5), who continued to be a Jew among Jews (1 Cor. 9:20), certainly saw it that way (Rom. 11)!

But should the role of Christ, and the consequent trinitarian experience and understanding of the mystery of God, be valid sources of mutual conflict, rather than mutual joy and mutual witness, between Jews and Christians, despite the sad history of our religious communities from the inception of Christianity? Both Jews and Christian Gentiles ought to rejoice that the Holy One of Israel elected to call all Gentiles to be His people through Christ. It is true that Jews and Christians have sharply clashing views regarding the dignity and role of Jesus, as well as the dignity and role of the Mosaic Law, in salvation history according to the deep religious experiences of their respective communities. But these transcendent claims on both sides *need not necessarily* lead to conflict but to profound spiritual meditation and theological thinking. Patriarch Athenagoras of blessed memory once, in the context of Christian ecumenism, defined theology as "a celebration of truth" rather than as "a weapon" to be used against others. This definition, filled with as much truth as beauty, is applicable as well to the dialogue between the Jewish and Christian communities. Jews and Christians, mindful of their primary faithfulness to the Lord God and His inscrutable mystery of salvation for all peoples, ought to rejoice and celebrate in utter humility and freedom, undefiled by proselytism, their mutual respect for and witness to one another and thus together to work toward the fulfillment of God's purposes in the world.

A Jew *qua* Jew ought to rejoice that a substantial part of the Jewish spiritual heritage is universally spread to the nations through the good news of Christ, notwithstanding the sins of Christians. A Christian *qua* Christian ought to rejoice that the Holy One of Israel is worshiped, praised, and obeyed by Jews all over the world, notwithstanding the sins of Jews. Who has not sinned? Who has not been disobedient? Who needs no repentance before the Lord God? Christians above all, on account of their numerous theoretical and practical expressions of anti-Judaism and anti-Semitism.[11] Yet if our primary faithfulness is truly to the Lord God, our Father in heaven, we would nurture "in fear and trembling," to use a Pauline expression from another context (Phil. 2:12), mutual respect toward one another and toward our respective deep religious claims. Conflict could arise, as it did arise, only if and when one community insists that the other must accept its claims, or when one community shows contempt and denigrates the claims of the other, contrary to the admonitions of the Apostle Paul (Rom. 11:13-21).

For example, appropriate respect and peace in the Name of the Lord God *could be maintained* even if a reflective Jew would say to a Christian, "Jesus of Nazareth was only a prophet, a charismatic rabbi, or perhaps even a radical son of Judaism who called for an unacceptable renewal of Judaism," but the same Jew would necessarily have to add humbly, *"for my community and me,"* that is, as we Jews understand the mysterious workings of the Lord God in history. Similarly, appropriate respect and peace *could be maintained* in the Name of the Lord God if a reflective Christian would say to a Jew, "the dispensation of the Mosaic Law has ended by being fulfilled by the dispensation of Christ," or even to say, "your view of God can be enriched through a trinitarian understanding," but the same Christian would have to add humbly, *"for my community and me,"* that is, as we understand the mysterious workings of the Lord God in history. Then they could say to each other, if interested: "Let us therefore discuss together these important matters in mutual love and respect, under mutual faithfulness to the Lord God, and see what we can learn about each other, and from each other, and even clarify our own ideas and convictions about our own respective faiths. Above all, let the truth itself, revealed in grace and love, draws us to itself and leads us in freedom."[12]

If we are strong and mature in our own personal faith, what true need is there to deny the revelatory experiences of one another's religious communities and the deep convictions of their members, and consequently to let conflicts arise? Where there is true faithfulness to and love for the living God, there is no such true need. But there are many false and pernicious needs at work in history: willful and ignorant zeal, wrong use of Scriptures, subtle psychological efforts to hold on to one's own weak or immature religious convictions by denying or attacking the religious convictions of others, and even a triumphalistic collective ego of a religious community stubbornly set to diminish, control, or even destroy another religious community. Add to this the all-too-human cultural, social, political, and economic self-interests, and you have the ugly soup of the painful tragedies of history, insofar as abuse of religion is concerned. In such cases we have placed "our religion" on the throne of the almighty God and presume to judge others, denying their God-given freedom of conscience and in the process committing idolatry, blasphemy, and injustice, all in the Name of God. A scandalous result is that religion, instead of being a liberating power inspiring cultures and people to mutual respect, justice, and peace, is perverted into a kind of satanic force to hate, slander, and destroy others. "And no wonder!" we might say with Saint Paul's words used in another context. For those who are fanatically and self-righteously blind to God's love and truth, "even Satan disguises himself as an angel of light" (2 Cor. 11:14).

If the sharpest theological disagreement between Jews and Christians can be faithfully treated and discussed in a humble and respectful manner, thus preserving continuity while working at renewal, it is obvious that the other important areas of our "roots" can be discussed with less difficulty. Due to the length of my paper, I offer only a few comments on the three remaining major areas of faithfulness and commitment. With regard to the ongoing community as the nurturing ground of our life and faith, faithfulness to our community does not need to deny the right of other people to be faithful to their own communities. In particular Christians ought to re-learn and be repeatedly reminded of the welcome and joyous fact of the continuity of the Jewish people in history, the bare fact of which shows that God has neither rejected nor abandoned His people, just as Saint Paul long ago categorically declared (Rom. 11:1,11).

Christian Orthodox theology ought to go at least as far as Saint Paul went in affirming that the Jewish people, despite their disobedience toward Christ, are still the elect people of God, and that Christian Gentiles are honorary citizens engrafted onto the rich tree of the Jewish heritage. Saint Paul severely warned Gentile Christians not to be haughty or boastful toward unbelieving Jews – much less to cultivate evil intent and engage in persecution against them – a critical warning largely and shamefully forgotten by Christians in history (Rom. 11:17-22). While it is true that, for the Apostle, the unbelieving Jews are in a state of disobedience regarding Christ, (that is, from the viewpoint of the Christian experience and understanding of salvation history, and in the case of Saint Paul, the specific conversion experience on the Damascus road), nevertheless he unreservedly affirmed both their continued electedness and existence. In fact, on account of the faithfulness of God Himself, Saint Paul could not possibly conceive of the end of the drama of salvation history without the participation of Jews as the climax of history by the hand of God Himself (Rom. 11:15,28-36). Christians have remembered the Jews as "enemies" but not as "beloved" of God (Rom. 11:28). Christians have taken to heart Saint Paul's critiques of the Jews, and used them viciously against Jews, but have forgotten Saint Paul's ineffable, sacrificial love for the Jews and their sacred traditions (Rom. 9:1-5).

Had Christian leaders heeded Saint Paul's vision and taught Christian people accordingly over the centuries, the history of Christian-Jewish relations would have been quite different. Christians in history would not have ironically proven themselves "superior" to Jews in unfaithfulness to the Lord God by denigrating and persecuting His people. Nicholas Berdyaev, the Russian Orthodox religious philosopher poignantly wrote: "Perhaps the saddest thing to admit is that those who rejected the Cross have to carry it, while those who welcomed it are often engaged in crucifying the other."[13]

Part of the commitment to the future toward renewal in this area means unreserved Christian affirmation of the theological validity of the continuity of the Jewish people as God's people, as well as the validity and continuity of the Sinai Covenant for Jews,[14] however disobedient they may be in His eyes, just as Christians are also His people, disobedient though they surely have been according to their own and many ways in His eyes. Moreover, God has given both of His peoples, Jews and Christians, a charge to fulfill. We have positive and constructive work to do in the world. We have forgotten that we are servant communities of God, not self-righteous critics or exploiters of society or of each other, being entrusted with a mission by God which as yet we are far from having rightly and fully accomplished.

As far our "roots" in terms of God's gifts to us from Abraham to Paul, from Moses to Christ, from the Sinai and Golgotha Covenants, from the Mosaic Law to the Sermon of the Mount, all these ought to be, as mentioned above, faithfully regarded with honor and awe as God's gifts. We disagree in our interpretation and application of them but surely in faithfulness to the Giver we must respectfully allow each community to witness to these gifts in its own way, on the basis of freedom and far from any shades of proselytism. Saint Paul was convinced that the period of the Mosaic Law had come to an end and had been fulfilled by Christ, according to his experience of Jesus of Nazareth as the risen Lord of Glory (Gal. 3:23-29; Rom. 10:4; 1 Cor. 2:8). However, he continued to regard the Mosaic Law as "holy," "good," and "spiritual" (Rom. 7:12-14) and did not hesitate to use it for Christian instruction (1 Cor. 9:8-9; cf. John 1:17; 4:22). Although the Apostle advocated freedom from the Mosaic Law for Gentile Christians, he neither expected nor preached that believing Jews in Christ – much less unbelieving Jews – had to abandon observance of the Law.[15] Moreover, as well known, the Orthodox Church reveres Abraham, Moses, the prophets, and many other figures in the Hebrew Scriptures as saints. We have so much to learn about each other and from one another. Orthodox Christianity long ago exorcized the ghost of the early Christian arch-heretic Marcion who renounced the Old Testament and reviled all things Jewish. Orthodox Christianity never fell into the Western temptation of contrasting Law and Gospel, free will and grace, works and faith, nor consequently into the inclination to "demonize" the Jewish heritage as being intrinsically legalistic and lacking grace. However, Orthodox cultures admittedly have developed frightful and noxious popular traditions denigrating Jews as an ongoing people on the basis of wrong inferences drawn from the Scriptures, liturgical texts, and popular customs.[16]

The fourth and final major area of "the roots" is the whole complex and variegated fabric of the innumerable institutions, rites, customs, teachings, values, offices, sacred documents, written rules, and oral traditions which express the actual life of our communities. On the one hand, faithfulness to these roots is vital because they represent the practical and frontline faith experience for all of us. On the other hand, to absolutize all of these faith expressions and put them on the same level of importance could prove to be an act of unfaithfulness to the very nature, spirit, and mission of our communities as servant communities of God. It is here that we must be especially careful not to give to these various traditions the kind of faithfulness that only belongs to God. We must not also identify our religious values with our ethnic self-interests, a potentially dangerous mixture, although religious values and ethnic interests can also have noble and liberating aspects. Differentiation between religion and ethnicity, at least in theory, is probably easier for Orthodox Christians than for Jews. However, with regard to this area of faithfulness and commitment toward renewal, each community must deal primarily with its own members. A general operating principle that we share is that of distinguishing the greater from the lesser, the constitutive from the useful, the irreformable from the reformable, as time marches on and the circumstances of life change.

Let me end with a telling example about both the possibilities and difficulties regarding continuity and renewal in my own Orthodox community on a practical level. Metropolitan Chrysostomos of the Ecumenical Patriarchate of Constantinople was one of the first Orthodox theologians to distinguish between Tradition and traditions as a principle of ecumenical change and renewal in a programmatic article published in 1960.[17] Thirty one years later the Metropolitan published another article dealing with the same issue but on a practical, popular level. An ordinary Orthodox Christian posed the occasional question to the Metropolitan: "Has the Church aged?" That is, has the Church become irrelevant to contemporary society?[18] The Metropolitan graciously sympathized with the question and used it to formulate a mild prophetic call for change in the Orthodox Church, offering several examples, among them the activation of the laity in the life of the Church. To those of us who live in the West, Orthodox Christians included, this subject appears frequently on our agenda. But the power of tradition in traditional Orthodox lands compelled the Metropolitan to focus enormous attention on defending and qualifying the concept of any change in the Church. The authority of traditional consciousness in which allegedly nothing changes, including a tradition of heavy clericalism in native Orthodox countries, the eminent and enlightened Metropolitan had to write ever so guardedly to justify such an obviously legitimate and welcome task as the activation of lay ministries in the Church! This is only one example of the dynamics of continuity and renewal in theory and practice. The possibilities of renewal are as many as they are wide, but the road ahead is long and difficult. But the good Lord, blessed be His Name, is merciful and patient.

NOTES

[1] The first officially sponsored dialogue between Jewish and largely Greek Orthodox scholars occurred in New York (1972) at the initiative of Archbishop Iakovos and the late Marc H. Tanenbaum. The papers of this meeting were published in the *Journal of Ecumenical Studies* 13 (4, 1976) and *The Greek Orthodox Theological Review* 22 (1, 1977). Two international consultations between Jewish and a wider circle of Orthodox scholars took place in Lucerne (1977) and Bucharest (1979). The papers of these meetings were published respectively in *The Greek Orthodox Theological Review* 24 (4, 1979) and in a book by the Romanian Patriarchate under the title *The Christian Orthodox-Jewish Consultation II* (no editor or date given). A third international conference, a larger gathering of Orthodox and Jewish scholars, occurred in Athens, March 21-24, 1993. The papers of this conference were edited by Malcolm Lowe and published under the title *Orthodox Christians and Jews on Continuity and Renewal – The Third Academic Meeting between Orthodoxy and Judaism* in the periodical *Immanuel* 26/27 (1994).
[2] The only documented conference between Orthodox and Muslims in modern times, known to me, occurred in March 1985 at Holy Cross Greek Orthodox School of Theology and its papers published under the title *Orthodox Christians and Muslims*, edited by N. M. Vaporis (Brookline: Holy Cross Press, 1986). There have been contacts between Orthodox and Muslims in Turkey and the Middle East but information about them is unavailable. In previous centuries, a few meetings between Orthodox and Muslims occurred in the form of debates and disputes.
[3] See note 1 for the bibliographical information.
[4] Shemaryahu Talmon, "Torah as a Concept and Vital Principle in the Hebrew Bible," *The Greek Orthodox Theological Review* 24 (4, 1979), p. 271.

⁵ In *The Christian Orthodox-Jewish Consultation II*, the article by Israel Singer, "The Individual and the Community in the Jewish Tradition," pp. 56-69 explains variegations within the larger Jewish community, including "the acute problem" between religious and non-religious Jews (p. 63).

⁶ See the different approaches of Demetrios J. Constantelos, "Greek Orthodox-Jewish Relations in Historical Perspective," *The Greek Orthodox Theological Review* 22 (1, 1977), pp. 6-16, and Zvi Ankori, "Greek Orthodox-Jewish Relations in Historic Perspective – The Jewish View," in the same volume, pp. 17-57. Constantelos emphasizes the tolerance toward Jews under the Byzantine Empire, while Ankori points up more sharply the conflicts without rejecting that there were also welcome periods of tolerance.

⁷ Ankori, especially pp. 28-46, analytically exposes the forces, sources, and areas of friction between Christians and Jews in the Byzantine Empire, including political and geographic interests which continue to the present. We can now add other Christian Orthodox-Jewish disputes in the Holy Land, including the murder of an Orthodox monk at the site of the Well of Jacob some years ago and the current occupation of Saint John's Hospice by Jews against the strong protests of the Orthodox Patriarchate of Jerusalem. In Israel and other lands of the Middle East there are Arab Orthodox Christians whose human rights are violated on a daily basis, a major factor in their own violent reactions as a people. The World Council of Churches has supported the rights of Palestinian Christians and Muslims numerous times, of course not without by Jewish objections and justifications.

⁸ The Jewish scholar Michael Wyschogrod, "Tradition and Society in Judaism," in *The Christian Orthodox-Jewish Consultation II*, p. 24, writes that from a certain viewpoint "the very attempt to distinguish between scripture and tradition is futile." A number of Orthodox Christians would agree but the majority of Orthodox scholars usually do not. See Elias Jones-Golitzin, "The Role of the Bible in the Orthodox Tradition," in the same volume, who writes, "although Scripture and Tradition cannot be separated, they can be distinguished," p. 39.

⁹ For example, the Jewish scholar Seymour Siegel, "Judaism and Eastern Orthodoxy: Theological Reflections," *The Greek Orthodox Theological Review* 22, (1, 1977), p. 64.

¹⁰ Jacob B. Agus, "Judaism and the New Testament," *The Greek Orthodox Theological Review* 22, (1, 1977), p. 86.

¹¹ Seymour Siegel, cited above (note 9), p. 65, rightly attacks the sin of anti-semitism and quotes the paradox of this sin by citing the Orthodox religious philosopher Nicholas Berdyaev, *Christianity and Anti-Semitism* (Aldington: Kent Publishing Company, 1952), p. 12.

¹² I trust that my words and line of argument clearly suggest that, contrary to a number of Western scholars, I do not in any way call for a diminishment of New Testament Christology or the classic Christology of the Church, which I view consistent and coherent, as a basis for the renewal of Jewish-Christian relations. In fact such diminishment of Christology neutralizes

and cancels authentic dialogue precisely because it is, on the part of Christians, a foolish and destructive expression of lack of faithfulness to Christ and to the Christian community. It also strikes at the heart of the enduring power of Christianity, especially the so-called mainline churches in our times.

[13] Quoted by Siegel (see above, note 11).

[14] An exceptional example of this Orthodox theological approach is by George C. Papademetriou, *Essays on Orthodox Christian-Jewish Relations* (Bristol: Wyndham Hall Press, 1990). I take this opportunity also to correct myself on an essential point made in my article, "New Testament Issues in Jewish-Christian Relations," *The Greek Orthodox Theological Review* 22 (1, 1977), p. 77, where I endorsed A. Roy Eckardt's critique of Saint Paul as teaching a "non-functional election" for Jews who do not believe in Christ. I no longer interpret Rom. 11 in this fashion. Rather, it is my judgment that, though disobedient regarding Christ, they are still the elect people of God, according to Saint Paul. Insofar as God continues to have plans for all Jews, even during the period of the call of the Gentiles, His election of Jews continues. There is no such thing as "non-functioning election" according to the Apostle Paul and certainly according to God whose faithfulness to the Jewish people could not be questioned according to the Apostle.

[15] For Jewish and Christian Orthodox perspectives on the Law, see S. Talmon, *The Greek Orthodox Theological Review* 24 (4, 1979), pp. 271-289, and Basilios Stoyiannos, "The Law in the New Testament from an Orthodox Point of View," in the same volume, pp. 309-322

[16] Popular examples of Christian Orthodox anti-Judaism and even anti-Semitism include the blood libel, the burning of the effigy of Judas during Holy Week in some lands, and anti-Jewish gestures of abuse or even persecution during Holy Week which long, uncritical tradition has carried with it.

[17] Chrysostomos Konstantinidis, "The Significance of the Eastern and Western Traditions within Christendom," in *Orthodoxy: A Faith and Order Dialogue* (Geneva: WCC Publications, 1960).

[18] Chrysostomos Konstantinidis, "Ekklesia gerasmene" (Has the Church Aged)?" in *Episkepsis*, February 1, 1991, a bulletin of the Orthodox Center of the Ecumenical Patriarchate in Geneva.